T0332394

Edge-AI in Healthcare

This book provides comprehensive research ideas about edge-AI technology that can assist doctors in making better data-driven decisions. It provides insights for improving the healthcare industry by examining future trends, simplifying decision-making, and investigating structured and unstructured data.

Edge-AI in Healthcare: Trends and Future Perspectives is more than a comprehensive introduction to Artificial Intelligence as a tool in healthcare data. The book is split into three sections covering the entire healthcare ecosystem. The first section is an introduction to edge-AI in healthcare. It discusses data usage, modeling, and simulation techniques as well as machine-learning and deep-learning approaches. The second section discusses the implementation of edge-AI for smart healthcare. The topics discussed in this section include Augmented Reality/Virtual Reality (AR/VR) and cloud computing, big data management, algorithms, optimization, and Internet of Medical Things (IoMT) techniques and methods. The third section covers the role of edge-AI in healthcare and the challenges and opportunities of the technologies. This section also provides case studies and discusses sustainability, security, privacy, and trust related to edge-AI in healthcare.

This book:

- provides comprehensive research ideas about edge-AI technology that can assist doctors in making better data-driven decisions and will provide insights to researchers about the healthcare industry, trends, and future perspectives.
- examines how healthcare systems of the future will operate by augmenting clinical resources and ensuring optimal patient outcomes.
- provides insights into how edge-AI is revolutionising decision-making, providing early warnings for conditions, and visual inspection in healthcare
- highlight trends, challenges, opportunities, and future areas where healthcare informatics deal with accessing vast datasets of potentially life-saving information.

This book is intended to benefit researchers, academics, industry professionals, R & D organizations, and students working in the field of healthcare, healthcare informatics, and their applications.

Edge AI in Future Computing

Series Editors:

***Arun Kumar Sangaiah, SCOPE, VIT University,
Tamil Nadu, India***
*Mamta Mittal, G. B. Pant Government Engineering College,
Okhla, New Delhi, India*

**Soft Computing Techniques in Engineering,
Health, Mathematical, and Social Sciences**
Pradip Debnath and S. A. Mohiuddine

**Machine Learning for Edge Computing:
Frameworks, Patterns, and Best Practices**
Amitoj Singh, Vinay Kukreja, Taghi Javdani Gandomani

Internet of Things
Frameworks for Enabling and Emerging Technologies
*Bharat Bhushan, Sudhir Kumar Sharma, Bhuvan Unhelkar,
Muhammad Fazal Ijaz, Lamia Karim*

Soft Computing
Recent Advances and Applications in Engineering and
Mathematical Sciences
Pradip Debnath, Oscar Castillo, Poom Kumam

For more information about this series, please visit: https://www.
routledge.com/Edge-AI-in-Future-Computing/book-series/EAIFC

Edge-AI in Healthcare

Trends and Future Perspectives

Edited by
Sonali Vyas,
Akanksha Upadhyaya,
Deepshikha Bhargava, and
Vinod Kumar Shukla

CRC Press
Taylor & Francis Group
Boca Raton London New York

CRC Press is an imprint of the
Taylor & Francis Group, an **informa** business

Designed cover image: © Shutterstock

First edition published 2023
by CRC Press
6000 Broken Sound Parkway NW, Suite 300, Boca Raton, FL 33487-2742

and by CRC Press
4 Park Square, Milton Park, Abingdon, Oxon, OX14 4RN

CRC Press is an imprint of Taylor & Francis Group, LLC

© 2023 selection and editorial matter, Sonali Vyas, Akanksha Upadhyaya, Deepshikha Bhargava, and Vinod Kumar Shukla; individual chapters, the contributors

Reasonable efforts have been made to publish reliable data and information, but the author and publisher cannot assume responsibility for the validity of all materials or the consequences of their use. The authors and publishers have attempted to trace the copyright holders of all material reproduced in this publication and apologize to copyright holders if permission to publish in this form has not been obtained. If any copyright material has not been acknowledged, please write and let us know so we may rectify in any future reprint.

Except as permitted under U.S. Copyright Law, no part of this book may be reprinted, reproduced, transmitted, or utilized in any form by any electronic, mechanical, or other means, now known or hereafter invented, including photocopying, microfilming, and recording, or in any information storage or retrieval system, without written permission from the publishers.

For permission to photocopy or use material electronically from this work, access www.copyright.com or contact the Copyright Clearance Center, Inc. (CCC), 222 Rosewood Drive, Danvers, MA 01923, 978-750-8400. For works that are not available on CCC please contact mpkbookspermissions@tandf.co.uk

Trademark notice: Product or corporate names may be trademarks or registered trademarks and are used only for identification and explanation without intent to infringe.

ISBN: 978-1-032-15448-0 (hbk)
ISBN: 978-1-032-15546-3 (pbk)
ISBN: 978-1-003-24459-2 (ebk)

DOI: 10.1201/9781003244592

Typeset in Times
by Deanta Global Publishing Services, Chennai, India

Dedication

This book is dedicated to family and friends...

Contents

Foreword

This book is a spectacular collection of chapters related to the Edge-AI in Healthcare, its trends, and future perspectives. Overall, there are 17 papers in this collection and all the authors claim responsibility for handling their subjects in a remarkable manner.

Through the book, readers will have the chance to explore the edge-AI concepts specifically in the healthcare sector, such as edge-AI tools and techniques, machine learning, blockchain and deep-learning approaches for healthcare, enhancing access of the visually impaired through the smart cane, automated wheelchairs for the physically challenged with Artificial Internet of Things (AIoT) modules, the role of edge-AI in Internet of Things (IoT) and Internet of Everything (IoE), the edge computing-based containerized deep-learning approach for intrusion detection in healthcare IoT, human mental experience through Chatbot, early diagnosis of cardiac disease, super-resolution in a world of scarce resources for medical imaging applications and edge-AI-empowered blockchain in medical tourism.

I congratulate the editors and the contributors who have put in a lot of time and effort in bringing out this book to address the edge-AI concept in healthcare to achieve a better understanding of the issues and future aspects.

We hope you'll like this book as much as I do.

Happy Reading!

Professor (Dr) Ajay Rana
Director General
Greater NOIDA Campus
Amity University Uttar Pradesh, India
&
Former Vice Chancellor-Deemed to be University

Preface

Edge-AI in Healthcare: Trends and Future Perspectives is an inclusive guide to the edge-Artificial Intelligence concept, with the emphasis on healthcare.

The purpose of this book is to make readers aware of the concepts and issues in edge-AI and the future developments of edge-AI with machine learning, deep learning, IoT, and blockchain. The organisation of the book covers the explanation of complex issues in a fairly easy-to-understand manner.

The book comprises 17 chapters and covers various facets of edge-AI, enhancing access of the visually impaired through the smart cane, an automated wheelchair for the physically challenged, intrusion detection in healthcare IoT, human mental experience through Chatbot, early diagnosis of cardiac disease, super-resolution in medical imaging applications, and medical tourism.

The book begins (Chapter 1) with an introduction to the edge-AI concept in healthcare, while Chapter 2 discusses the different edge-AI tools and techniques for healthcare. In addition, different machine-learning and deep-learning approaches to edge-AI are highlighted in Chapters 3 and 4, respectively. Further chapters include case-specific problem statements and address different edge-AI solutions, such as support for the visually impaired through the development of the Smart Cane, authentication of the edge-AI-based Smart Health Care System, development of an automated wheelchair for the physically challenged with AIoT modules, early diagnosis of cardiac disease using feature optimisation, and solution to intrusion detection and stroke prediction. The chapters in the latter half of the book highlight the contemporary role of edge-AI in IoT and IoE in healthcare and digital marketing. The last few chapters cover the human mental experience through Chatbot, and human engagement with evidence-based cognitive-behavioral techniques. The book concludes with legal and ethical implications of an edge-AI-enabled IoT healthcare monitoring system and the use of blockchain for edge-AI.

Editor Profiles

Dr Sonali Vyas
Ph.D. (Computer Science), SMIEEE
Dr Vyas has been serving as an academician and researcher for more than a decade. Currently, she is working as Associate Professor (Selection Grade) in the School of Computer Science at the University of Petroleum and Energy Studies, Uttarakhand, India. Her research interests include healthcare informatics, blockchain, database virtualisation, data mining, and big data analytics. She has authored many research papers, articles, and book chapters in refereed journals, conference proceedings, and books. She authored a book on "*Smart Health Systems*", published by Springer. She is also an editor of "*Pervasive Computing: A Networking Perspective and Future Directions*", by Springer Nature, and "*Smart Farming Technologies for Sustainable Agricultural Development*", by IGI Global". She acted as a guest editor in a special issue of "Machine Learning and Software Systems" in *Journal of Statistics & Management Systems*" (Thomson Reuters). She has also been awarded three patents in the area of smart and sustainable systems. She has also acted as a Resource Person on the AICTE-ISTE Faculty Refresher Course on "Embedded Systems, IoT, Pervasive Computing" and delivered many talks at reputable international and national conferences. She is also a member of the editorial boards and reviewer boards for many refereed national and international journals. She has also been a member of organising committees, national advisory boards, and technical program committees at many international and national conferences. She has also chaired sessions in various renowned international and national conferences. She has been awarded the "National Distinguished Educator Award 2021" and "International Young Researcher Award 2021", instituted by the International Institute of Organized Research (I2OR), which is a registered MSME, Government of India, and Green ThinkerZ. She was also awarded the "Women Researcher Award 2021" in Engineering, Science, and Medicine, by VDGOOD Professional Association in International Conference, and was also awarded the "Best Academician of the Year Award (Female)" in the Global Education and Corporate Leadership Awards (GECL-2018). She is a professional member of IEEE (Senior Member), ACM-India, CSI, IFERP, IAENG, ISOC, SCRS, and IJERT.

Dr Akanksha Upadhyaya
Ph.D. (Computer Science)
Dr Upadhyaya is working as an Associate Professor and Head, AI Cell, at Rukmini Devi Institute of Advanced Studies (RDIAS), Delhi, India. She has been associated with RDIAS for more than nine years, with an overall experience of more than 13 years, as an academician. She has teaching experience in the fields of information technology, computer science, and management sciences. She holds a Ph.D. from Amity University, Noida, in the field of data authentication and fraud

detection. She was awarded the Outstanding Thesis award in 2020 by GRF. With her vast experience, she has presented papers at various national and international conferences and received several best paper awards. She has written more than 25 research papers, some of which have appeared in journals and conferences with Scopus indices from publishers like IGI Global, IEEE, Springer, Inderscience, and Elsevier, to name but a few. She has chaired sessions at several international and national conferences organized by IIM and other premier institutions, served as a guest editor for renowned international book publications, and reviewed articles for peer-reviewed journals, published by Springer Nature, Inderscience, and other reputable international publishers. She has two patents to her name and is currently serving as a guest editor for three edited books by CRC Press, Apple Academic Press, and Nova Science Publisher. She has been an invited speaker and resource person in the field of research methodology and data authentication in several research workshops and faculty development programs.

Professor (Dr) Deepshikha Bhargava
Ph.D. (Computer Science), Banasthali Vidyapith, Rajasthan
SMIEEE, LMCSI, MIE, M.Tech. (CS), MCA, M.Sc. (CS)
Professor Bhargava has a rich experience of more than 22 years as an academician, working at present as Professor and Head of Institution, Amity University Uttar Pradesh, Greater Noida (An Atulyam Campus), India. She has authored 16 books and 14 book chapters, edited two Books, and published more than research papers in journals and conference proceedings. She was recently nominated as a member of the Project Review Steering Group (PRSG), Ministry of Electronics & IT (MeitY), Government of India. She has also served as visiting fellow at Université des Mascareignes (UDM), Ministry of Education and Human Resources, Tertiary Education and Scientific Research, Mauritius. She has been nominated by MeitY, Govt. of India, to visit the Drone Application and Research Center (DARC), Information Technology Development Agency (ITDA) Department of Information Technology, (Government of Uttarakhand). She is also empaneled among PaperVest Press scientific advisors, PaperVest University Publisher of Centro Universitário Facvest (UNIFACVEST), Brazil. Recently she was included as Reviewer for the 2022 NSF Graduate Research Fellowship Program (GRFP) by the National Science Foundation (NSF), USA. Prof. Bhargava has also received the following awards: "Active Participation Woman Award", "Best Faculty of the Year" under subcategory "Authoring Books on Contemporary Subjects", to name but a few. She was also awarded the MHRD, Govt. of India, in 1992, for academic excellence. She is a member of the UN Online Volunteering, Institute of Engineers (IE), ACM-W, Senior Member-IEEE, ACM-CSTA, Computer Society of India (CSI), Project Management Institute (PMI), Indian Society of Lighting Engineers (ISLE) and Vigyan Bharti (Vibha). Overall, four PhDs have been completed under her guidance. Her areas of research interest are artificial intelligence, soft computing, bio-inspired computation, and Healthcare informatics.

Dr Vinod Kumar Shukla
Ph.D. (Computer Science)
Dr Shukla is currently working with Amity University, Dubai, UAE, in the capacity of Associate Professor, Information Technology and Head of Academics, Engineering Architecture Interior Design, Amity University, Dubai, United Arab Emirates. He has more than 14 years of experience. He completed his Ph.D. in the field of semantic web and ontology. He is an active member of IEEE. He has published many research papers in various reputable journals and conferences. He has also completed the "General Management Program" from the Indian Institute of Management Ahmedabad (IIM-A). He is also a certified Network Trainer, CCNI (Cisco Certified Network Trainer). He has conducted many training programs, including training programs for the employees of Delhi Transco Limited (D.T.L), Indian Postal Department in Megdoot Bhawan, Delhi, and Directorate General Resettlement (DGR), an inter-service organisation functioning directly under the Ministry of Defence. (DGR). He has also written a case study on "Online Retail in UAE: Driven to Grow" and "Modi's Visit to UAE: Uncovering New Areas of Cooperation", which are hosted by the European Case Clearing House (ECCH), UK. He received the "Inquisitive Award" in Unanimity, 2020, organised and hosted by Amity University Dubai, UAE. He was awarded the "Star Supporter Award 2019", which was presented by Manzil Center, Sharjah, UAE. Her Highness Sheikha Chaica S. Al Qassimi and Dr. Ayesha Saeed Husaini, Director, Al Manzil Center, Sharjah, UAE, presented the "Appreciation Certificate and Star Supporter Award 2019" to Amity University, Dubai, which was received by Dr Shukla for continuous support to community engagement and volunteerism. He has also received Memento for Amity University Dubai, from Mrs. Gloria Gangte, Deputy Chief of Mission, Embassy of India, Sultanate of Oman, for Guidance Seminar 2016.

Contributors

Anand Deshpande
Department of Electronics &
   Communication Engineering,
   Angadi Institute of Technology and
   Management, Belagavi, Karnataka,
   India

Aditi Gupta
Manipal University Jaipur, India

Akanksha Upadhyay
Rukmini Devi Institute of Advanced
   Studies (RDIAS), Delhi, India

Amitabh Bhargava
Amity University, Greater Noida, UP,
   India

Ankita Kashyap
Manipal University Jaipur, India

Ashima Bhatnagar Bhatia
Vivekananda Institute of Professional
   Studies, New Delhi India

Ashish Kumar
Bennett University, Greater Noida,
   India

Atishi Jain
Manipal University Jaipur, India

Ayon Datta
Department of Pharmaceutical
   Technology, Global College of
   Pharmaceutical Technology, West
   Bengal, India

Bhajneet Kaur
Fortune Institute of International
   Business, New Delhi, India

Bhupendra Prajapati
Shree S K Patel College of
   Pharmaceutical Education and
   Research, Ganpat University, India

Biswajit Basu
Department of Pharmaceutical
   Technology, Global College of
   Pharmaceutical Technology, West
   Bengal, India

Deepshikha Bhargava
Amity University, Greater Noida, UP,
   India

Devesh Kumar Srivastava
Manipal University Jaipur, India

Disha Garg
Rukmini Devi Institute of Advanced
   Studies (RDIAS), Delhi, India

G. V. Kallimani
Angadi Institute of Technology and
   Management, Belagavi, Karnataka,
   India

Jigna B. Prajapati
Computer Applications, Ganpat
   University, Gujarat, India

Ketan Gupta
Research Scientist, University of the
   Cumberlands, USA

Komal Tahiliani
Sagar Institute of Science &
   Technology, Bhopal, MP, India

Manan Pruthi
Bharati Vidyapeeth's College of
   Engineering, New Delhi, India

Nivedita Singhal
Deutsche Bank, India

Manaswini Pradhan
Department of Computer Science,
    Fakir Mohan University, Odisha,
    India

Mann Bajpai
Manipal University Jaipur

Mayank Singhal
Bharati Vidyapeeth's College of
    Engineering, New Delhi, India

Nasmin Jiwani
Research Scientist, University of the
    Cumberlands, USA

Nidhi Singh
Rukmini Devi Institute of Advanced
    Studies (RDIAS), Delhi, India

Nisha Solanki
Maharaja Surajmal Institute of
    Technology, Delhi, India

P. Patavardhan
RV Institute of Technology and
    Management, India

Pawan Whig
Vivekananda Institute of Professional
    Studies, New Delhi India

Preetha V K
Department of Computing, University
    of Stirling, RAK, United Arab
    Emirates

Preeti Nagrath
Bharati Vidyapeeth's College of
    Engineering, New Delhi, India

Priyanka Mishra
Indian Institute of Information
    Technology, Kota, India

Rachna Jain
Bhagwan Parshuram Institute of
    Technology, Delhi India

Rahul Nijhawan
Thapar University, Patiala, India

Ridoan Karim
School of Business, Monash
    University Malaysia, Malaysia

S.Prabavathy
G. Narayanamma Institute of
    Technology and Science,
    Hyderabad, Telangana

Sanatan Shrivastava
The University of Texas at Dallas,
    Texas, US

Shama Kouser
Department of Computer Science,
    Jazan University, Kingdom of
    Saudi Arabia, Saudi Arabia

Shaurya Gupta
UPES University, Dehradun, India

Sonali Vyas
UPES University, Dehradun, India

Sunil Gupta
UPES University, Dehradun, India

Sunpreet Bhatia
UPES University, Dehradun, India

Syeda Fizza Nuzhat Zaidi
Department of Engineering and
    Architecture Amity University,
    Dubai, U.A.E

Uday Panwar
Sagar Institute of Science &
    Technology, Bhopal, MP, India

V. V. Estrela
Department of Telecommunications
    at Federal Fluminense University
    (UFF), Brazil, South America

Vinod Kumar Shukla
Department of Engineering and
    Architecture Amity University,
    Dubai, U.A.E

1 Introduction to edge-AI in healthcare

Atishi Jain, Mann Bajpai, Aditi Gupta,
Ankita Kashyap, Devesh Kumar Srivastava

CONTENTS

1.1 INTRODUCTION

In models, the algorithms are proposed and processed locally without dependence on the cloud, internet, etc. They use the data that they have generated themselves for training purposes, storing it locally and taking quick decisions when needed. Such techniques are model trains on various client devices. The model updates and the curated data are then sent to the remote server periodically. The implementation of such models saves backhauling costs and bandwidth requirements. In a field such as healthcare where even a second's delay can result in death, reduced latency is a major point to be considered. The analytics methods utilised by the edge-AI (edge-artificial intelligence) techniques to locally curate, analyse, and produce results, include advanced analytics methods like artificial intelligence and machine learning, edge computing techniques like machine vision, video analytics, and sensor fusion, and methods incorporating location intelligence. The hardware support consists of electronics and devices that enable edge computing. The power efficiency and scalability reduce costs, increase real-time performance, and achieve accurate analytics which, along with the greater

DOI: 10.1201/9781003244592-1

1

reach, make this technique more lucrative. Such techniques can enable medical workers to obtain information about critical patients even in regions where the connectivity is inadequate. Detection, identification, and diagnosis of musculo-skeletal injuries, fractures, cardiovascular abnormalities, and even some neu-rological diseases will be possible, even in remote locations, with the help of edge-AI. The impact of AI and its applications in various industries all over the world has significantly improved. Nowadays, cloud computing is being used in almost every field in the face of the growing data needs of the corporate world, thereby becoming an integral part of AI. Edge-AI, regarded as the future of AI, is a combination of AI and edge computing that uses machine learning to deploy intelligent solutions on hardware devices. These hardware devices are known as edge devices and use machine-learning algorithms to sort, filter, and analyse data which are generated by this device, and make decisions in real time. Edge AI processes data locally, directly on a server or device, which reduces time latency as the data doesn't have to be transferred to the cloud. This shift from the cloud to the edge is quite beneficial. Another advantage of edge AI is that it doesn't need internet connectivity to analyse data in real time. The role of AI in improving the systems and enhancing technology in different industrial sectors in recent years is commendable. Healthcare is one of the leading industries driven by AI technology and edge computing (Fasciano & Vitulano 2020). AI has the potential to automate processes and has become extremely useful in enabling autonomous monitoring of hospital rooms and patients, enhanced by edge-AI. This is achieved by various AI algorithms which use a host of sensors to gather and process data in order to respond appropriately. There have been a lot of different innovations and developments in transforming the present-day healthcare landscape by auto-mation of cardiovascular tests like X-rays, and much more. The increasing global population brings many problems and challenges surrounding the quality of life for people of all ages. This is mainly affecting the healthcare sector. With the help of AI-based techniques directly on the edge, a faster, more private, and more precise result is enabled which directly works on edge computing.

With the growth of technology and the increased longevity of human life, patients require more sophisticated and faster results, which help them to achieve rapid treatment of any conditions. The exploitation of AI technology, aiming to promote improved health in society, which is very necessary in today's world, is a challenge because of poor knowledge, social and economic issues, and lack of communication. In this chapter, we focus on the architecture, framework, and models for edge-AI tools and techniques in healthcare. AI-based techniques will help us to achieve a more empowering society and community, using edge-AI, which has the potential to impact millions of patients and health providers by improving health systems and reducing costs. From better analysis to improved decision support, edge-AI can achieve wonders when it is adopted.

With the help of simulation, we can have an environment and a model which will help us identify which healthcare systems are useful and will help to take better care of patients. By integrating the AI models with our healthcare system, we can identify and analyse the problem swiftly, and can also help propose good solutions which can help save the lives of patients. We can train models in such a way that they can derive insights with regard to the level of disease risk from the datasets of a patient's medical and social history. The models will also be also useful as they will allow the technical team to evaluate and modify the model and workflow to normal clinical practice. Edge-AI is going to be prove extremely useful to patients and doctors as it ensures affordable prices and healthcare.

1.2 DATA USAGE, ANALYTICS, AND APPLICATIONS OF EDGE-AI IN HEALTHCARE

Edge systems can be thought of as real-time control engines or deterministic embedded communication systems present at the ends of a network, in proximity to the physical world and the industrial environment. One of the main contributors to the advent of edge-AI was the momentous advances of the Internet of Things (IoT) devices with which the web partners transmit data and information between the device and the cloud.

Data collection is achieved through devices like motion controllers, programmable logic controllers, sensors, etc., residing at the boundary of the network. All these devices have analytic capability which enables them to perform analysis and produce results at the edge itself, being connected to the running system as close as possible to the site where the data are being produced, instead of the cloud. Integration of AI at the edge nodes only allows real-time operations, decision-making, data creation, and storage within the same device. Using an inferencing model, AI models are shifted from the cloud to closer to the edge by edge-AI. If any action needs to be taken, the device takes care of it, based on the analysis that it performs. In order to analyse the larger picture, transmission of the relevant data takes place from the devices at the edge to the cloud which are then aggregated.

Machine-learning methods are used by the edge-AI systems for processing the data generated at the local level by the hardware devices. Based on the data collected by the device, AI algorithms are proposed on the hardware devices locally. The devices store the results locally and afterward the information is sent to the cloud for further processing and storage. The llocal computing resources and devices used in edge-AI are optimised for AI and integrated directly. This makes it ideal to analyse and process vast amounts of data in real time on site The reduced amount of data that must be transmitted further reduces the cost of data communication. The vulnerability arising from the privacy perspective can also be avoided as data do not have to be transmitted and stored in the cloud. Let's take the example of sensor data generated to monitor and analyse the status of equipment at some remote healthcare facility. Millions of data points can be created in such an environment per second. It will be impractical to transmit the raw data to a remote data center without filtering and processing it first. The situation gets worse if there's poor network connectivity or inconsistent bandwidth. There are a few cases where, in the absence of edge technology, the data must be collected in storage media and physically shipped via trucks to the data centers. This adds latency which, in turn, results in the loss of signals which might prove to be useful in finalising the procedure for a patient's diagnosis or a medical instrument's need for immediate repair or replacement. All this can be avoided as, in edge-AI, the latency and bandwidth requirements are dramatically reduced because much of the process takes place next to the sensors. IoT devices have limitations when it comes to on-device AI as they usually can't store, compute, label, and analyse large amounts of data. Furthermore, for the outcomes to be accurate and usable, massive amounts of aggregated data from several devices need to be executing the machine-learning algorithms. It is not feasible to rely on the cloud to analyse and process data for real-time decision-making. When big data analytics are held at the end device, only the updates to the algorithms are sent back to the cloud to keep the multiple sites in sync, saving expensive backhaul and cloud storage costs.

Machine-learning and intelligence processes are quite resource heavy. Deep learning algorithms need to be fed data, ultimately to train the deep neural network (DNN). After a DNN framework is established, it is deployed at the edge device for inference. So, basically, the computer collects all the data on an object from the sensors and then utilises it to make accurate predictions. Generally, edge-AI is used for inferencing, whereas, for training new algorithms, the cloud is used. The processing power and capability required for inferencing algorithms is significantly less than that required for training algorithms (Vyas 2023). Hence, at times, the inferencing algorithms are run on Central Processing Units (CPUs) or less efficient microcontrollers on edge devices. In some cases, the inference power is improved along with a reduction in power by using highly efficient AI chips. A proper edge-AI microchip can make autonomous decisions based on the data it acquires even in the absence of the cloud or even internet connection. These microchips can even have a sub-millisecond latency as the data are processed inside the device itself. Machine-learning algorithms can run autonomously due to the decentralised nature of technology. The risk of internet outages or poor network reception is eliminated. The data that the cloud receives has already been highly processed by the edge device, reducing energy consumption by 30–40%. With the 5G rollout, edge technology is becoming integral, with many network providers incorporating edge-AI in the towers themselves, improving speeds and eliminating the requirement for external servers. Some of the analytic tools widely used in the industry today include the following:

- IBM Watson IoT edge analytics.
- Intel IoT Developer Kit.
- Cisco SmartAdvisor.
- Dell Statistica.
- Oracle Edge Analytics.
- Microsoft Azure IoT Edge.
- ASW IoT GreenGrass.

Edge-AI usage is multiplying by leaps and bound, and investment in the edge computing semiconductor industry grew by 74% over the past year, making the total investment equal to $5.8 billion. Its applications can be in various industries, ranging from healthcare to security and surveillance, from navigation to computer vision, etc. It plays a crucial role in data creation, decision-making, and performing other real-time operations where milliseconds matter. Healthcare is one such industry where on-demand insights help paramedics make immediate and crucial decision regarding patients.

A study suggests that 30% of all globally stored data comes from life sciences and healthcare. Considering the amount of data coming in from the healthcare industry, collection and derivation of insights in real time becomes imperative in order to make quick decisions. Technologies powered by edge-AI are already making an impact in the healthcare sector. Surgeons can focus on finding anomalies to be removed, tracking surgical tools, monitoring organs which must be preserved, making automatic measurements, and detecting real-time bleeding, using ultra-low-streaming of surgical videos into AI-powered data-processing workflows. Edge-AI is being integrated into smart hospitals in technologies like patient screening, improved medical image acquisition and reconstruction, heart rate estimation, surgical therapy guidance, real-time visualisation and monitoring, conversational AI, etc. Many different medical and life science instruments, including ultrasound devices, CT and MRI scanners, cryo-electron microscopy, ultrasound devices, and DNA sequencers, benefit from edge-AI too. Some of the most severe diseases can be easier to treat as a result of early diagnosis. Early screening can be brought to a higher level with the implementation of AI-powered diagnostic tools. Google's support in the early diagnosis of diabetic retinopathy with AI-powered bots in India is a good example. Edge-AI can be used in image recognition, predictive maintenance, visual search and object recognition and tracking. Edge-AI can notify the nursing staff if it identifies a patient at risk of falling out of a hospital bed. Also, many wearable devices come with specific hardware these days which can detect if a person falls suddenly. With training, edge-AI systems in these wearables detect falls in a fraction of a second and notify the caregivers; the Apple watch's fall detection feature is an example of the same. Edge-AI is of immense help in the monitoring of vital signs too. AI can be leveraged to detect any abnormality at any given instant by the use of medical devices recording data like temperature, heartbeat, blood pressure, oxygen level, respiration rate, etc. (Slomka et al. 2017); these can be used to alert hospital staff. DICOM (Digital Imaging and Communications) images are quite common in radiology. Their transmission to the cloud or a central server can be costly and time consuming, but edge-AI implementation enables analysis to happen locally, resulting in a faster diagnosis.

Advanced imaging using edge-AI has several applications in the healthcare industry. Cardiovascular abnormalities, fractures, and musculoskeletal injuries can be detected using edge-AI. The integration of AI with the concept of imaging data can also help in the identification of changes in overall flow, thickening of muscle structure, soft tissue injury, detection of hairline fractures, dislocations, and so on. Sets of diagnostic processes can be streamlined by algorithms which flag images containing anomalies in the case of neurological diseases. Large chip manufacturers like Intel, Nvidia, and Qualcomm have invested heavily in edge-AI. Nvidia introduced its reference edge application, Clara Federated Technique. This application creates an AI training module which can be used for preventive care, better imaging, predictive diagnosis, real-time analysis, and so on. Intel's Pentium and Atom x6000E series and Celeron's N and J series processors have been designed specifically for enhancement of the edge workloads. In the healthcare industry, it will facilitate service robots, medical displays, and entry-level ultrasound machines requiring edge-AI (Wan et al. 2020).

1.3 EDGE-AI TOOLS AND TECHNIQUES FOR HEALTHCARE

1.3.1 TOOLS AND TECHNIQUES OF EDGE-AI

Traditionally, AI solutions were cloud-driven due to the high demand for high-quality hardware able to execute deep learning, computing jobs, and the ability to scale-up the resources in the cloud. But there are certain limitations to the cloud, which could be obviated by the need to move computing tasks closer to the data generation site, i.e., to the edge of the network. The impact of AI and its applications to various industries all over the globe have significantly improved. Today, numerous applications make use of AI, which raise the technical requirements of the data center, generating high costs. The cloud may not always be a feasible option. This ushers in the need for cloud computing which helps minimise service delivery latency and yields the required computing power. In today's data-centric landscape, cloud computing is being used in almost every field to match the growing data needs of the corporate world, becoming an integral part of AI. Edge-AI is an amalgamation of edge computing and AI, which uses machine learning to deploy intelligent solutions on hardware devices and which has innumerable potential uses.

Edge computing comprises numerous techniques, like collection, analysis, and processing, that help bring data to the edge of a network instead of at remote locations, hence reducing time latency. Basically, processes are dispersed and take place in a more sensible physical location. A much-needed rise in the need for greater intelligence, computing power, and advanced services at the network edge to help boost the role of edge devices has been enabled by the Internet of Things (IoT) and cloud computing. Edge devices use machine-learning algorithms to sort, filter, and analyse data generated by this hardware device and makes decisions in real time. It controls data flow at the extremities between two networks. Transmission, routing, processing, monitoring, filtering, translation, and storage of data passing between networks are some of the functions of edge devices. Edge-AI offers great flexibility, which allows for smart devices to support various industries. Since data are handled at the local level on an edge computer, this diminishes the possibility of the data being at risk of manipulation, a risk which would be increased were it to be sitting somewhere in the cloud. This also makes the computers more responsive. The most significant advantage of real-time data processing makes it possible to utilise AI applications directly on field devices. Edge inference and training is another advantage as the application of training models and inference happens directly on edge devices. Edge-AI also provides improved levels of automation. Automatic tasks can be performed by machines trained at the edge. Industrial automation and edge-AI technology is rapidly growing and is being employed extensively worldwide. From self-driving vehicles like Tesla to automation of cardiovascular tests, like X-rays, the use of artificial intelligence is expanding at an exponential rate in various sectors.

1.3.2 IMPLEMENTATION IN HEALTHCARE

One such sector is healthcare. An up-and-coming technology is the development of healthcare service robots. Dealing with patients suffering from chronic or psychological illnesses requires the long-term, around-the-clock attention of a nurse or caregiver. Scientists are exploring ways to provide constant chaperoning to provide "a mobile healthcare robot". These robots hold the potential to learn and gain experience from human medical professionals and experts, and go on to give an even more accurate diagnosis than a human caregiver as it will not be prone to any human errors. The mobility of the robot gives an added advantage. The sensor-equipped robot does not miss the minutest details about the environment and the patient and allows the robot to be more dexterous in repetitive work. This helps to capture important information about the patient, which might help them recover faster. The sensor acts as a dispatcher of direct information to some other edge device or to the cloud, when required (Islam et al. 2022), thus allowing each edge device to process information and carry out its role rather than sending all its data to a centralised server. AI has boomed in the cardiovascular imaging field, helping radiologists and pathologists with medical imaging to identify and diagnose a range of conditions. MRI, CT scans, and X-ray images allow doctors to see the inner workings of the human body. However, it can be difficult and time consuming for anyone to evaluate the huge amount of complex data which these images often contain. AI tools can act as clinical decision supports and hence help enhance care delivery by supporting the workflow of radiologists and pathologists (Mazzanti et al. 2018). A clinical cardiac MRI (CMR) scan calls for approximately one hour of imaging time, followed by significant time for post-processing the image obtained. Although clinical use of completely automated methods for analysing CMR analysis has not yet materialised, CMR stands to benefit much from automated segmentation because of the current latency of manual image post-processing. Various CMR pulse chronologies, scanning variables, and imaging protocols – each of which needs to be fashioned according to each patient and the medical issue – are a barrier to automation of scanning and analysis. There is a lot of ongoing research work underway to overcome these challenges, despite such limitations. The use of edge-AI in the healthcare sector has demonstrated great potential in the near future to provide doctors and physicians with completely automated and accurate tools for both diagnostic purposes and to improve patient treatment.

1.4 ARCHITECTURES, FRAMEWORKS, AND MODELS FOR EDGE-AI IN HEALTHCARE

1.4.1 Architecture of edge-AI (Xu et al. 2020)

Edge-AI enables visual, location, and analytical solutions for various industries like healthcare, manufacturing, energy, etc. These solutions are deployed on edge devices which help to reduce latency, allowing offline and online execution, and providing strong results and security. Edge-AI leverages the fact that training and deployment processes for a machine-learning (ML) model are completely decoupled. It allows a trained ML model to be embedded in devices with limited memory and computational resources – enabling their execution in an offline fashion. The architecture of edge-AI is shown in Figure 1.1.

Edge-AI is an architecture which is a distributed on the cloud.

1) Cloud layer. The cloud layer is one of the most important layers as it stores all the edge-AI data which may be required presently or in the future. The cloud helps us to access data remotely and from anywhere. Edge-AI is based upon the principles of AI, machine learning, Internet of Things, and cloud computing. I n healthcare, we use these principles to achieve precise results.

2) Edge layer. This layer comprises of the devices, sensors, Local Area Networks/Wide Area Networks (LANs/WANs), etc. In this layer, the data are collected and stored for further processing. They have the functionality of internet bandwidth, storing the memory, processing ability, and computing resources to collect, process, store, and analyse data with very little help from other parts of the network.

3) Device layer. This is one of the most important layers of any edge-AI network. We need to collect various components that will serve the

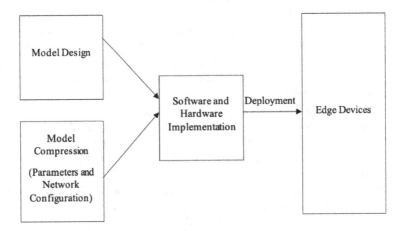

FIGURE 1.1 Architecture for edge-AI.

unique needs of a network for a given problem. However, a network happens to comprise many devices, like cloud service, servers, sensors, etc. Some examples are medical devices, ambient devices, interactive devices, etc.

1.4.2 EDGE-AI BENEFITS

1) Low latency. Running AI models on the cloud means a round-trip latency of at least a few milliseconds, which can potentially go up to a few seconds, depending on network connectivity.
2) Privacy. Processing data locally, on the device itself, implies that we do not need to send it back to the cloud for processing. This becomes increasingly relevant as smart devices (e.g., cameras, speakers) start being deployed in shops, hospitals, offices, factories, etc., coupled with growing user distrust pertaining to how enterprises are storing and processing their personal data, including images, audio, video, location, and shopping history.
3) Reduced costs. Real-time processing at the edge not only enables low latency and achieves privacy protection, but it also acts as a "filter", ensuring that only relevant data gets transmitted to the cloud for further processing, saving bandwidth. Fewer data transferred to the cloud also implies less storage and processing costs on the cloud.

1.4.3 FRAMEWORKS FOR EDGE-AI

While ML models have traditionally been embedded in cameras, mobiles, drones, self-driving cars, etc., the growing adoption of edge-AI has led to the development of specialised devices capable of performing AI inferencing efficiently. The framework for edge-AI is represented in Figure 1.2.

1) Model design and model compression. The goal is to reduce the model's inference time on the device. Deep neural networks (DNNs) often require storage of and access to many parameters that are used to describe the architecture of the edge model. Edge devices have limitations not only in terms of computational resources, but also memory. There are mainly two ways to perform neural network (NN) compression: lowering precision or fewer weights (pruning).
2) Software and hardware implementation. This is further forwarded to the software and hardware phase. Based upon the model design and parameter, we design software/hardware which is further forwarded for deployment.
3) Deployment of edge device. Based upon information and deployment, the hardware and software are deployed in devices, which are further used in various industries.

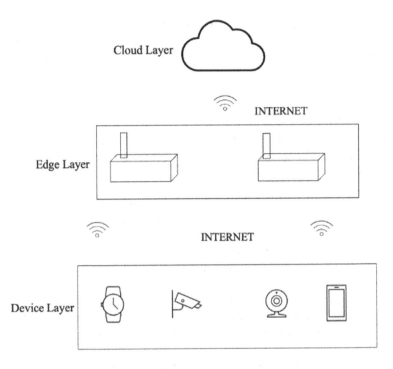

FIGURE 1.2 Framework for edge-AI.

1.4.4 MODEL FOR EDGE-AI

To address these challenges, we present the Model Audit Toward Endorsement framework (as shown in Figure 1.3). It provides extensible engines, platform-independent libraries, and validation tools capable of guaranteeing the algorithm functionality across different platforms.

Model normalisation includes adapting a chosen model to provide a standard interface toward the integration layer tools. Model Audit Toward Endorsement framework can be accessed through the interface and assessment of these models, which are accessed using their original framework, usually working on a laptop/PC or on cloud services. It can also work on their microprocessor built using components for custom processing libraries. This evaluation of the process may lead to retraining of these models. It may also provide recommendations in terms of these important extensions and optimisations on the microprocessor. For example, rehabilitation can be improved upon by evaluating the model or the collected data. The models which are generally available are trained on these datasets which may require adjustment for these special parameters in an application. As discussed, model modification for better speed of execution of these models on embedded devices can be another reason for model rehabilitation.

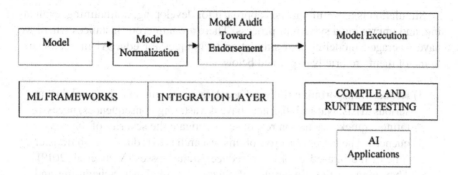

FIGURE 1.3 Model for edge-AI.

1.5 MODELING AND SIMULATION TECHNIQUES FOR EDGE-AI IN HEALTHCARE

Our healthcare institutions are in economic turmoil and are facing numerous challenges. They are compelled to come up with new innovative methods to improve their operations and make constructive use of their limited resources. The need of the hour is to increase service quality and cut costs, so we need viable alternatives to old healthcare systems. The need for intelligent decision-making techniques is increasing. Researchers are working hard to solve complex systems with the help of AI. They know that even a single miscalculation can result in the loss of lives. Modeling and simulation techniques have been extensively examined to address various decision-making problems in the healthcare sector.

Nowadays, we are focusing on using technology to make smart cities. Smart healthcare and healthcare facility are among the major components of smart cities. Healthcare thrives on utilising its resources efficiently. The most expensive resource in this area is human capital. If we can put this resource to good use, we can take a step toward a fully automated smart healthcare system. Healthcare is bombarded with data every single second of the day; to manage such a huge amount of data, we need reliable and safe sources. To make this possible, we need to use cloud and edge computing. Distributed cloud-fog-based healthcare systems are not only helping us to manage enormous amounts of data but also to keep them secure. Cloud computing has significantly reduced the cost of establishing a networked healthcare system, while efficiently maximising the usage of cloud resources provided. The use of cloud computing stems from the requirement for convenient computational power, storage, and networking resources with high operational and maintenance expenses. Cloud computing can readily be coupled with IoT and thus this has further pushed it forward. Edge-AI is playing a key role in disease diagnosis, cure prognosis, social media analytics for a specific condition, and medical imaging. Smart devices with sensors, such as smartphones or smart watches, and gateway devices, such as microcontrollers, can both be utilised as edge nodes.

Simulation is a useful analysis approach for developing, maintaining, evaluating, and improving a system or process. There are numerous instances where we have leveraged modeling and simulation techniques for edge-AI in healthcare. Some of them are briefly explained below.

1) Reduce transportation time and accelerate assignment to hospital during serious crisis. Natural disasters have devastating consequences, necessitating a quick evacuation response to mitigate the severity of the consequences. The major objective of this research is to reduce overall transfer time of the injured in order to reduce human losses (Vyas et al. 2019). They manage the "Integrated Problem of Ambulance Scheduling and Resource Assignment", also known as IPASRA, in case of a disaster. They present a mathematical model to succeed by a branch and cut algorithm under the CPLEX solver, with a resolution that performs better than the meta-heuristic method and is based on grounding of a hybrid algorithm based on tabu search and "Greedy Randomised Adaptive Search Procedure", also known as GRASP. The problem is divided into two subparts: the first is concerned with treating and scheduling the problem statement, wheras the second one focuses on resource assignment for the problem. Tabu search works on the principle of penalising movements that transport the solution to previously searched areas. GRASP is a meta-heuristic method which is often used to solve combinatorial optimisation issues. It can generate optimal solutions within seconds, and this speaks for its capability and reliability.

2) Carbon footprints in emergency departments. By considering shortening the standby time and length of stay as limits to leveling up patient satisfaction, the OptQuest optimisation approach has been used to reduce greenhouse gases and carbon footprint in patient flow to the emergency department. Evaluation and optimisation of the Carbon Foot Prints (CFP) in the patient flow is the main motivation for this research, so medical supplies and the time spent using medical practices at every care unit are considered during the treatment process. Discrete-event simulation (DES) is used to make decisions about patient flow in the examined hospital, and the Arena14.0 package is used to simulate the system.

3) Distinct event representation in healthcare system. This is one the most powerful and versatile tool for examining a variety of challenges in healthcare systems, involving dimensioning of capacity, flow management of patients, allocation of staff, and scheduling of activities. However, in practice, it is facing failure due to the features and environment of implementation. The focus of it in healthcare is on healthcare features that are sources of uncertainty.

4) A robust operating theater scheduling algorithm. In order to assist operating room administrators in creating reliable schedules, this study developed a robust bi-objective algorithm that takes into consideration the uncertainty of surgery and recovery times. It is susceptible to data inconsistency to a small extent. It allows minimisation of two goals

simultaneously. The first goal is to reduce the importance of the initial scenario's criterion. The second goal is to minimise the difference between the value of the criterion in all disrupted situations and the value in the starting scenario. The purpose of this evaluation function is to come up with a good solution that isn't too sensitive to data uncertainty.

These new developments have enormous potential for improving clinical workflows, lowering costs, and improving patient care. As healthcare moves into the data-driven decade, there is a growing demand for data storage and computing on the device, not to mention other benefits, such as speed and privacy, which allow physicians to make faster, more educated judgments while remaining secure. Many medical technology businesses recognise that edge-AI is the next wave of AI in healthcare. Edge computing extends data processing, analytics, and storage closer to the end source.

1.6 EDGE-AI, MACHINE LEARNING, AND DEEP LEARNING APPROACHES FOR HEALTHCARE

Machine learning (ML) can be defined as the study of algorithms which can improve autonomous training and use of data. It comes under the aegis of AI. ML and deep learning (DL) are preferred due to their superior performance and use in predictions to diagnose various diseases. ML/DL techniques have shown tremendous results as they require less input and less time to process data, making them incredibly fast. It is expected that soon ML/DL are going to help doctors and nurses during major surgery and scanning (Plastiras et al. 2018). Some of the research even shows that ML models have surpassed human physicians on average. ML can give us predictive outcomes that are highly accurate and can even attain human-focused intelligence (Vyas et al. 2019). We can now think of providing healthcare services in remote rural areas because of ML. A huge amount of clinical data was ignored in the past, because of the complexity and size of these data, and because there was no way for storing such data. Hence, these data were undervalued and not used. ML provides much-needed options to tackle this problem of storage and analysis. Some of the applications of machine-learning techniques in healthcare are as follows:

1. Classification.
2. Clustering.
3. Prediction.
4. Anomaly detection.
5. Recommendation.
6. Automation.
7. Ranking.

To save time (and lives, in healthcare) we need smart devices. The application of IoT to the healthcare industry is rapidly increasing. The IoT helps connect with the patients proactively. Many researchers are in the process of making devices that involve both IoT and machine learning to obtain accurate results rapidly. One of the main reasons for using machine learning in the healthcare industry is to eliminate the human element, resulting in a decrease in the probability of human error. ML will automate all the tasks in a hectic routine process which would be expected to increase human error. Some of the examples where ML has been adopted in the healthcare industry are as follows:

- Clinical decision-support systems.
- Personalised medicine.
- Data collection.
- Behavior adjustments.
- Major and repetitive surgery.
- Clinical research.
- Drug discovery.

To abide by privacy regulations and avoid making flawed decisions when using ML, we need to follow some ethics. Some of them are listed below:

- Privacy and data security.
- Transparency and informed consent.
- Representation and inclusiveness.
- Addressing autonomy issues.

Machine learning and deep learning are driving major transformations in the healthcare industry. Time is not far away when ML is going to replace every human task in the healthcare industry.

REFERENCES

Fasciano, C., & Vitulano, F. (2020). Artificial intelligence on edge computing: A healthcare scenario in ambient assisted living. *Proceedings of the Artificial Intelligence for Ambient Assisted Living* (AI* AAL. it 2019).

Islam, M., Karim, R., & Vyas, S. (2022). Challenges of robotics: A quest for an integrated action. In V. Skala, T. P. Singh, T. Choudhury, R. Tomar, & B. Abul (Eds.), *Machine Intelligence and Data Science Applications* (pp. 227–238). Singapore: Springer.

Mazzanti, M., Shirka, E., Gjergo, H., & Hasimi, E. (2018). Imaging, health record, and artificial intelligence: Hype or hope?. *Current Cardiology Reports*, 20(6), 1–9.

Plastiras, G., Terzi, M., Kyrkou, C., & Theocharides, T. (2018, July). Edge intelligence: Challenges and opportunities of near-sensor machine learning applications. In *2018 IEEE 29th International Conference on Application-Specific Systems, Architectures and Processors (ASAP)* (pp. 1–7). IEEE.

Slomka, P. J., Dey, D., Sitek, A., Motwani, M., Berman, D. S., & Germano, G. (2017). Cardiac imaging: Working towards fully automated machine analysis & interpretation. *Expert Review of Medical Devices*, 14(3), 197–212.

Vyas, S. (2023). Extended Reality and Edge AI for Healthcare 4.0: Systematic Study. In *Extended Reality for Healthcare Systems* (pp. 229–240). Academic Press.

Vyas, S., Gupta, M., & Yadav, R. (2019, February). Converging blockchain and machine learning for healthcare. In *2019 Amity International Conference on Artificial Intelligence (AICAI)* (pp. 709–711). IEEE.

Wan, S., Gu, Z., & Ni, Q. (2020). Cognitive computing and wireless communications on the edge for healthcare service robots. *Computer Communications*, 149, 99–106.

Xu, D., Li, T., Li, Y., Su, X., Tarkoma, S., Jiang, T., ... Hui, P. (2020). Edge intelligence: Architectures, challenges, and applications. arXiv preprint arXiv:2003.12172.

2 Edge-AI tools and techniques for healthcare

Rahul Nijhawan, Sunpreet Bhatia

CONTENTS

2.1 INTRODUCTION

Smart health monitoring frameworks provide services in many fields, such as hospitals, workplaces, and residences, to drastically reduce the cost of doctor visits while also improving overall patient care quality. Innovative healthcare services enable doctors to forecast, detect, diagnose, and treat diseases through intelligent remote handling and response to medical requests, reducing hospitalisation and supporting patients. Artificial intelligence (AI) can be used to prevent and control the spread of dangerous illnesses like as Ebola, avian influenza, and, most recently, the COVID-19 epidemic. Given the challenges, the development of effective, innovative healthcare services will surely promote the health of our society (Akmandor & Jha 2017). Intelligent healthcare systems integrate a variety of smart devices to meet the demands of many consumers. As a result, a vast volume of medical records created by smart devices must be accurately analysed. For this to happen, there needs to be effective communication between the intelligent healthcare data centers, so as to provide real-time responses to health

DOI: 10.1201/9781003244592-2

emergencies as quickly as possible. High response times in data centers are key hazards in smart health systems that might result in irreparable damage. In light of these facts, Internet of Things (IoT) and artificial intelligence (AI) are the most useful solutions to these problems. Adopting a hybrid of these two technologies, in particular, can help address a variety of problems in the field of smart healthcare (Gaba & Raw 2020; He et al. 2014; Kruse et al. 2016). With the Internet of Things, it is possible to generate and exchange data across a network device. In terms of medical facility improvement, this means that a traditional hospital can be transformed into an innovative hospital (Azimi et al. 2017). Instead of transmitting all data to cloud data centers, edge technology allows smart healthcare systems to execute procedures and store data closer to end users. As a result, smart healthcare systems would simply need to transfer raw data to cloud data centers located far away (Azimi et al. 2017; Bierzynski et al. 2017). Furthermore, by imitating human intellect in data processing by using intricate algorithms, AI can smooth the process of calculating conclusions without the direct involvement of humans (Chiang & Zhang 2016). Based on patient data, AI oversees looking into the associations between illness treatment, prevention, and detection measures. Because of the resource limits at the edge, new and lightweight approaches are required to execute them there (Abdellatif et al. 2019)

2.2   EDGE COMPUTING

Edge computing falls under a system that puts business use closer to IoT devices and local edge servers. At its inception, this closeness to data can provide significant business benefits, such as faster insights and shorter response times. Connected devices generate a vast quota of untapped data. With edge computing, you can maximise their potential by discovering new business options to serve our consumers with services that are quicker, more consistent, and more dependable (Zhang et al. 2019; Hao et al. 2019) It was the IoT devices that connected to the internet in an increasingly exponential way that led to edge computing. Additionally, many IoT devices generate a great deal of data when they are in use. Consider a webcam that transmits live video from a remote location or a device that monitors manufacturing equipment on a factory floor. Edge computing is a critical component for achieving speedier connectivity. Cloud services will be brought closer to edge devices, reduce latency, and provide users with new applications and services. It will disseminate AI capabilities and move them away from the cloud. It will also provide the basis for future hybrid computing, in which processing choices may be made in real-time locally, on the cloud, or on the device, depending on latency, power, and overall storage and performance needs (Uddin 2019; Hossain et al. 2017).

Edge architecture consists of the *cloud*, which stores container-based workloads such as apps and machine-learning models. Apps that manage and manage multiple edge nodes are also stored and run in these clouds. These cloud workloads interact with edge workloads, including on-premises and device workloads. The cloud also serves as the source and destination for all the data needed by other nodes. *Edge devices* are devices with built-in computing capabilities. Exciting tasks can be performed by edge devices, such as manufacturing machines, ATMs, smart cameras, and automobiles. Edge devices often have limited computing resources and are often motivated by economics. Edge devices can be more powerful but, for now, they are exceptions, rather than rules.

Edge node is a general term for edge devices, edge servers, or gateways that can perform edge computing. *Edge cluster* is an IT computer installed in remote operation facilities, such as factories, hotels, and banks. Edge clusters/servers are often built in the form of industrial PCs or rack computers. *Edge gateway* is a cluster that not only hosts business application workloads and shared services but also provides network services, such as protocol translation and wireless connectivity.

2.3   UNDERSTANDING EDGE-AI

The processing of artificial intelligence algorithms on the edge, that is, on the devices of users, is referred to as edge-AI. Its concept is founded on the same premise as edge computing: data are stored, processed, and managed directly at IoT endpoints. Because the data are processed locally for machine learning, the device does not need to be connected to edge-AI. The cloud model's communication costs are considerably reduced as a result of this. In other words, it moves data and processes them to the user's nearest point of dealings, whether it's a computer, an IoT device, or an edge server (Gaba & Raw 2020; He et al. 2014; Kruse et al. 2016). An example of this technology is The Google Homepod, Alexa, and Apple Homepod speakers. They use machine learning to learn words and phrases, which they then save locally on the device. When a user speaks with an AI assistant, such as Siri or Google, the audio recording is transferred to an edge network, where it is transformed to text, using AI algorithms, and returned to the user. Edge-AI addresses the privacy concerns associated with transmitting and storing massive amounts of data on the cloud platform and the bandwidth and latency limitations that limit data transmission capability. Many industries rely on edge technology; for example, driverless cars will reduce power usage by improving battery durability. It will also work with robots and surveillance systems (Azimi et al. 2017; Bierzynski et al. 2017). Artificial intelligence is transforming and improving a variety of essential processes in healthcare, and the potential is even more diversified and astounding. Chatbots and computer-aided detection (CAD) for diagnosis and analysis can assist physicians in better understanding illnesses and managing patients' health. Healthcare systems will be able to execute AI algorithms locally on end-user devices where data are generated, but traditional healthcare systems will not be able to do so.. This integration allows data to be processed on edge devices in a matter of milliseconds, resulting in real-time outcomes. Because healthcare services are so closely linked to human health, providing services and outcomes is important in emergency situations (Chiang & Zhang 2016). The inference component of the AI workflow has lately been moved to edge devices, according to researchers.

So, let's see how AI can contribute to the advancement of healthcare in the coming years. Incomplete medical records and ineffective sequencing frequently cause human errors. Advanced machine-learning algorithms can arrive at the proper diagnosis when papers are loaded into a computer, decreasing mistakes and enhancing the efficiency of medical institutions. Drug production in the conventional sense can be prohibitively expensive and time consuming. This is a significant impediment, particularly when a pandemic threatens the entire world and immediate action is required. Clinical trials typically cost $2.6 billion, with just 10% of medicines making it to market. Modern AI is beneficial in applications where there's a lot of data and repetitive actions, making the drug industry a prime candidate for AI. Many years of test data and repeated tests have been accumulated and have become a difficult part of drug discovery. In a computer simulation, AI can perform the same experiments that a scientist could, running a lot of tests in a short amount of time. These discoveries ensured technology's sustained and expanding importance in medicine, resulting in speedier drug manufacture at a fraction of the cost. Daily, congested healthcare facilities, rising numbers of reports, and insurance difficulties create a chaotic environment. Under such circumstances, AI has emerged as a savior, skimming through data quickly, generating reports, and allowing patients to know precisely where to go and who to call. AI is at the heart of some of the most complicated digital systems, allowing for connection and dialogue, as well as precise time updates, report availability, appointment scheduling, and more. The protection of sensitive patient data is critical in healthcare. They're constantly upgrading AI algorithms to help encrypt personal information, clinical reports, diagnostic findings, and more, keeping it safe from hackers and securely storing it in the cloud for patients and professionals to access from anywhere. Complex and life-saving procedures require a great degree of focus, precision, and expertise. The number of successful treatments conducted using AI-enabled robots is increasing. The robots include cameras, mechanical arms, and surgical equipment. They may be made to reach any area of the body and offer a crisp, magnified picture of the surgical site that is significantly superior to human vision. These treatments are less painful, require less time, and help patients recover more quickly. Connecting devices can save lives by utilising real-time monitoring of events such as heart attacks and asthma episodes. IoT networks are used by remote monitoring devices to connect and track activities in the human body. Data can be retrieved through wearable devices or mobile applications, and AI can make quick choices.

AI enables healthcare practitioners to go through simulations based on an extensive database of scenarios, assisting trainees in making judgments and learning from prior replies to achieve training requirements. Pattern recognition is used to determine a patient's risk of developing a specific disease by delivering significant insights, while machine learning in healthcare aids fast decision-making and actions. Insurance firms can use connected devices to collect health data for underwriting, health claims, and risk management. Insurance companies and customers are better able to communicate, and bogus claims are reduced.

As a result of intelligent medical devices, real-time alerts, tracking, and monitoring are possible, allowing hands-on treatment, greater accuracy, faster doctor intervention, and better overall health outcomes. Sensors can be used to track wheelchairs, scales, nebulisers, pumps, and monitoring devices, making it easier for personnel to keep track of them.

Despite such significant improvements, AI usage in healthcare is still in its early stages. Continuous research adds additional capabilities to the technology, resulting in more critical advances in the coming years across a wide range of industries. Healthcare is undergoing one of the most rapid digital transformations of all time, so AI and machine learning have a lot to offer. These facilities can make the world a safer and better place for everyone by improving customer service, creating new digital lines of business, and meeting research targets faster.

2.4 SCOPE OF EDGE-AI IN HEALTHCARE

The modern healthcare industry is being shaped by edge computing technology. As previously stated, there are various advantages to implementing edge-AI. It can be highly beneficial for patients, healthcare practitioners, and workers in the healthcare industry.

- *Autonomous monitoring of hospital rooms.* The potential to automate tasks is one of AI's most fascinating selling points in general. Artificial intelligence programs may collect data from various sensors and analyse them to choose the best course of action. This is where edge AI comes in. It allows autonomous monitoring of hospital rooms and patients by combining computer vision and data from various sensors. Consider the case of fall detection. Many wearables now include the capacity to detect if a person falls suddenly by utilizing specific technology. The edge-AI of these devices can be trained to detect falls in real time and even notify caregivers. In most circumstances, this can save a person's life. The fall detection feature on Apple Watch is an example of this.
- *New applications in radiology.* DICOM (Digital Imaging and Communications) images in radiology are pretty huge. As a result, sending these photos to the cloud or a central server for processing and receiving machine-learning inferences can be quite costly and time consuming. On the other hand, edge-AI allows the analysis to take place locally, resulting in a considerably faster diagnosis.
- *Cardiovascular abnormalities detection.* The total automation of cardiovascular abnormalities in routine imaging tests, such as chest X-rays, should mean faster decision-making and fewer diagnostic errors. The application of artificial intelligence to the notion of imaging data can also aid in detecting significant issues such as muscle thickening, monitoring changes in total blood flow in the heart, and so on. Detection of fractures and other musculoskeletal injuries, using artificial intelligence to detect hairline fractures, soft tissue injuries, and dislocations, can help surgeons feel more confident about their treatment options.
- *Rural medicine.* Providing high-quality healthcare in rural regions has always been difficult. Despite advances in telemedicine and more

publicly available health information, medical practitioners have struggled to offer timely, high-quality care to patients who live far from hospitals and have restricted internet connection. Traditional healthcare databases have significant challenges in this area, owing to connection limitations, but combining IoT medical devices and edge computing apps makes such problems easier to overcome. Overall, using AI approaches to analyse medical data at the network's edge can help to provide better healthcare services with faster reaction times, more privacy, higher accuracy, greater dependability, and increased bandwidth use. By reducing the amount of data sent to cloud servers, it can also reduce the load on the network.

2.5 EDGE-AI AND THE INTERNET OF THINGS (IOT)

Edge-AI works with other digital technologies such as 5G and the Internet of Things. IoT may create data for edge-AI systems to exploit, and 5G technology is required for the future progress of both edge-AI and IoT. IoT is a network of smart gadgets that are linked together via the internet. These devices produce data, which can be sent to the edge-AI device, which can also be used as a temporary storage unit for the data until they are synced with the cloud. The data-processing method offers additional flexibility. To say that contemporary medicine is struggling is an understatement. Every day, "without remorse", progress is made, altering all known medical techniques (Hossain et al. 2019). Healthcare advances in the world are based on the latest discoveries of the world's brightest minds, as well as on the potential of self-learning, autonomous technology solutions. However, with such rapid progress comes the unavoidable requirement to keep up. The incredible thing is that modern technologies are integrated into all medical sectors, from diagnostics to medicines, pediatrics, and tricky surgery. With multiple technologies, artificial intelligence, and machine learning, what specific technology concepts or combinations of concepts can provide the monitoring and management capabilities needed for such a fast-growing global niche? The answer lies in the Internet of Things (IoT). Despite its youth, the term is already deeply intertwined with healthcare. It is called the "medical internet". Regular hospitals can be transformed into smart hospitals by way of improving medical facilities (Ahmed et al. 2017). A smart hospital a sophisticated facility where everything is recorded and managed at the same time, and all data are gathered in a centralised database. Such technical traits open up a multitude of chances for modern hospitals to improve their comfort, efficiency, and even cost-cutting choices. The benefits of IoT applications in healthcare aren't limited to that. Technology has several uses in medicine.

2.6 EDGE-IOT SMART HEALTHCARE ARCHITECTURE

Diagnostic, sensitive, and preventative healthcare systems may be implemented using edge-based IoT frameworks, which utilise several types of smart sensors. To offer real-time patient data, health experts have been researching methods for remote patient monitoring and transmission of health reports for many years (Miraz et al. 2015; Pazienza et al. 2019). Basic computer-based monitoring devices for patients, such as ECG and heartbeat sensors, were recommended by (Liu et al. 2019) To further analyse these physiological data, sophisticated ECG sensors are used (Verma et al. 2017). Thanks to recent developments in IoT technology, intelligent solutions based on software platforms and system designs may now be developed and deployed with ease. Static or dynamic patient monitoring is possible. The patient would be tracked in an outside environment via dynamic patient monitoring (Zhang et al. 2019). A generic edge/fog computing-based method employs a multi-level architectural design to achieve its goals. Each of the three basic levels includes the following elements:

- Data is gathered via IoT body sensors at the edge node level. Devices, such as smart watches, smartphones, and tablets, perform low-level processing.
- This level includes fog nodes, which collect data from IoT field sensors and edge devices.
- Servers and PCs are used for storage and local processing. where all the information is captured and stored on the cloud. In this area, high-level processing occurs.

Edge architecture does not have to be always contained in the same architecture. Fog nodes can be used in non-dynamic systems to gather data directly from sensors, with the help of cloud service providers. When a fog level cannot be imposed, edge devices communicate directly with cloud providers (Yang et al. 2016; Hartmann et al. 2022). Processing of data is relocated closer to the network edge using edge and fog-based solutions, resulting in quicker reaction times and improved energy efficiency. Instead of sending data to the cloud on a constant basis for computational operations, which costs energy, data may be processed locally on devices and servers. Because of the reduced latency offered by edge and fog technologies, emergency medical aid may be reached promptly in cases involving health monitoring. Because of the large volumes of data transferred to cloud services, privacy and security are still major concerns, particularly when a patient's medical information is at risk (Hao et al. 2019; Chen et al. 2018). Instead of concentrating critical information in one part of the network, spreading it throughout a fog might allow greater privacy. As outlined below, there are specifics on how a combination of edge- and fog-based technologies might help meet future medical device needs: *low cost, low latency, high security, high privacy, low cost, low latency.*

2.7 BIG DATA AND BLOCKCHAIN IN IOT-BASED HEALTHCARE FRAMEWORKS

Every second, a massive quantity of data is created, especially in an IoT network. Analysing such a vast volume of data necessitates high-performance processing skills. To achieve this, a variety of big data analytics approaches have been proposed. Machine-learning and deep-learning approaches work along with IoT to improve large data processing capabilities, and sophisticated deep-learning models are particularly useful for managing such data (Verma et al. 2017; Ahmed et al. 2017). Using big data analytics, healthcare can better detect illnesses early, gain insights into disease processes, assess the quality of medical and healthcare facilities, and improve treatment methods. Using data mining techniques on Electronic Health Records (EHRs), online, and social media data, hospitals may find the most practical recommendations, identify association rules in EHRs, and reveal disease monitoring and health-related trends. Blood pressure, glucose, pulse, and other vital signs can all be monitored with new IoT smart sensors. Patients are able to stay out of hospitals with the aid of big health data analytics, which offer diagnostics and enhanced healthcare services at home. Big data has also benefited IoT healthcare systems in cutting total treatment costs by reducing manpower and travel requirements. It has also enabled healthcare practitioners to identify those who are at high risk and give them specialised treatment. It has also reduced mistakes caused by human factors, resulting in increased trust in artificial intelligence. To address the problems associated with large data, IoT health systems can use blockchain to protect data privacy and the interests of patients (Hossain et al. 2019; Amin et al. 2019). Blockchain is primarily used in healthcare to regulate access to and storage of confidential medical data.

A blockchain is a continuously increasing collection of encrypted and connected data called blocks. Blocks are linked to each other by encryption. In short, blockchain is a simple yet great way to move data from point A to point B in a fully automated and secure way. At the start of the process, a block is created on one side of the transaction. This block has been validated by thousands of computers around the world. The validated block is added to the chain maintained throughout the Internet, making it a record that is not only unique, but also has a unique history (Xie et al. 2019) Blockchain is a peer-to-peer network that reduces the cost of setting up and maintaining centralised clouds, data centers, and network devices by distributing computing and storage requirements across all network devices (Makhdoom et al. 2019). The blockchain contains all medical records of the patient. This vast amount of data is stored in a data lake that can contain a variety of health data. Intelligent edge-based algorithms, such as deep learning, access data lakes and enable a wide range of data searches. In addition, these data are encrypted and validated. When the data are stored, a pointer is created on the blockchain with the patient's unique ID (Hossain, & Muhammad 2017). Patients will be notified when new data related to the patient are uploaded. Patients can securely upload validated health data to the data lake using edge devices, such as smartphones and body sensors.

2.8   EDGE INTELLIGENCE IN IOT HEALTHCARE FRAMEWORKS

The goal of edge computing is to unite various types of edge devices and servers that can work together to achieve effective processing of locally produced data (Mutlag et al. 2019). The Internet of Everything (IoE) is already a reality thanks to advances in IoT devices. For processing so much data, edge intelligence is more important than ever because cloud data centers are located all over the world. With edge computing, AI techniques can be implemented on a wide range of new platforms. When the environment is managed by these agents, it is automatically monitored and controlled, and users receive help (Hossain et al. 2019). Patients can get therapy, illness prevention and detection, and medical assistance via intelligent edge platforms. A smart healthcare framework based on fog-based data analytics was also presented in recent research (Xie et al. 2019). Real-time data gathering, processing, and transmission architecture for healthcare is challenging. This system sheds light on how fog nodes and servers are used in a Healthcare 4.0 context. The suggested edge computing system is made wiser by cognitive intelligence, which allows for better resource utilisation. As a result, edge intelligence is now a part of cutting-edge IoT healthcare designs aimed at increasing intelligence and dependability.

2.9　MACHINE LEARNING AND IOT IN HEALTHCARE FRAMEWORKS

Machine Learning (ML) has been used by a variety of researchers all around the world for a variety of applications and areas. Machine learning has recently attracted the interest of researchers in the healthcare IoT. ML is a phenomenon in the field of artificial intelligence. ML allows a machine to automatically analyse and interpret a set of inputs as an experience without the need for any further assistance (Amin et al. 2019; Qadri et al. 2020). In recent years, machine-learning algorithms have become popular in healthcare applications. To improve medical applications, some clinical decision-support systems use machine-learning techniques to create advanced learning models. These models are used in many cancer classification applications to enable accurate cancer type detection. These algorithms analyse data collected from sensor devices and other data sources and identify patient behavioral tendencies and health problems (Tuli et al. 2020). Machine learning is gaining in popularity by using IoT-based smart sensors to diagnose and predict cardiac arrest in patients with heart disease. For patients with heart disease, ECG data are continuously monitored, noise is filtered out, and then the data are sent to a machine-learning algorithm for feature extraction (Qadri et al. 2020). Using edge and cloud computing architectures, ML has been used to detect patient falls. Researchers in the AI field use ML to track patient sleep patterns. A multimodal dataset consisting of electrocariogram (EEG), elektrokardigram (EKG), or electroocoulogram (EOG) is used to analyse sleep patterns. With advances in prostheses, ML is currently being utilised for post-accident and injury assistance. It is also used to recognize and classify emotions, enabling robots to recognize human emotions (Hossain & Muhammad 2016). This allows people to control the robot with their own mind without doing anything. As a result, machine learning-based healthcare solutions are being deployed to help patients with severe disabilities lead a normal life.

2.10   EMERGING EDGE TECHNOLOGY IN SMART HEALTHCARE

Most of the healthcare organisations have turned to cloud computing to provide cost-effective solutions for processing and storing of the vast volumes of data collected by various biosensors. As a result, cloud-based healthcare systems cannot meet emergency and real-time medical needs. Furthermore, the massive volumes of data generated by sensors must be transmitted to the cloud regularly to be analysed and stored, resulting in significant energy consumption and expense.

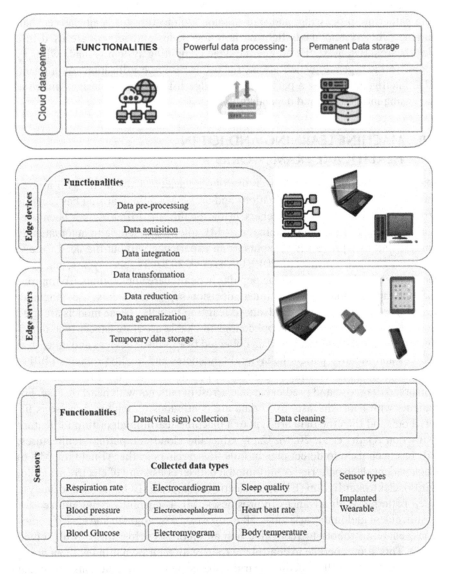

FIGURE 2.1   Edge-assisted smart healthcare functionality flow.

Furthermore, most patients demand low-cost mobile settings, which cloud-based solutions do not offer (Abdellatif et al. 2019; Tuli et al. 2020). Edge computing acts as a layer between end-user devices and cloud data centers. It is an intelligent gateway that serves as a channel between gadgets and data servers (Abdellatif et al. 2019).

2.11 EDGE-ASSISTED SMART HEALTHCARE FUNCTIONALITY FLOW

Figure 2.1 represents edge-assisted smart healthcare functionality flow. Edge processing also improves security, privacy, mobility, dispersion, location awareness, and online diagnostics and analytics, all of which minimise clinic and hospital visits (Vyas et al. 2022; Vyas & Gupta 2022). As a result, edge technology helps to establish smart healthcare services by allowing for faster, more thorough, and more accessible treatments. Sensors, edge devices, edge servers, and cloud data center layers are the four levels that make up edge computing architecture in smart healthcare applications (Vyas 2023; Vyas & Bhargava 2021).

The sensor layer contains a variety of sensors that capture patients' vital signs and data. (Azar et al. 2019; Al-Rakhami et al. 2020). We've included some of the types of data that sensors may collect for a smart healthcare system. The sensor and edge device layers interact via a short-range, low-power wireless communication technology like ZigBee, Bluetooth, or Wi-Fi. The edge device layer includes users' gadgets such as smartphones, tablets, and smartwatches that can perform some functions and store data in the short term. Bluetooth, Wi-Fi, or the internet are used to transport data from the devices to the edge servers' layer. The edge servers' layer is made up of tiny data centers that can handle and store more data. The sole difference between the devices and the servers is that the server layer has more storage capacity than the device layer. Cloud data centers at this tier have more powerful Central Processing Units (CPUs) and can store massive volumes of data (Hosseini et al. 2020).

2.12 CONCLUSION

This chapter explains how edge technology, in conjunction with AI approaches, might improve smart healthcare systems. The combination of AI and edge technologies makes smart healthcare systems smarter and provides several benefits. We present here a revolutionary smart healthcare framework that employs several AI approaches in parallel mode, using edge technology. The suggested approach moves processes from sensors to cloud servers. As a result of using a lightweight AI approach to sensors, the parameters latency, complexity, and network load are all reduced. There are security and privacy considerations for all aspects of smart healthcare, including sensitive medical data and network connections, as well as user access. Simple models for data collection, pre-processing, transmission, and analysis are being replaced by complex and intelligent systems capable of heavy processing and distant data analytics. Due to the complexity of these models, deep learning (DL) techniques must be applied with care to improve computing power without increasing resource usage. Due to the massive amount of data generated by real-time smart sensors, such models may only be deployed on the cloud layer at times. According to researchers, such techniques have several limitations, such as data availability, quality problems, and real-time processing in an environment where disease prevention and early detection of symptoms are the most important considerations. Healthcare systems employ personal and private information. Therefore, data security and storage are a key problem for these systems as well. Several researchers have also advocated the use of edge and fog nodes in distributed DL models, allowing them to minimise training and processing times. The edge nodes were tasked with local decision-making, whereas the cloud layer was tasked with model training. Edge nodes gained relevance due to the GPU devices being integrated at the edge level. They were also used to improve the model's computational capacity and data processing capabilities at a fog level by using Graphic Processing Unit (GPU)-powered nodes.

REFERENCES

Abdellatif, A. A., Mohamed, A., Chiasserini, C. F., Tlili, M., & Erbad, A. (2019). Edge computing for smart health: Context-aware approaches, opportunities, and challenges. *IEEE Network*, 33(3), 196–203.

Ahmed, E., Yaqoob, I., Hashem, I. A. T., Khan, I., Ahmed, A. I. A., Imran, M., & Vasilakos, A. V. (2017). The role of big data analytics in Internet of things. *Computer Networks*, 129, 459–471.

Akmandor, A. O., & Jha, N. K. (2017). Smart health care: An edge-side computing perspective. *IEEE Consumer Electronics Magazine*, 7(1), 29–37.

Al-Rakhami, M., Gumaei, A., Alsahli, M., Hassan, M. M., Alamri, A., Guerrieri, A., & Fortino, G. (2020). A lightweight and cost-effective edge intelligence architecture based on containerization technology. *World Wide Web*, 23(2), 1341–1360.

Amin, S. U., Alsulaiman, M., Muhammad, G., Mekhtiche, M. A., & Hossain, M. S. (2019). Deep learning for EEG motor imagery classification based on multi-layer CNNs feature fusion. *Future Generation Computer Systems*, 101, 542–554.

Amin, S. U., Hossain, M. S., Muhammad, G., Alhussein, M., & Rahman, M. A. (2019). Cognitive smart healthcare for pathology detection and monitoring. *IEEE Access*, 7, 10745–10753.

Azar, J., Makhoul, A., Barhamgi, M., & Couturier, R. (2019). An energy efficient IoT data compression approach for edge machine learning. *Future Generation Computer Systems*, 96, 168–175.

Azimi, I., Anzanpour, A., Rahmani, A. M., Pahikkala, T., Levorato, M., Liljeberg, P., & Dutt, N. (2017). HiCH: Hierarchical fog-assisted computing architecture for healthcare IoT. *ACM Transactions on Embedded Computing Systems (TECS)*, 16(5s), 1–20.

Bierzynski, K., Escobar, A., & Eberl, M. (2017, May). Cloud, fog and edge: Cooperation for the future?. In *2017 Second International Conference on Fog and Mobile Edge Computing (FMEC)* (pp. 62–67). IEEE.

Chiang, M., & Zhang, T. (2016). Fog and IoT: An overview of research opportunities. *IEEE Internet of Things Journal*, 3(6), 854–864.

Chen, M., Hao, Y., Hu, L., Hossain, M. S., & Ghoneim, A. (2018). Edge-CoCaCo: Toward joint optimization of computation, caching, and communication on edge cloud. *IEEE Wireless Communications*, 25(3), 21–27.

Gaba, P., & Raw, R. S. (2020). Vehicular cloud and fog computing architecture, applications, services, and challenges. In R. S. Rao, V. Jain, & O. Kaiwartya (Eds.), *IoT and Cloud Computing Advancements in Vehicular Ad-Hoc Networks* (pp. 268–296). IGI Global.

Hao, Y., Miao, Y., Hu, L., Hossain, M. S., Muhammad, G., & Amin, S. U. (2019). Smart-Edge-CoCaCo: AI-enabled smart edge with joint computation, caching, and communication in heterogeneous IoT. *IEEE Network*, 33(2), 58–64.

Hartmann, M., Hashmi, U. S., & Imran, A. (2022). Edge computing in smart health care systems: Review, challenges, and research directions. *Transactions on Emerging Telecommunications Technologies*, 33(3), e3710.

He, W., Yan, G., & Da Xu, L. (2014). Developing vehicular data cloud services in the IoT environment. *IEEE Transactions on Industrial Informatics*, 10(2), 1587–1595.

Hossain, M. S., & Muhammad, G. (2016). Cloud-assisted industrial internet of things (iiot)–enabled framework for health monitoring. *Computer Networks*, 101, 192–202.

Hossain, M. S., & Muhammad, G. (2017). Emotion-aware connected healthcare big data towards 5G. *IEEE Internet of Things Journal*, 5(4), 2399–2406.

Hossain, M. S., Amin, S. U., Alsulaiman, M., & Muhammad, G. (2019, February) Applying deep learning for epilepsy seizure detection and brain mapping visualization. *ACM Transactions on Multimedia Computing, Communications, and Applications*, 15(1s), 1–17.

Hossain, M. S., Rahman, M. A., & Muhammad, G. (2017). Cyber–physical cloud-oriented multi-sensory smart home framework for elderly people: An energy efficiency perspective. *Journal of Parallel and Distributed Computing*, 103, 11–21.

Hosseini, M. P., Tran, T. X., Pompili, D., Elisevich, K., & Soltanian-Zadeh, H. (2020). Multimodal data analysis of epileptic EEG and rs-fMRI via deep learning and edge computing. *Artificial Intelligence in Medicine*, 104, 101813.

Kruse, C. S., Goswamy, R., Raval, Y. J., & Marawi, S. (2016). Challenges and opportunities of big data in health care: A systematic review. *JMIR Medical Informatics*, 4(4), e5359.

Makhdoom, I., Abolhasan, M., Abbas, H., & Ni, W. (2019). Blockchain's adoption in IoT: The challenges, and a way forward. *Journal of Network and Computer Applications*, 125, 251–279.

Miraz, M. H., Ali, M., Excell, P. S., & Picking, R. (2015, September). A review on Internet of Things (IoT) Internet of everything (IoE) and Internet of nano things (IoNT). *2015 Internet Technologies and Applications (ITA)* (pp. 219–224). Wrexham, UK. doi: 10.1109/ITechA.2015.7317398.

Mutlag, A. A., Abd Ghani, M. K., Arunkumar, N. A., Mohammed, M. A., & Mohd, O. (2019). Enabling technologies for fog computing in healthcare IoT systems. *Future Generation Computer Systems*, 90, 62–78.

Pazienza, A., Polimeno, G., Vitulano, F., & Maruccia, Y. (2019, October). Towards a digital future: An innovative semantic IoT integrated platform for industry 4.0, healthcare, and territorial control. In *2019 IEEE International Conference on Systems, Man and Cybernetics (SMC)* (pp. 587–592). IEEE.

Qadri, Y. A., Nauman, A., Zikria, Y. B., Vasilakos, A. V., & Kim, S. W. (2020). The future of healthcare internet of things: A survey of emerging technologies. *IEEE Communications Surveys & Tutorials*, 22(2), 1121–1167.

Tuli, S., Basumatary, N., Gill, S. S., Kahani, M., Arya, R. C., Wander, G. S., & Buyya, R. (2020). HealthFog: An ensemble deep learning based Smart Healthcare System for Automatic Diagnosis of Heart Diseases in integrated IoT and fog computing environments. *Future Generation Computer Systems*, 104, 187–200.

Uddin, M. Z. (2019). A wearable sensor-based activity prediction system to facilitate edge computing in smart healthcare system. *Journal of Parallel and Distributed Computing*, 123, 46–53.

Verma, S., Kawamoto, Y., Fadlullah, Z. M., Nishiyama, H., & Kato, N. (2017). A survey on network methodologies for real-time analytics of massive IoT data and open research issues. *IEEE Communications Surveys & Tutorials*, 19(3), 1457–1477.

Vyas, S. (2023). Extended Reality and Edge AI for Healthcare 4.0: Systematic Study. In *Extended Reality for Healthcare Systems* (pp. 229–240). Academic Press.

Vyas, S., & Bhargava, D. (2021). *Smart Health Systems: Emerging Trends*. Singapore: Springer.

Vyas, S., & Gupta, S. (2022). Case study on state-of-the-art wellness and health tracker devices. In S. S. Iyer, A. Jain, & J. Wang (Eds.), *Handbook of Research on Lifestyle Sustainability and Management Solutions Using AI, Big Data Analytics, and Visualization* (pp. 325–337). IGI Global.

Vyas, S., Gupta, S., Bhargava, D., & Boddu, R. (2022). Fuzzy logic system implementation on the performance parameters of health data management frameworks. *Journal of Healthcare Engineering*, 2022, 1–11.

Xie, J., Tang, H., Huang, T., Yu, F. R., Xie, R., Liu, J., & Liu, Y. (2019). A survey of block-chain technology applied to smart cities: Research issues and challenges. *IEEE Communications Surveys & Tutorials*, 21(3), 2794–2830.

Yang, X., Zhang, T., Xu, C., Yan, S., Hossain, M. S., & Ghoneim, A. (2016). Deep relative attributes. *IEEE Transactions on Multimedia*, 18(9), 1832–1842.

Zhang, Y., Ma, X., Zhang, J., Hossain, M. S., Muhammad, G., & Amin, S. U. (2019). Edge intelligence in the cognitive Internet of things: Improving sensitivity and interactivity. *IEEE Network*, 33(3), 58–64.

3 Edge-AI, Machine-Learning, and Deep-Learning Approaches for Healthcare

Pawan Whig, Nasmin Jiwani, Ketan Gupta,
Shama Kouser, Ashima Bhatnagar Bhatia

CONTENTS

3.1 INTRODUCTION

Personalised treatment is increasingly dependent on the analysis of medical data. For instance, customised cancer therapy aims to give the proper care to the right patient by considering a variety of patient-specific variables, including genetic variation, the patient's surroundings, imaging, genetics, existing medications, and lifestyle. A vast and complicated quantity of health data was collected in

DOI: 10.1201/9781003244592-3

the past ten years by current technologies like genomics, imaging, and lifetime monitoring, enabling researchers to give patients improved therapies. Despite the abundance of data, however, we still lack a comprehensive knowledge of illnesses and effective patient treatments. Given the complexity of the data, it has become more appealing to apply machine-learning (ML) and data-mining techniques, such as deep neural networks (DNN), to evaluate such data (Whig et al. 2022). The development of reliable analytic techniques founded on information-determined approaches and machine-learning simulations is hampered particularly by the basic challenge of recognising the relationships between the many forms of patient data (Alkali et al. 2022).

Over the past ten years, a range of AI and ML approaches have been used to efficiently analyse the vast amounts of data generated by the healthcare industry. For instance, a model of prediction based on logistic regression was used to automate the early diagnosis of cardiac disease (Whig et al. 2022). Medical imaging has also used machine learning to automatically identify object attributes. DNN-based approaches are attracting a lot of interest among the many ML models, especially when it comes to the analysis of large datasets. Data is filtered via a cascade of layers using deep-learning (DL) techniques, which involve numerous phases in the learning process. DNN models surpass many traditional machine-learning models because they grow increasingly precise after processing vast amounts of data. DNN-based methods have also shown excellent results in the analysis of images and natural language (Whig et al. 2022). There has been considerable growth in AI requests and facilities because of deep-learning advances. Millions of bits of information are generated by the billions of mobile and Internet of Things (IoT) devices linked to the internet as a result of the rapid advances in mobile calculations and the IoT. The success of IoT and artificial intelligence technologies has accelerated the need to extend the boundaries of artificial intelligence to their full advantage to fully realise the promise of big data. Control computation is a potential idea to achieve calculations based on artificial intelligence applications to realise this trend (Whig et al. 2022). Edge-intelligence, also known as edge-AI, is a hybrid of artificial intelligence and edge computing that allows ML algorithms to be beneficially deployed to where the data are created. Superiority intellect can offer artificial intelligence to every individual and business, wherever they may be (Whig et al. 2022).

3.2 EDGE COMPUTING

Edge computing defined the idea behind edge calculation, in order to gather, store, process, and analyse information closer to the point of use to speed up reaction times and conserve bandwidth. Edge computation is a dispersed calculation system that enables requests to be run closer to data sources such as edge servers, IoT devices, and local endpoints, as shown in Figure 3.1. The idea behind edge computing is that processing should take place close to the data sources (Whig et al. 2022). Therefore, we believe that edge computing might have a similar significant influence on society as cloud computing has had.

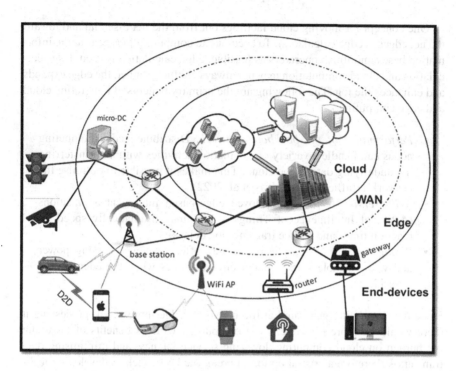

FIGURE 3.1   Edge computing connection with the cloud.

At the network edge, data are generated. Big data has lately seen a drastic change in information sources from fog information centers to the more common end plans, such as mobile and IoT plans, as it serves as a vital driver for the advancement of AI. Big data was traditionally created and stored in mega-scale data centers, and included internet shopping records, social media material, and corporate informatics (Jupalle et al. 2022). However, the tendency is currently changing because of the development of mobile computing and IoT. Massive volumes of data are being produced nowadays by a vast number of sensors and smart devices, and rising processing control is pushing most calculations and facilities to the cloud, to the network's advantage (Vyas & Gupta 2022). Currently, there are approximately 50 billion IoT devices linked with each other (Tomar et al. 2021). By 2021, according to Cisco's Worldwide Cloud Index, approximately 850 Zettabytes (ZB) of data would be produced annually outside of the cloud, compared to a predicted 20.6 ZB for global data center traffic. This shows that the bases of information are changing, moving away from massive cloud data centers and toward an expanding variety of edge devices. Cloud computing, meanwhile, is becoming unable to control this widely dispersed processing capacity and to analyse the data. Wide-area network (WAN) capacity and the computational capability of cloud computing infrastructures are seriously hampered by the massive volume of data that must be moved through them (Whig et al. 2022).

One concept for moving cloud facilities out from the net essential and toward the net edges is edge calculation. To accumulate computing jobs near to the information bases and finish operators as feasible, edge calculation is used. Edge calculation and cloud computation may not always conflict. Rather, the edge expands and enhances the fog. The following are the primary benefits of integrating cloud and edge computing:

- *Performance of the backbone network.* Distributed edge computing nodes can handle a variety of calculation activities without transferring the underlying data to the cloud. This makes it possible to optimise the network's traffic burden (Vyas et al. 2022).
- *Agile service response.* Deployed edge-based intelligent applications (Artificial Intelligence of Things, AIoT) may dramatically speed up reaction times and reduce transmission delays.
- *Strong cloud backup.* The cloud may offer strong processing power and vast, scalable storage under circumstances when the edge cannot afford it.

Since data are being generated at the network's edge more often, processing it there would be more effective. Edge computing, with its benefits of lessening the burden on cloud computing, lowering service latency, and minimising data transfer, is therefore a crucial option to break the bottleneck of developing technologies (Anand et al. 2022).

3.3   EDGE-AI OR EDGE INTELLIGENCE

What is edge-AI or intelligence at the edge? Edge intelligence, sometimes known as "edge-AI", is a new field of study that emerged from the convergence of edge computing and AI. Without completely relying on the cloud, edge intelligence takes advantage of the accessible edge capitals to enable AI applications. Although the name "edge-AI" is new, techniques in this area have existed for some time. For example, in 2009, Microsoft developed an edge-based prototype to facilitate mobile voice command recognition. There is still no official definition for edge intelligence (Alkali et al. 2022). Edge intelligence is categorised as an emerging technology by the Gartner Hype Cycles, which predicts that it resolves to reach peak productivity in the next ten years. The benefits of edge computing in bridging the concluding mile of AI have been confirmed by several significant businesses and technological pioneers, including Google, Microsoft, IBM, and Intel (Chopra & Whig 2022). Deep-learning applications need more than the cloud to run due to the tremendous benefits of deep learning in the disciplines of computer vision (CV) and natural language processing (NLP). Intelligent services and apps based on artificial intelligence and deep learning have revolutionized many parts of people's lives. The existing cloud calculation facility building, however, is insufficient to supply AI for each individual and each enterprise wherever owing to efficiency and latency difficulties. *Cost*: Using devices or users to transfer enormous volumes of data to the cloud is necessary for the training and inferences of deep learning models. A significant quantity of network bandwidth is used for this. *Latency*: The time it takes to access cloud services isn't always guaranteed to be quick enough for many time-sensitive applications. *Reliability*: Most cloud computing applications link consumers to services through wireless communications and backbone networks. Intelligent services need to be extremely dependable in many industrial contexts. *Privacy*: DL frequently uses a vast quantity of sensitive data. Smart manufacturing, smart homes, and smart cities are all at risk of AI privacy problems. Even the transfer of sensitive data may fail in specific circumstances.

3.4   DEEP LEARNING

Artificial neural networks (ANN), with two or more concealed coatings, that aim to improve prediction accuracy are referred to as a deep-learning architecture. The definition of higher-level features makes use of each lower-level feature. DL has been used for a variety of purposes, including speech recognition, picture analysis, text mining, health monitoring, and drug development.

Convolutional neural network (CNN) is an architecture for supervised deep learning. Applications involving image processing are its principal use cases, as shown in Figure 3.2. Convolutional, pooling, and fully linked layers are the three types of layers used in CNN. The input picture is processed by kernels or filters in the convolutional layer to produce various feature maps.

Each feature map's size is decreased in the pooling layer to minimise the number of weights. This method is often referred to as subsampling or down-sampling. There are several types of pooling techniques, including average, maximum, and global pooling. To extract significant aspects from medical data and identify any

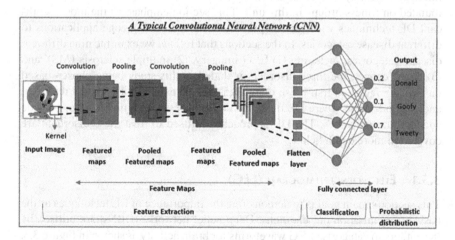

FIGURE 3.2   Typical convolutional neural network (CNN).

anomalies, a revolutionary end-to-end DL, dubbed "deeper learning", was proposed. A convolutional neural network is used to predict unexpected readmission after discharge by applying it to a series of discrete components. The convolution operator was used for the patient EHR matrices' time dimension in the second layer of the proposed DL. To include the temporal smoothness of EHR into the learning process, early, late, and slow fusion are used as temporal fusion strategies in the model (Sharma et al. 2015).

The structure of RNN has a cyclic connection. These cyclic connections of hidden units carry out recurrent computations to process the input data sequentially. Each of the preceding inputs is saved in a state vector in hidden units, and the outputs are computed using these state vectors. RNNs compute the new output by considering both the current and prior inputs. The fundamental issue with RNN, despite its promising performance, is the diminishing gradient during data training. The use of long short-term memory (LSTM) networks is one way to address this issue. Deep belief networks (DBNs) are capable of learning high-dimensional data manifold. Directed and undirected connections are seen in DBNs, a hybrid multi-layer neural network. Whereas all other connections between levels are directed, the link between the top two layers is undirected. DBNs may be thought of as a stack of greedy layerwise trained restricted Boltzmann machines (RBMs). The RBM layers communicate with one another and with earlier levels. A feed-forward net and multiple layers of RBM serve as feature centrifuges in this model. There are just two layers in an RBM: a hidden layer and a visible layer.

3.5   HEALTHCARE WITH DEEP LEARNING

In this part, we will go through various DL procedures used in healthcare schemes to distinguish between healthy and unhealthy people. To accomplish this, the replicas for certain illnesses are made. Finally, we emphasize how well DLs can distinguish unhealthy people from healthy people. We examine several approaches founded on illness groups in this unit. This section emphasises the most significant DL techniques with various presentations and cutting-edge applications to different disease categories. In the sections that follow, we examine nine different disease categories, including (1) EEG imagery, (2) multiple sclerosis (MS), and (3) breast cancer, the three disorders included in this study being chosen based on two key factors. First, those that have received extensive DL model research, and, second, those where DL models were used to address problems or provide encouraging outcomes. The DL approaches utilised to treat these disorders are covered in more depth below.

3.5.1   ELECTROENCEPHALOGRAM (EEG)

This section's main goal is to demonstrate the importance of DL techniques as the basis of organisation presentations. Deep belief networks (DBNs) are utilised by the authors to categorise EEG waveforms for brain activity as shown in Figure 3.3.

The DBN findings show that, even on raw data, this model's prediction task requires less time than those of support vector machine (SVM) and k-nearest

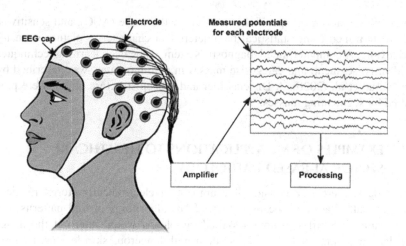

FIGURE 3.3 Electroencephalogram (EEG) demonstration.

neighbour (KNN) classifiers. Later, brand-new method was proposed for categorising electrocardiogram (ECG) data based on deep learning. In this model, a regression coating was put on the highest of the resultant image coating to produce a deep neural network following the feature learning phase. Less expert participation and a quicker online retraining phase boosted this novel method's accuracy compared with previous approaches. The classification of mitotic and non-mitotic nuclei in breast cancer images was presented using a unique data-balancing approach utilizing a CNN model. In this model, the strong similarity between mitoses and non-mitoses is addressed to deal with a classification case. The blue ratio histogram-based K-means were developed in the second stage to under-sample the majority class skewness with minimal information loss. The study's findings showed that the model decreased training time while also increasing the CNN's mitotic detection rate.

3.5.2   Multiple sclerosis (MS)

To categorise a mental effort, a stacked de-noising auto-encoder (AE) was created. This novel organisation was then likened to standard cerebral effort classifiersusing different machine learning models. Later, images of hidden MS damage were extracted from baseline images using a CNN technique. This technique demonstrated a deep network of faith with random forests used on axonal and T1-weighted MRI images to find MS symptoms in brains that seemed healthy on scans such as MRI.

3.5.3   Breast cancer

A two-layer deep learning architecture was developed to distinguish between benign and malignant breast cancers using shear wave elastography. Both a point-wise gated Boltzmann machine and a limited Boltzmann machine were included.

The method's accuracy, specificity, area under the curve (AUC), and sensitivity were determined using statistical parameters that characterise picture intensity and texture. A computer-aided diagnostic system, using deep learning techniques to identify, segment, and categorise masses in mammograms, was described by the Masud et al. (2020). A DL classifier and a deep structure output were presented for segmenting masses.

3.6 EXAMPLES OF ML APPLICATIONS TO HEALTHCARE SECTOR AI-BASED RADIOLOGY

These days, there is a considerable amount of electronically stored medical imaging data that could be used to feed DL algorithms to find patterns and abnormalities. Similar to how a skilled radiologist would interpret the imaging data, machines and algorithms could find dangerous skin lesions, tumors, and bleeding in the brain. As a result, the use of AI/ML tools and platforms to aid radiologists is set to grow rapidly. This method addresses a significant issue in the healthcare industry because it is getting increasingly difficult to identify radiologists with the necessary training. Due to the flood of digital medical data, such trained individuals are typically under a great deal of pressure. To keep up with demand, a typical radiologist must deliver interpretation findings for one image every 3–4 seconds. Microsoft's Scheme InnerEye, which uses ML techniques to section and locate cancers using 3D radiological pictures, is a great test case. It can aid in accurate navigation, tumor contouring for radiation planning, and operation planning. ML algorithms are being added to MRI and other sophisticated imaging systems, which are increasingly being employed for early cancer diagnosis. In this regard, the following section (Section 3.7) offers a comprehensive summary.

3.7 ML AND DATA KNOWLEDGE FOR LEGAL UNDERSTANDING

Exabytes of medical data are currently being digitised at several healthcare facilities. Sadly, this material is frequently disordered and unstructured. Patient data, in contrast to typical transactional business data, is less susceptible to straightforward arithmetical models and analytics. The essential required is for robust and flexible AI-enabled schemes that can link to several patient databases and evaluate a complicated mix of data types. These schemes must also be effective in thoroughly selecting finished examinations and finding any hidden trends. Medical robots can also provide traditional surgeons with special aids, increasing vision and navigational skills throughout treatment, and making small, accurate incisions and minimising discomfort with ideal stitch and wound shape. The potential applications of AI/ML for such digital surgical robots are fascinating. Robot cooperation focused on software, using widely distributed processor insights and recommendations derived from historical data on surgeries and their results in a virtual reality environment created by AI, providing instant instruction and advice for telemedicine and remote surgery, may be used for very basic treatments.

3.7.1 AI FOR PATIENT EXPERIENCE AND CONTROL OF HEALTHCARE OPERATIONS

The cost and accessibility of quality healthcare for the general population in the United States have been hotly debated for a very long time. AI and related data-driven approaches are particularly positioned to address some of the issues that have been identified as the core causes – lengthy lines, concern over exorbitant bills, arduous and confusing appointment procedures, and difficulty in accessing the appropriate healthcare provider. Traditional businesses have faced similar sets of issues for decades, and AI/ML approaches are already a part of the answer. Enormous records and sophisticated hunt procedures, which are a strength of AI schemes, are excellent at solving these pattern-corresponding challenges, which explains the potential significance of AI in healthcase.

3.7.2 DRUG DISCOVERIES

Big names in the pharmaceutical business are increasingly turning to AI and ML approaches to tackle the excruciatingly challenging issue of effective drug development. Several well-known cases involvE Sanofi, Genentech, and Pfizer. These case studies span a wide range of therapeutic areas, including therapies for cancer, immuno-oncology medications, and metabolic illnesses.

3.7.3 AI IN SYSTEMS FOR PUBLIC HEALTH

Such potent strategies may be used for both individual patient care and large-scale public health systems. Digital pandemic monitoring and AI-assisted health data analytics are primed for growth. How crucial it is to conduct hundreds of similar hearings for inoculation growth and medical investigation initiatives has been demonstrated by the current COVID-19 pandemic. With typical statistical modeling approaches, which are geared toward small-scale trials, it is hard to use data to identify patterns from all these diverse bases, frequently generating conclusions with a high grade of doubt. Such planetary-scale issues require the use of AI technology.

3.8 CASE STUDY

A characteristic magnetic resonance (MR) copy categorisation and prediction approach is studied. This model contains feature extraction for classification and prediction, along with pre-processing stages like filtering, skull stripping, and so forth. Most contemporary research papers with "classification" and "prediction" in the title employ this technique. The primary drawbacks of this method are that it takes a lot of time and produces sub-optimal results.

The unique technique developed in Vyas and Gupta's (2022) study employs the DL procedure, removes preprocessing stages, reduces computing difficulty, and improves presentation. The deep-learning algorithm doesn't need any pre-processing if we can supply the essential and appropriate strictures to examine, using the bottomless knowledge perfectly. Deep learning has a high accuracy rate, making it cutting-edge. Utilising deep-learning technology, accuracy levels significantly increased after 2012. ML is the study of teaching processers to learn from diverse types of information, as the name suggests. A simpler definition is offered by Arthur Samuel, who describes machine learning as "the study of how computers may learn without being explicitly taught". People manually coded all algorithms, mathematical formulas, statistical formulas, etc. to complete machine-learning tasks. The process was therefore laborious, time consuming, and ineffective. However, it is now simpler and more effective than it was in the past because of the numerous Python libraries, frameworks, and modules. One of the most used computer languages for this purpose nowadays is Python. It has replaced a lot of other languages in the industry, in part because of its enormous library system. Python's vast ecosystem of data-centric Python tools makes it an excellent language for data analysis. One of these apps, Pandas, greatly eases the import and analysis of data. A bar plot is a type of graph that uses rectangular bars with lengths according to the values they represent to depict categorical data. Comparisons between several groups are shown using a bar plot. One axis of the figure represents the numerous groups to be compared, whereas the other represents a measured value. The bar chart presented in Figure 3.4 demonstrates that there are more girls than males who are not suffering from dementia.

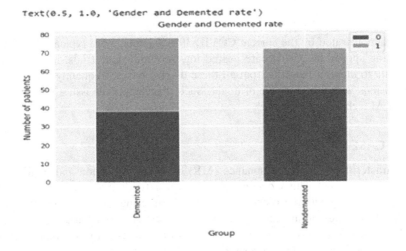

FIGURE 3.4 Frequencies of demented and non-demented categories.

3.8.1 Seaborn FacetGrid

It typically produces charts known as "lattice", "trellis", or "small-multiple" visuals. The values of a third variable may also be represented by the color hue parameter, which displays different data subsets in a variety of hues. To resolve elements in a third dimension, color is used. However, unlike axes-level functions that get a hue, it essentially superimposes subsets and does not tailor the hue parameter to the visualisation. Then, one or more graphing techniques are applied by repeatedly using FacetGrid.map(). ASF Atlas Scaling Factor, ITV Projected Total Intracranial Capacity, and WV Regularized Whole Brain Capacity for the assumed data set is intended and planned to be used for the next instructions. The inconsistent sample has a greater attention of 70- to 80-year-olds in the affected role than the nondemented consistent group.

3.9   RESULTS AND DISCUSSION

It has been shown that men are far more likely than women to get dementia, such as Alzheimer's disease. Additionally, demented patients had fewer years of education than healthy individuals. Additionally, it has been found that non-demented individuals had larger brains than demented individuals. Compared with the non-demented adult sample, the sample of those people with dementia has a larger percentage of people in their 70s and 80s.

3.9.1 Performance measures

The area under the curve (AUC) of the receiver operating characteristic (ROC) curve serves as one of our performance metrics. We believe that a high actual positive rate is essential to quickly identify everyone with Alzheimer's disease, when conducting diagnostic procedures for non-life-threatening incurable diseases, such as the majority of neurodegenerative disorders. However, since we do not want to wrongly label a healthy adult as having a mental disorder and start medical therapy, we must make sure that the false positive rate is as low as is practical. Therefore, ROC appeared to be a strong contender for a performance metric as shown in Table 3.1.

TABLE 3.1

Comparison of accuracy recall area under the curve (AUC)

	Model	Accuracy	Recall	AUC
0	Logistic Regression (w/ imputation)	0.763158	0.70	0.766667
1	Logistic Regression (w/ dropna)	0.805556	0.75	0.750000
2	SVM	0.815789	0.70	0.822222
3	Decision Tree	0.815789	0.65	0.825000
4	Random Forest	**0.868421**	0.80	0.872222
5	AdaBoost	0.86S421	0.65	0.825000

3.10 CONCLUSION AND FUTURE SCOPE

The main objective of the program is to predict Alzheimer's disease. The Freely Accessible Sequence of Archiving Studies project provided the "MRI and Alzheimer's" dataset, which was used to predict thinking in elderly people. The dataset is shown, and the blanks have been filled in with appropriate values. Pre-processing of the data has removed some unnecessary features. To make sure that the variables would fit perfectly into the ML models, they were standardised. Models, including support verctor machine (SVM), logistic regression, decision tree, and random forest, were then trained using the dataset. As evaluation criteria, accuracy, recall, AUC, and a confusion matrix were used. To improve the performance of the system, all models created were refined using the mesh technique. The system achieving the best results used SVM. A more intricate model, with the random forest classifier, exhibited overfitting. When the results are compared, it is found that the random forest model gives roughly 87% of the best results, followed by the Deep Learning Ludwig Classifier with 95% accuracy. In summary, we find that the DL-based hybrid and ensemble methods outperform single strategies in terms of accuracy. By integrating two or more procedures concurrently, and without regard to the type of datasets, these methods result in an enhancement of the process. Deep-learning techniques require a lot of memory and time, which is a drawback. Designing and implementing the best practices in healthcare systems is thus a significant task. In conclusion, given the magnitude and complexity of health data, we think there is an enormous potential in DL models and their involvement in health care schemes. The researchers in this sector will find this research study useful and this book chapter will be very useful for researchers working in the same field.

REFERENCES

Alkali, Y., Routray, I., & Whig, P. (2022). Strategy for reliable, efficient and secure IoT using artificial intelligence. *IUP Journal of Computer Sciences*, 16(2), 16–25.

Anand, M., Velu, A., & Whig, P. (2022). Prediction of loan behaviour with machine learning models for secure banking. *Journal of Computer Science and Engineering (JCSE)*, 3(1), 1–13.

Chopra, G., & Whig, P. (2022). Smart agriculture system using AI. *International Journal of Sustainable Development in Computing Science*, 4(1).

Jupalle, H., Kouser, S., Bhatia, A. B., Alam, N., Nadikattu, R. R., & Whig, P. (2022). Automation of human behaviors and its prediction using machine learning. *Microsystem Technologies*, 1–9. Springer.

Masud, M., Eldin Rashed, A. E., & Hossain, M. S. (2020). Convolutional neural network-based models for diagnosis of breast cancer. *Neural Computing and Applications*, 1–12.

Sharma, A., Kumar, A., & Whig, P. (2015). On the performance of CDTA based novel analog inverse, low pass filter using 0.35 Mm CMOS parameter. *International Journal of Science, Technology & Management*, 4(1), 594–601.

Tomar, U., Chakraborty, N., Sharma, H., & Whig, P. (2021). AI-Based smart agriculture system. *Transactions on Latest Trends in Artificial Intelligence*, 2(2).

Vyas, S., & Gupta, S. (2022). Case study on state-of-the-art wellness and health tracker devices. In S. S. Iyer, A. Jain, & J. Wang (Eds.), *Handbook of Research on Lifestyle Sustainability and Management Solutions Using AI, Big Data Analytics, and Visualization* (pp. 325–337). IGI Global.

Vyas, S., Gupta, S., Bhargava, D., & Boddu, R. (2022). Fuzzy logic system implementation on the performance parameters of health data management frameworks. *Journal of Healthcare Engineering*, 2022, 1–11.

Whig, P., Kouser, S., Velu, A., & Nadikattu, R. R. (2022). Fog-IoT-assisted-based smart agriculture application. In *Demystifying Federated Learning for Blockchain and Industrial Internet of Things* (pp. 74–93). IGI Global.

Whig, P., Nadikattu, R. R., & Velu, A. (2022). COVID-19 pandemic analysis using application of AI. *Healthcare Monitoring and Data Analysis Using IoT: Technologies and Applications*, 1, 1–25.

Whig, P., Velu, A., & Bhatia, A. B. (2022). Protect nature and reduce the carbon footprint with an application of blockchain for IIoT. In *Demystifying Federated Learning for Blockchain and Industrial Internet of Things* (pp. 123–142). IGI Global.

Whig, P., Velu, A., & Naddikatu, R. R. (2022a). The economic impact of AI-enabled blockchain in 6G-based industry. In *AI and Blockchain Technology in 6G Wireless Network* (pp. 205–224). Singapore: Springer.

Whig, P., Velu, A., & Nadikattu, R. R. (2022b). Blockchain platform to resolve security issues in IoT and smart networks. In *AI-Enabled Agile Internet of Things for Sustainable FinTech Ecosystems* (pp. 46–65). IGI Global.

Whig, P., Velu, A., & Ready, R. (2022). Demystifying federated learning in artificial intelligence with human-computer interaction. In *Demystifying Federated Learning for Blockchain and Industrial Internet of Things* (pp. 94–122). IGI Global.

Whig, P., Velu, A., & Sharma, P. (2022). Demystifying federated learning for blockchain: A case study. In *Demystifying Federated Learning for Blockchain and Industrial Internet of Things* (pp. 143–165). IGI Global.

4 Transforming healthcare with machine-learning and deep-learning approaches

Komal Tahiliani, Uday Panwar

CONTENTS

4.1 TRANSFORMING HEALTHCARE WITH AI

It seems like, wherever you turn, artificial intelligence (AI) is in the news. From self-driving vehicles to savvy collaborators, AI (and the promotion that accompanies it) is starting to pervade the innovations we utilise each day (Rong et al. 2020). Computer-based intelligence innovations are advancing into clinics, care offices, and specialist workplaces all over the planet – and medical care suppliers and patients are now reaping the rewards. Because of these useful assets, suppliers are seeing smoothed-out processes and decreased costs, and patients are

DOI: 10.1201/9781003244592-4

receiving more customised consideration and on-request care. In the healthcare world, the discussion about computerised brainpower (AI) has been expanding in recent years. AI is revolutionising the healthcare industry by providing a powerful helping hand (Secinaro et al. 2021).

4.2 ARTIFICIAL INTELLIGENCE AND ITS APPLICATIONS IN HEALTHCARE

When we consider this generation of technology, companies and industries around the world are talking about artificial intelligence (AI), machine learning, and deep-learning techniques. It is important to understand that all these compositions are part of the umbrella concept of artificial intelligence (AI) (Secinaro et al. 2021). AI is an umbrella term which covers each and everything which makes machines smarter. Machine learning (ML) is commonly used along with AI, but it is a subset of AI. Machine learning corresponds to an AI system that can achieve self-learning based on an algorithm. Systems that get smarter with time without human interference involve ML. The deep-learning technique is a machine-learning strategy applied to a large number of datasets. Most AI tasks involve machine learning because intelligent behavior needs knowledge (Manne & Kantheti 2021). The relationship between AI, machine-learning, and deep learning is represented in Figure 4.1.

AI, deep-, and machine-learning techniques go hand in hand with respect to improving a patient's condition and for diagnosis of disease in healthcare. Figure 4.2 shows the relationship between deep learning, machine learning, and artificial intelligence (Secinaro et al. 2021). At present, deep learning is ready to take over the machine learning space because of its greater importance and performance. Brainpower in medical care corresponds to the use of detailed calculations intended to roll out specific undertakings in a robotised design. At the point when specialists and researchers introduce information onto PCs, the recently concluded calculations can audit, decipher, and even recommend answers for complex clinical issues (Bajwa et al. 2021). Man-made brainpower in this medical field depends on the investigation and translation of measures of data collections to guide specialists to make decisions on better choices, oversee patient informational data, making customised and individualised medication plans from complicated and complex data, and to find new strategies and treatments (Bajwa et al. 2021). At its most elevated level, here is a snapshot of the current uses of AI in medical services which we should know about.

- *Medical diagnostics.* The utilisation of artificial intelligence to determine which patients have specific medical conditions.
- *Drug discovery.* There are many well-being organisations and pharma companies at present utilizing artificial intelligence to assist with drug discoveries, working to shorten the extended timetables and cycles Any plans(Chen & Decary 2020).

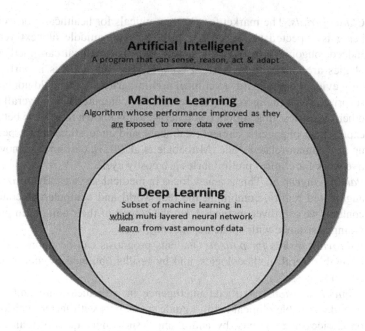

FIGURE 4.1   Relation between concepts of artificial intelligence, deep learning and machine learning.

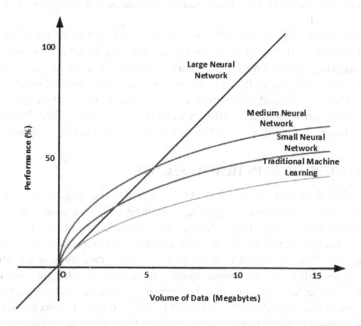

FIGURE 4.2   Scaling machine-learning techniques with increases in quantity of data.

- *Clinical trials.* The market for pharmaceuticals for healthcare for well-being is expected to exceed \$35 billion by the middle of next year. Indeed, ongoing investigations have shown that medical care methodologies are changing because of computerisation, and this is particularly evident with regards to clinical preliminaries. This should not be a surprise, given the increasing importance of computerisation overall in other industries. In addition, computerisation is known to achieve better experiences of specific clinical treatments, and unquestionably to speed up any human-related cycle (Mirbabaie et al. 2021); customary innovative work for clinical preliminaries is a costly cycle.
- *Pain management.* This is a new focus in medical services. By utilizing augmented reality, combining the real world and computer-generated content, we can divert patients from the source of their pain, even providing assistance with opiate dependency.
- *Improving results for patients.* Patients prognosis can be improved on through several methodologies, and by results obtained by man-made consciousness.
- *Clinical decisions.* Artificial intelligence in a medical care unit can provide valuable clinical help to guide specialists with faster decisions on choices and options, by addressing issues more quickly than can be achieved by the human mind (Kononenko 2021). The more rapid response and the standard of decisions made are incomparable in an industry where the time taken and choices made can change the life of the patient.
- *Data management (both doctor and patient).* Artificial intelligence in the medical field is an extraordinary expansion to the data and the executives for both doctor and patient. With opportunity to the patients having time to specialists quicker, or not under any condition when telemedicine is utilized, removing the strain from medical services experts (Davenport & Kalakota 2019). Specialists can facilitate their learning and increase their capacities through AI-driven interactive modules,

4.3   FUTURE OF AI IN HEALTH SECTOR

Considering the future advances in AI for investigating images, it is possible that most radiology and pathology images will be inspected sooner or later by a machine (Thompson & Brailer 2004). Text acknowledgment are of no use for undertakings like patient correspondence and clinical notes, and their utilisation will increase. The first check to AI in these scientific care units is not whether the advances will be useful enough to be valuable, but whether they should be used in everyday scientific practice. For global acceptance of AI to happen, AI frameworks must be supported with the aid of using controllers, coordinated with EHR frameworks, normalised to an ok diploma that comparative gadgets paintings likewise, accessible to clinicians, paid for by private payer associations, and continuously optimised in the field. These problems will ultimately be solved, but they may take drastically longer to do so, delaying the time taken for the real improvements to develop.

4.4   ROLE OF MACHINE LEARNING IN HEALTHCARE

Machine learning is a subclass of synthetic intelligence in which algorithms analyse enormous datasets to pick out designs and trends independently without being advised on exactly how to solve the issue. Machine learning is complicated, and advanced mechanical application of machine learning has turned into a closed pattern in the industry. Machine learning is an Omni gift and is extensively used in unique ways. It is assumed to be a crucial component in lots of fields like finance, medical technological know-how, and in security (Bhardwaj et al. 2017). Machine learning is implemented to get designs from clinical information sources and to achieve incredible capabilities to predict diseases.

First, it permits healthcare experts to zero-in on quiet considerations instead of investing their energy in data searching. Second, an important job of machine learning in the medical field is the incremental increase in diagnostic precision (Collins & Varmus 2015). For instance, machine learning has proven to be 92% precise in predicting mortality of COVID-19 patients. Third, utilising machine learning in medicine can assist with fostering a more exact treatment plan. Many clinical cases are one of a kind and require an exceptional methodology for treatment. In addition, although a medical care expert and a machine-learning algorithm will no doubt come to a similar decision in light of similar informational input, using machine learning will attain the outcome a bit quicker, so that therapy can start sooner (Collins & Varmus 2015). Accuracy in prescribing appropriate medicinal drugs depends on identifying which remedies will be effective on a given patient, and that is determined with input from the health record of the patient (Collins & Varmus 2015; Murphy 2012). This kind of decision-making from past learning will require training the model by utilising datasets, and this approach is called supervised learning.

4.4.1   SEMI-SUPERVISED MACHINE LEARNING

This is the strategy of identifying the first-class classifier from every unlabeled and marked statistic. By making use of unlabeled statistics, it carries out advanced execution of actions. This approach is achieved based on a number of essential suppositions.

4.4.2   UNSUPERVISED MACHINE LEARNING

In unsupervised machine learning, no preparation is given to the names. The strategies utilised for unsupervised learning is grouping, fluffy bunching, various leveled bunching, K- mean grouping, or affiliation rule mining of the calculations. These algorithms are utilised for creating a structure with the support of information tests.

4.4.3 Reinforcement Machine Learning

In this type of machine learning, permission is given by the computer program for playing out a particular aim. Feedback is given to the program as it explores its downside.

4.5 APPLICATIONS OF MACHINE LEARNING TO HEALTHCARE

The algorithms of machine learning are very helpful in analysing examples involving enormous volumes of data. Machine learning is particularly appropriate to medical applications, especially those which depend on cutting-edge genomics. It is often used in diagnosing numerous illnesses. In scientific applications, the algorithms developed will produce better selections of treatments for patients. These models use factors like patient data, exigency charts, and even the design of the clinic room itself (Murphy 2012).

4.6 VARIOUS MODELS USED IN MACHINE LEARNING

- *Support vector machine.* To achieve machine learning (ML) undertakings, the support vector machine (SVM) can be used, a supervised learning model with associated learning algorithms that analyze data for classification (Sharma & Bhatia 2012). For the most part, the SVM is used for classification and relapse issues.
- *Naïve Bayes classifier (NBC).* Statistical classifiers are nothing but the model for Bayesian classifiers. NBC recognize and identify the class enrollment probabilities with respect to a given class name. It performs filtering of information; consequently, order is simple to achieve (Bishop 1995).
- *Decision tree.* Decision trees generally involve a strategy for order containing an inside hub and one leaf hub with a class name. The top hubs of the decision tree are called root hubs. The tree selected is valuable in that the development is very basic and will not need any boundaries (Bishop 1995).
- *K-nearest neighbor.* The k-nearest neighbor algorithm is commonly used for classification of samples. By making use of this technique, we can calculate the distance measure from a number (N) of training samples (Zimmermann 2011).
- *Fuzzy logic.* Fuzzy Logic is an advanced form of fuzzy set theory; the values lie between 0 and 1. It is a well-known technique which is utilized in designing applications (Learning 2017).
- *CART.* CART stands for classification and regression tree methodology. In classification and regression trees, the target variables are represented as categorical or continuous variables. The roles of variables are used to assume and predict values in the tree (Hazra et al. 2012).

Different machine learning approaches respond differently depending on the amount of data. Figure 4.2 depicts a comparison graph showing how different techniques respond in different networks.

4.7   DEEP LEARNING AND ITS ROLE IN HEALTHCARE

Deep learning is an AI method that trains PCs to solve problems. Deep learning is a fundamental development of driverless vehicles, allowing them to recognise a "Stop" sign. It is the method which allows voice manipulation in consumer devices like telephones, tablets, TVs, and hands-free speakers (Xu et al. 2014). In the case of deep learning, a computer can learn to perform tasks from pictures, text, or sound. Models are organised by using an association of marked statistics and neural networks that comprise many layers (Xu et al. 2014). The word "deep" generally shows the amount of stowed away layers in the neural association. Regular neural associations usually have two or three layers, whereas deep associations can have as many as 150. Deep-learning models are trained by using large guides of movement of stamped facts and neural affiliation systems that consist of immediate facts without the prerequisite for guide element extraction. Deep-learning models can become increasingly more precise as they execute more content, basically learning from history to refine their ability to develop relationships and associations (Mishra & Shukla 2018).

Normally, the math associated with growing models of deep learning is uncommonly complicated, and there are various classes of organizations that influence different sub- procedures within the field. The handling capacity of deep-learning models offers fast, precise and viable undertakings of clinical benefit. Deep-learning networks change patients' cognition and they have a major impact in clinical practice. Computer vision technique, natural language processing, and reinforcement learning strategy are the most typically implemented deep-learning techniques with clinical benefits.

4.8   COMPUTER VISION

Computer vision is a discipline of artificial intelligence (AI) that empowers computer systems and frameworks to derive enormous amounts of information from superior images, recordings, and different visual sources and generate responses in view of that information. AI can empower computer systems to think and respond. Computer vision surpasses human imagination and persistence (Xu et al. 2014).

4.9   NATURAL LANGUAGE PROCESSING

Natural language processing (NLP) is important for regular day-to-day existence, and it is crucial for our lives at home and at work. Without really thinking about it, we send voice orders to our virtual home partners, our cell phones, and surprisingly our vehicles. Voice-empowered applications, like Alexa, Siri, and Google Assistant, use NLP and machine-learning algorithms to address our inquiries, add exercises to our schedules, and call the contacts that we list in our voice orders. NLP isn't just making our lives simpler, also altering the way in which we work, live, and play (Xu et al. 2014). AI is an umbrella term for machines that can reproduce human knowledge, while NLP and machine learning (ML) are two subsets of AI. In the healthcare world, there are many applications of natural language processing. NLP, through the utilization of query interfaces, can greatly enhance the distribution of factual information and semantic understanding by providing a vast amount of relevant facts (Vyas 2023).

4.10 REINFORCEMENT LEARNING (RL)

The use of machine learning in medical care has numerous extraordinary outputs, although there is tremendous room for error in diagnosing conditions or anticipating results. RL has performed well at learning the ideal strategies in similar (video/tabletop games) settings, although it has generally been untested under real-world conditions like healthcare (Murphy 2012).

4.11 FRAMEWORKS OF DEEP LEARNING

Machine learning is a universally beneficial approach to man-made reasoning that could make valuable connections from data gathered. Conventional techniques comprise of a solitary, directed, change of the space and are limited in their capacity to handle normal data and information in their structure. Certainly, deep learning is central to computational models that are produced to deal with layers reflecting neural relations to accept groups of information with different degrees of thought. Artificial neural networks are typically depicted with three layers, but they can be tailored and optimized specifically for complex tasks, rather than being generalized models (Mishra & Shukla 2018).

- *Deep convolutional neural networks.* A convolutional neural network consists of three layers – input layer, hidden layers and an output layer. Figure 4.3 presents a view of a convolutional neural community with three convolution and pooling (csnv+pool) layers and a pair of fully connected (FC) layers in any feed-ahead neural organisation; any central layers are known as "hidden" because their elements of feedback and consequence are hidden with the aid of the actuation capability and final convolution. As the convolution element slides along the information grid for the layer, the convolution activity creates an element map, which thus adds to the development of the subsequent layer. This is followed by different layers, for example, pooling layers, completely associated layers, and standardisation layers (Masci et al. 2011).
- *Deep neural networks.* A deep neural network (DNN) is an artificial neural organisation with various layers between the input and output

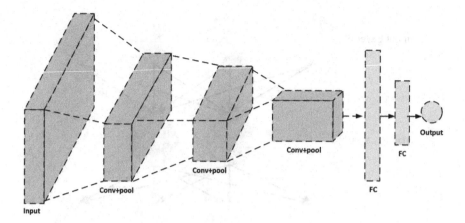

FIGURE 4.3   Structure of convolutional neural network.

layers. There are numerous types of neural networks, but they generally comprise of similar elements: neurons, synapses, loads, predispositions, and capacities. DNNs can show complex non-linear connections. DNN models create composition models in which the item is communicated as a layered arrangement of nodes as shown in Figure 4.3.

The additional layers empower the arrangement of elements from lower layers, conceivably displaying complex information with fewer units than a correspondingly performing shallow network (Coronato et al. 2020). Deep neural networks are conventionally feed-forward networks in which data moves from the data layer to the outcome layer. The information sources are copied and return an outcome at some point in the range 0 to 1. In case the network didn't definitively develop a particular model, a computation is required for changing heaps.

- Recurrent neural networks (RNN). RNNs are used by Apple's Siri and Google's voice assistant. It is the predominant calculation that remembers its input, due to an internal memory, which makes it particularly suitable for AI problem solving, that consists of consecutive statistics. An expansion in computation power to deal with the enormous volumes of data with which we deal and the innovation of long short-term memory (LSTM) during the 1990s has truly carried RNNs to the forefront (Alzubaidi et al. 2021)

The data move straight through the network and never touch a hub twice. Feed-forward neural networks have no memory of the input they get and are poor at foreseeing what is approaching. In a RNN, the information spins through a circle. At the factor whilst information is based on choice and predicts the output on the basis of inputs received earlier.

1) *Deep autoencoders*. This encoder is used for feature extraction and has equal numbers of input and output nodes. Deep autoencoder is a neural network architecture shown in Figure 4.4, which works on

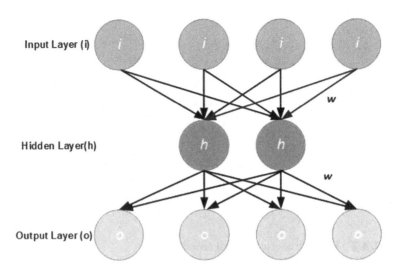

FIGURE 4.4   Autoencoder structure, showing all three layers.

the unsupervised learning technique to reorganise the input values. In simple terms, we recreate the input value X to a neural network with minimum error. In autoencoder, the input data that we provide is basically compressed through a bottleneck in the architecture as we impose a smaller number of neurons in the hidden layers. As in the above diagram, the network accepts unlabeled information as info X and trains it to yield $\hat{X}$, a reproduction of a unique contribution, by outlining it as an administered issue. The principal thought of the network is to limit the recreation blunder L (X, $\hat{X}$), which is fundamentally the distinction between the unique input to the reproduced output (Hinton et al. 2006). As we limit the number of layers in the hidden layer, limited amounts of data move through the network, otherwise, if we give similar number of neurons in the hidden layer, the model will retain the input information alongside the network without learning significant characteristics about the input. Restricting neurons in the hidden layers will compel the network to refresh the loads by effectively being punished for remaking the error (Hinton et al. 2006).

2) *Deep belief network.* The deep belief network (DBN) is a community, which essentially incorporates the stack layers of the constrained Boltzmann machine. It is a feed-forward community with many hidden nodes. DBN may be applied to deal with unsupervised mastering responsibilities to decrease the dimensionality of elements and may likewise be applied to address supervised mastering undertakings to manufacture grouping fashions or relapse fashions.

To put together a DBN, there are stages, layer-by-layer learning and first-rate tuning. Layer-by-layer learning pertains to unsupervised coaching of every Restricted Boltzmann Machine (RBM), and first-rate tuning pertains to the use of back-propagation error algorithms to calibrate the bounds of DBN after the unsupervised learning is done. Deep neural networks are retrained by using calculations called Greedy calculations. This computation uses layer-by-layer procedures to realise the entire top-down system and analyse enormous generative loads. These connected loads choose how all factors in a solitary layer depend upon various elements in the layer above (Liu et al. 2014). Recently, DBNs have gained increased popularity in the field of AI due to their promising advantages. DBNs offer fast analysis and have the ability to model complex network structures effectively.

- *Deep Boltzmann machine.* A deep Boltzmann machine (DBM) is a kind of pair-wise uneven Markov field with various dissimilar layers. It is a network of coupled equal stochastic units. The structure of two layers is confined to a DBM. DBMs can study intricate and dynamic inner portrayals of the input in projects, Like DBNs, i.e, signal recognition, using partial, categorised data to adjust the portrayals made using a huge arrangement of uncategorized tangible input information. Nevertheless, unlike all Boltzmann machine and deep convolutional neural networks, they seek after the deductive and preparative technique in the two arrangements, top-down and bottom-up, which authorisation the DBM to more readily divulge the portrayals of the input architecture. Be that as it may, the restricted performance of DBMs due to their slow speed also reduces their usefulness. In the process of data decision-making, mean field determination is used to assign subpositions and Markov chain Monte Carlo (MCMC) is employed to obtain satisfactory estimations (Liu et al. 2014). This derivation, that must be completed for every test input, is somewhere between 25 and multiple times slower than a solitary base up pass in DBMs. This makes joint development irrational for vast data collections and limits the use of DBMs to projects like element portrayal and extraction. Figure 4.5 clearly illustrates a descriptive summary of healthcare applications of deep-learning methods.

4.12   CASE STUDIES OF DEEP-LEARNING TECHNIQUES IN HEALTHCARE

Nevertheless, deep learning is continuously discovering its path into applications to the real-world clinical environment. There are numerous use cases that involve visionary patient-centric applications, as well as several techniques aimed at enhancing the well-being of IT clients and fostering future growth.

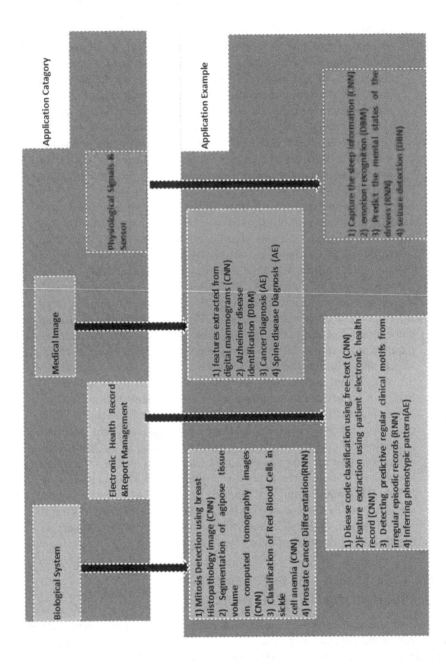

FIGURE 4.5 Summary of health and biomedical applications.

- *Imaging analytics and diagnostics.* Convolutional neural networks (CNNs) are one of the deep-learning strategies, particularly suitable for classifying images, such as MRI and X-rays, etc., as shown by specialised software engineers at Stanford University, allowing the networks to work even more efficiently and to store bigger images. Subsequently, some CNNs are approaching more to – in some cases, outperforming – the accuracy and precision of human diagnosticians, while acknowledging significant highlights in indicative imaging studies (Cheng et al. 2016). Researchers have created a deep neural network with the potential to diagnose severe neurological conditions, such as stroke and brain hemorrhage, 150 times more quickly than that achieved by human radiologists.
- *Purpose of natural speech signal processing.* Nowadays, for achieving huge improvements in the healthcare industry in terms of analysing and interpreting documentation, neural networks and deep-learning policies are support considerably by natural speech signal processing tools. Meanwhile these neural networks can differentiate distinct etymological or syntactic components by "gathering" comparable words together and comparing these words to one another, supporting the network to make accurate sense of complex semantics. It can be difficult to understand the nuances of public speech and communication, i.e., words that generally show up close to one another in an informal expression may wind up being something altogether different than equivalent words which show up in unique situations. Although sufficiently accurate language-to-text translation has turned into a reasonably normal skill for correspondence apparatuses, producing solid and noteworthy translation from free-message clinical information is essentially a really testing exercise (Cheng et al. 2016).
- *Electronic health record (EHR) for tracking patients' health.* Deep learning has been applied to process-added EHRs, dealing with both systematised (i.e., dosage, medication, and research center tests) and formless information (i.e., free-text clinical notes). The best examples of this system dealt with the EHRs of a medical services framework based on the specialised engineering of a frequently supervised predictive clinical task. Especially for the typical methodology, deep learning can achieve an outcome superior to the ordinary AI models. To learn detailed descriptions of clinical concepts, such as illnesses, prescriptions, and research center tests, that might be used for diagnosis and prediction, neural language deep learning models have also been applied to EHRs (Cheng et al. 2016; Vyas 2023). Suppliers, scientists, and insurance companies will soon use EHR information to track down patterns in terms of infections and medication. AI unravels the crucial information that is frequently buried deep inside such text script in the many health records. Long Short-Term Memory (LSTM) neural networks are one of the best-known models used for NLP.

- *Drug discovery.* Deep-learning engineers have more plans involving precision medicine and medication discovery. The two assignments require analyzing incredibly large volumes of genetic, clinical, and population-level data in order to identify the previously hidden connections between symptoms, medications, and health conditions. The universe of genetic medication is new, so that startling revelations are typical, making this an invigorating demonstration area for creative ways to deal with issues (Xu et al. 2014).
- *Clinical decision support and analytics.* In clinical decision support and predictive analysis, businesses have expanded expectations for the role of deep learning. Deep learning will soon become a convenient analytic buddy in the ongoing setting, where it can provide awareness of changes in conditions like Sepsis Respiratory Disorder. Similarly, eye care professionals examine eye issues using optical coherence tomography (OCT) sweeps. These 3D images depict a description of the back of the eye, although they are difficult to read and demand close inspection for interpretation. The process of analyzing these outputs, combined with the large number of scans that healthcare professionals have to review, can lead to significant delays between the scan and treatment when prompt action is needed. These delays may even result in people losing their sight if they result in an unanticipated problem, such a channel at the back of the eye (Alzubaidi et al. 2021; Cheng et al. 2016).

4.13 CHALLENGES FACING THE DEEP- LEARNING STRATEGY IN THE HEALTHCARE WORLD

- Occasional lack of information brings about low precision.
- Interpretability issue with deep-learning models provides it with the state of a "black box".
- Shortage of explicit disease-related information on uncommon diseases.
- Those occasions where raw data cannot be used straightforwardly as input for DNN.
- DNN can be misled by adding little changes to the information tests, resulting in misclassification.

4.14 CONCLUSION

In view of all the research carried out on deep learning by various scientists, obviously deep learning can be a component for improving interpretation of biomedical information to expand human healthcare. The most recent advances in deep learning innovations give new helpful developments to demonstrate the start-to-finish learning models for complex information structures. Deep learning will almost certainly take on a critical role in providing the highest-quality care possible to patients for decades to come, thanks to an incredibly large number of promising case studies, speculation from key stakeholders in the business, and a developing amount of information to help frontline investigations. People need to stop thinking of AI as a futuristic concept and, instead, embrace the tools and beneficial opportunities it is presenting to us. It's interesting to imagine where the field of medicine might go in the future as a result of how AI is moving the industry into a completely new area.

REFERENCES

Alzubaidi, L., Zhang, J., Humaidi, A. J., Al- Dujaili, A., Duan, Y., Al-Shamma, O., & Farhan, L. (2021). Review of deep learning: Concepts, CNN architectures, challenges, applications, future directions. *Journal of Big Data*, 8(1), 1–74.

Bajwa, J., Munir, U., Nori, A., & Williams, B. (2021). Artificial intelligence in healthcare: Transforming the practice of medicine. *Future Healthcare Journal*, 8(2), e188.

Bhardwaj, R., Nambiar, A. R., & Dutta, D. (2017). A study of machine learning in healthcare. *IEEE 41st Annual Computer Software and Applications Conference (COMPSAC)*, 2, 236–241.

Bishop, C. M. (1995). *Neural Networks for Pattern Recognition*. Oxford University Press.

Chen, M., & Decary, M. (2020). Artificial intelligence in healthcare: An essential guide for health leaders. In *Healthcare Management Forum* (Vol. 33, No. 1, pp. 10–18). Los Angeles, CA: SAGE Publications, National Academy of Medicine. *JAMA*, 323(6), 509–510.

Cheng, Y., Wang, F., Zhang, P., & Hu, J. (2016). Risk prediction with electronic health records: A deep learning approach. In *Proceedings of the 2016 SIAM International.*

Collins, F. S., & Varmus, H. (2015). A new initiative on precision medicine. *New England Journal of Medicine*, 372(9), 793–795.

Coronato, A., Naeem, M., De Pietro, G., & Paragliola, G. (2020). Reinforcement learning for intelligent healthcare applications: A survey. *Artificial Intelligence in Medicine*, 109, e101964.

Davenport, T., & Kalakota, R. (2019). The potential for artificial intelligence in healthcare. *Future Healthcare Journal*, 6(2), 94–98.

Hazra, A., Mandal, S. K., & Gupta, A. (2012). Study and analysis of breast cancer cell detection using Naïve Bayes, SVM and ensemble algorithms. *International Journal of Computer Applications*, 145(2), 39–45.

Hinton, G. E., Osindero, S., & Teh, Y. W. (2006). A fast learning algorithm for deep belief nets. *Neural Computation*, 18(7), 1527–1554.

Kononenko, I. (2021). Machine learning for medical diagnosis: History, state of the art and perspective. *Artificial Intelligence in Medicine*, 23(1), 89–109.

Learning, M. (2017x(. Heart disease diagnosis and prediction using machine learning and data mining techniques: A review. *Advances in Computational Sciences and Technology*, 10(7), 2137–2159.

Liu, S., Liu, S., Cai, W., Pujol, S., Kikinis, R., & Feng, D. (2014). Early diagnosis of Alzheimer's disease with deep learning. In *2014 IEEE 11th International Symposium on Biomedical Imaging (ISBI)* (pp. 1015–1018).

Manne, R., & Kantheti, S. C. (2021). Application of artificial intelligence in healthcare: Chances and challenges. *Current Journal of Applied Science and Technology*, 40(6), 78–89.

Masci, J., Meier, U., Cireşan, D., & Schmidhuber, J. (2011). Stacked convolutional auto-encoders for hierarchical feature extraction. In *Artificial Neural Networks and Machine Learning–ICANN 2011: 21st International Conference on Artificial Neural Networks, Espoo, Finland, June 14-17, 2011, Proceedings, Part I 21* (pp. 52–59). Berlin, Heidelberg: Springer.

Mirbabaie, M., Stieglitz, S., & Frick, N. R. (2021). Artificial intelligence in disease diagnostics: A critical review and classification on the current state of research guiding future direction. *Health and Technology*, 11(4), 693–731.

Mishra, A., & Shukla, A. (2018, December). From machine learning to deep learning trends and challenges. *CSI Communications*, 41(8), 10–12.

Murphy, K. P. (2012). *Machine Learning: A Probabilistic Perspective*. MIT Press.

Rong, G., Mendez, A., Assi, E. B., Zhao, B., & Sawan, M. (2020). Artificial intelligence in healthcare: Review and prediction case studies. *Engineering*, 6(3), 291–301.

Secinaro, S., Calandra, D., Secinaro, A., Muthurangu, V., & Biancone, P. (2021). The role of artificial intelligence in healthcare: A structured literature review. *BMC Medical Informatics and Decision Making*, 21(1), 1–23.

Sharma, P., & Bhatia, A. P. R. (2012). Implementation of decision tree algorithm to analysis the performance. https://www.ijarcce.com/upload/december/24-Implementation%20of%20Decision.pdf

Thompson, T. G., & Brailer, D. J. (2004). *The Decade of Health Information Technology: Delivering Consumer-centric and Information-rich Health Care*. Washington, DC: US Department of Health and Human Services.

Vyas, S. (2023). Extended Reality and Edge AI for Healthcare 4.0: Systematic Study. In *Extended Reality for Healthcare Systems* (pp. 229–240). Academic Press.

Xu, R., Li, L., & Wang, Q. (2014). dRiskKB: A large-scale disease-disease risk relationship knowledge base constructed from biomedical text. *BMC Bioinformatics*, 15(1), 1–13.

Zimmermann, H. J. (2011). *Fuzzy Set Theory—And its Applications*. Springer Science & Business Media.

5 Enhancing access of the visually impaired through the smart cane

Syeda Fizza Nuzhat Zaidi, Vinod Kumar Shukla, Shaurya Gupta, Preetha V K

CONTENTS

DOI: 10.1201/9781003244592-5

5.1 INTRODUCTION

Human–computer interaction has been a continuous issue of concern for accessing computer systems by people with visual impairment, hearing impairment,
speech impairment, dyslexia, autism, etc. The three groups of disability, which
are *blindness and visual impairment, deafness and hearing impairment*, and
autism spectrum disorders, affect different organs of the body and their functioning and have extremely different outcomes and impacts on the individual during
social events and life in general. But they also have two factors in common. They
all affect the sensory system and are only sometimes immediately apparent. The
sensory system is the body's system of sense organs. The five important and major
senses are vision, hearing, taste, smell, and touch (Smith et al. 2018). To come up
with solutions, using technologies, for the visually disabled, we must first understand the challenges people with this disability face and the frequency of these
disabilities across the planet. With the growth of technology and its implementation in every field possible, the scale of human interactions with technologies has
increased greatly. Thus, human–computer interaction comes into play in a multitude of fields. Human–computer interaction, or HCI, is a multidisciplinary field of
study that focuses on the design of computer technology and the interaction of the
users (humans) with the technology. Initially, this field only focused on computers
but has expanded its scope to cover all types of technology design and is a part of
every field, whether small or huge. The field of HCI ranges from wearable devices
to household gadgets to architectural devices. HCI not only increases our chances
of accessing our gadgets more easily, making life easier, but also increases the
chance of changing the lives of millions of people with disabilities on this planet.
The aim of HCI is to produce usable and advanced technology which can serve its
purpose for every individual: highly advanced technology for people who do not
need assistance and highly assistive technology interactions for those who need
assistance and support.

5.2 GLOBAL STATISTICS OF DISABILITIES FACED BY PEOPLE

As of 1 December 2020, there are around one billion people around the globe
who live with a disability. This is around 15% of the world's population; there
are around 190 million people, or 3.8%, who are 15 years of age and older, and
who require health care for their disabilities (World Health Organization (WHO)
2022) (Figure 5.1).

Globally, it is said that two in ten adults live with a disability. As of 7 April
2020, the most common disability was seen to be difficulty walking/climbing
stairs (30.6 million) which could be due to old age or a physical disability of some
sort. This is followed by disabilities where people require constant assistance

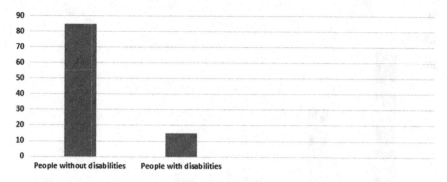

FIGURE 5.1   World populations of people with and without disabilities (2020).

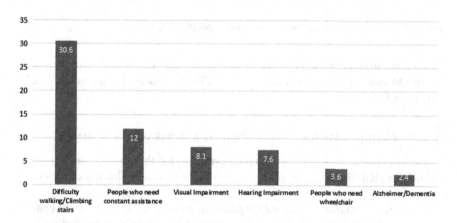

FIGURE 5.2   Most common disabilities in the world (2020).

from others for daily tasks (12.0 million), suffer from visual impairment (8.1 million), hearing impairment (7.6 million), need a wheelchair (3.6 million), or with Alzheimer's disease or dementia (2.4 million) (Figure 5.2) (Disabled World 2022).

5.3   GLOBAL STATISTICS OF VISUAL IMPAIRMENT

5.3.1   Visual impairment and blindness

According to the WHO, as of 8 October 2020, at least 1 billion people around the globe have a near or distant vision impairment which could have been prevented. The top leading causes of visual impairment and blindness currently are uncorrected refractive errors and cataracts. The report also found that most people who have visual impairment or blindness are over the age of 50 years. These one billion people include those with moderate or severe distance vision impairment or blindness due to unaddressed refractive errors (123.7 million), cataracts (65.2 million), glaucoma (6.9 million), corneal opacities (4.2 million), diabetic retinopathy

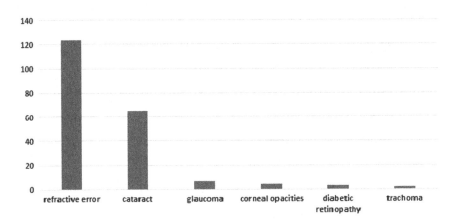

FIGURE 5.3   Visual impairment in one billion people (2020).

(3 million), and trachoma (2 million), as well as near-vision impairment caused by unaddressed presbyopia (826 million) (World Health Organization 2022) (Figure 5.3).

5.3.2 NEED FOR ASSISTIVE TECHNOLOGIES FOR PEOPLE WITH A DISABILITY

There are several assistive technologies available for the disabled society with the help of HCI; these assistive technologies fall under the following categories:

- *Assistive products required for personal medical treatment.* These can include any personal medical equipment required by the disabled user without the help of another person.
- *Assistive products for training in skills.* These can include technological devices and gadgets used by the disabled user for improvement training regarding his/her personal, mental, or social abilities.
- *Orthoses and prostheses.* Orthoses are devices applied externally and are used for modifying the structure or functions of the neuro-muscular and skeletal systems. Prostheses, on the other hand, are external devices used to replace a body part wholly or partially.
- *Assistive products which can be used for personal care and protection.* These can include assistive technology, which helps the disabled user dress, eat, or drink.
- *Assistive products for mobility.* These can include technology required for moving from one place to another and gadgets required to move one object from one workplace to another.
- *Assistive products for communication and information.* These can include technological devices for communication, using sight, hearing, speech, etc.

- *Assistive products for recreation.* These can include user-friendly devices for the disabled which can be used for playing games, watching videos, listening to music, etc.
- *Assistive products for housekeeping.* These can include technological gadgets that help around the house, for example, cooking and cleaning, switching on the lights or the fan, etc.
- *Assistive products for environmental improvement.* These can include gadgets that help in getting familiar with the environment the disabled person is in, to help them navigate around it.
- *Assistive products for employment and school.* These can include technological gadgets that help in learning for the disabled and help in carrying around and accomplishing tasks in the workplace or at school.

5.4   DESIGNING FOR PEOPLE WITH VISUAL DISABILITIES

Visual disabilities are by far the most challenging of challenges to overcome when designing a technological gadget that is suitable for these types of users. The results of various studies are available to improve the various aspects of disability, such as low vision (Shukla & Verma 2019), with help of smart glasses (Nazim et al. 2022). Technology plays an important role to deliver these services, such as the Internet of Things, which combines the real world and computer-generated content (Trayush et al. 2021; Komal et al. 2021) and blockchain technologies (Vyas et al. 2022). Some inventions and ideas for technology for the visually disabled are described in the following subsections:

5.4.1   Using data that make a specific sound when
a task is underway or accomplished

Every website component should make a specific sound and include metadata. For example, every image, graphic, heading, etc., should contain all text, a comment, or a piece of text describing the shown image or graphic. This is important because visually disabled users use screen readers, and it becomes easy for them to understand when such descriptions are present for every image and graphic.

5.4.2   Adopting the Braille code

Braille is a widely used form of obtaining information for the visually disabled society from technological gadgets. This could make the keyboard easily understandable for the visually impaired user and be used by someone with no visual impairment, thus following the principle of design for all. This is where the refreshable braille display comes into play. This electronic braille display is a great example of using haptics or touch in HCI design for the visually impaired (UX Collective 2022).

5.4.3 Using speech recognition

This involves recognising speech by technological devices using various methods, such as pattern recognition, Hidden Markov Model (HMM), neural networks, etc.

5.4.4 Using standard HTML to design websites

This allows screen readers to navigate easily through the website and understand the text. It is also important to use the right structure: H1 for the heading, H2 for the subheading, and the headings in the heading tab, etc., so that the screen reader can easily understand and communicate such information to the impaired user.

5.4.5 Using Screen Readers such as Job Access with Speech (JAWS)

These are the devices most widely used by those who are visually impaired. They work by using a text-to-speech engine, which reads out all the textual data and the menus present on the device. It also repeats all the keystrokes the user makes so they know what they are clicking on. These can be even more useful when used along with the braille code mentioned above so the user can hear and feel the data, giving the user the best experience.

5.4.6 Using auditory icons

With auditory icons, every action performed can have a specific sound associated with it. For example, when deleting something, it can have the sound of glass smashing, or, when closing a tab, it can have a whoosh sound. The SonicFinder for Macintosh has specific sounds for a variety of tasks like folders having a papery sound, moving the files having a dragging sound, big files having a louder sound than small files, etc.

5.4.7 CAPTCHA (Completely Automated Public Turing test to tell Computers and Humans Apart)

CAPTCHA tools could be used with an audio function present on every site. Nowadays, every site requires us to prove we are not a robot, and this becomes difficult for the visually impaired. Hence, the CAPTCHA option should come with audio for every website present.

5.4.8 Website design

Website design should avoid too many scattered links on their pages because this makes it difficult for the screen reader to identify what the data are. The links should come with a description before them, so that the visually impaired user will know what the link leads to when he/she uses the screen reader on that page.

5.4.9 USE EARCONS

Earcons are brief descriptive sounds used to describe or communicate an event. They are synthetic sounds that convey information (Banerjee et al. 2020).

5.4.10 ZOOM OPTION

The devices should have the option to zoom into text and change its colour so people with low vision can see the larger text and colour-blind people can change the colour to see the text. iPhones have an accessibility feature that makes all the icons larger. Keyboards exist where we can zoom into the keypad to see the tiny letters and easily recognise them.

5.4.11 THE BIONIC EYE

This is one of the most advanced and expensive HCI devices designed yet for the visually impaired and must be surgically implanted into the user's eye (Kasowski & Beyeler 2022).

5.5 SMART CANE PROTOTYPE FOR THE VISUALLY IMPAIRED

The field of human–computer interaction has come up with various devices for the disabled society. The device or prototype we have put forward in this chapter is a smart cane for the visually impaired, using infrared sensors and speakers to alert the visually impaired user to the obstacle in front of them. When the visually impaired user points this stick while moving around and the sensor detects an object, it sends a signal to the buzzer, which sets off an alarm and alerts the user to the obstacle in front of them. This lets the user stay safe and gives them a sense of independence because they don't need to ask for help from anyone or require assistance. It is also an effective and excellent device that can be used by anyone, regardless of age or ability, when it is dark, or when the power source is not working. We can easily use this device to indicate any obstacles in case we need to go from one room to another (Vyas & Bhargava 2021)

5.5.1 INTRODUCTION TO PROXIMITY SENSORS

Proximity sensors have been successful in industrial, medical, aerospace, and other fields, and now they have witnessed another success in the consumer electronics market. Proximity sensors, based upon their fundamental principle, have been divided into inductance type, capacitive type, magnetic inductive type, photoelectric type, and ultrasonic type, etc. Traditional practice is to use a large current to drive LEDs and increase the luminous intensity of LEDs, or keep the chip working under low temperature, thus inevitably increasing the power or limiting the chip's scope (Treeratanaporn et al. 2021). Based on the environmental noise problems of background light and dark current of the infrared (IR) proximity sensor, this chapter puts forward the application of proximity IR sensors into making an automatic device that is lightweight and useful for visually impaired people worldwide.

The working of an IR-based proximity sensor is conducted by an object detection-based method. In this type of detection of objects, any second when an object is detected within the line-of-sight (LOS) of the sensor working on IR, there will be a reflection using a signal in the direction of the infrared sensor. This type of reflected signal is often known as an echo signal (Junsheng 2013). Now, if we use a proximity sensor that works on IR and which is used for a working model for object detection, the presence of the object when it comes near the sensor will disturb or block the LOS of the IR signal, which will then give an echo signal, showing that an object has been detected and will trigger the 5V buzzer attached inside the dispenser to give off an alarm and inform the user of the obstacle. Similarly, the absence of an object here will not give out an echo-based signal. Thus, this method uses proximity-based sensors working on IR to detect the presence of an object to warn the visually impaired user of an obstacle in their way (Siraj & Shukla 2020).

5.6 HARDWARE REQUIRED FOR A SMART CANE PROTOTYPE

5.6.1 INFRARED SENSOR

The sensor used in this chapter is a proximity IR sensor (Figure 5.4) which can be used for obstacle detection and avoidance. The module light of this sensor is easily adaptable to any surroundings and the working voltage to be used here is to be above 3.3 V and below 5 V. This sensor has two IR transmitters and a tube for receiving. The range of its effectiveness is in the range 2–80 cm.

5.6.2 18650 DOUBLE BATTERY HOLDER

The battery holder required here should be able to hold two 18650 batteries in it to be able to provide the required power.

FIGURE 5.4 Proximity infrared sensor.

FIGURE 5.5   Round speaker.

5.6.3   V BUZZER/MINI SPEAKER-PC MOUNT

This is a small 12-mm diameter speaker (Figure 5.5) that operates around the audible range.

5.6.4   CANE/STICK

The stick or cane is where the circuit will be mounted. The stick can be of any sort and length but preferably lightweight so it is easy to carry, with an approximate length of 2.5–3 feet or the cane's length should be adjustable.

5.6.5   18650 BATTERIES

There are two 18650 batteries required here. The 18650 batteries are lithium-ion batteries and can be used in various appliances such as flashlights, laptops, vaporisers, cameras, electrical devices, etc. The 18650 describes their size, which means they are 18 mm by 65 mm.

5.7   CIRCUIT DIAGRAM FOR THE PROPOSED PROTOTYPE (SENSOR-BASED SMART CANE)

Figure 5.4 shows a circuit diagram, where the round speaker, proximity sensor and battery relates to wires, to test the functioning of one part of the smart cane.

5.7.1   TESTING OF INFRARED PROXIMITY SENSOR

Infrared light (IR light) is based on the principles of optics in physics. The IR proximity sensors apply a certain voltage to a pair of IR LED (light-emitting

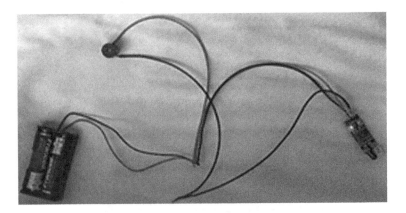

FIGURE 5.6   IR Sensor without an object detected.

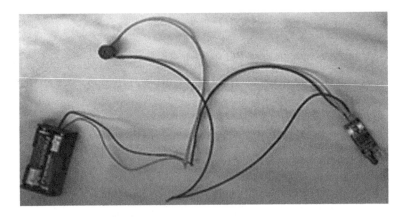

FIGURE 5.7   IR Sensor with an object detected.

diodes). These will, in turn, emit infrared or IR light. If the object is close by, the reflected light will be stronger than if the object is farther away from the sensor. The testing should be done to ensure the IR proximity sensor is working properly and that the LEDs are working properly (Figures 5.6 and 5.7). This testing can be done by setting up the connection for the circuit diagram and then testing the sensor by bringing an object or your hand closer to the sensor. If the light is emitted, the sensor works and can be used in the circuit for the model.

The sensor lights up and works properly, showing that the circuit is connected properly and has no loose connections in any set devices. The circuit is then attached to the stick and is put in such a way that it is presentable and does not lead to a short circuit at any point, especially when used, which could cause a shock to the person using it.

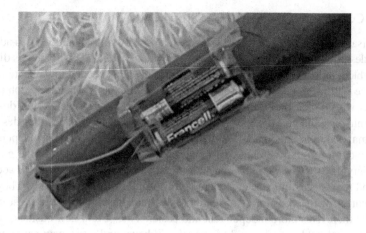

FIGURE 5.8 Overview of the smart cane set-up

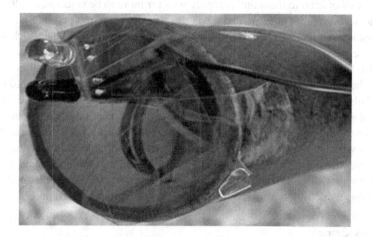

FIGURE 5.9 Working of the smart cane

5.7.2 RESULT OF A WORKING PROTOTYPE

The entire circuit is set up on the cane, and the testing is done again for object detection. It is found that, every time an object is encountered, the buzzer gives off an alarm, indicating that the device works perfectly and can be used by the person whenever they need it. Figure 5.8 showcases the cane in the ready state, with the completion of the final setup, and Figure 5.9 displays the working of the smart cane.

5.8   CONCLUSION AND FUTURE WORK

The disabled society is the world's largest minority and should be considered when designing and producing every new technical gadget. This society is differently abled and can remember the procedures and steps needed to navigate using a device within hours, if taught properly. The challenge is when they don't find devices with which they can be compatible. This is where several HCI designs come into play and give disabled people the technological advantage they deserve. The smart cane is thus made for them to make sure they can feel independent while moving around without assistance or supervision. Thus, with the growth of society day by day, we must consider the huge growth in this disabled society too, and their needs must be considered when implementing new ideas. They are one-quarter of the consumers of technological advances but need it most of all to make their lives more independent and easier. Thus, every new business in the technological field, every new designer of a website, and every new game developer must ensure that they tend to the needs of these differently abled users. This ensures that every single consumer of the technological world is satisfied with the technology offered to them and can only wait for more to be consumed. Although this device serves its purpose and helps the visually impaired people find out all the obstacles in their way, in our future work we could upgrade this in such a way that it serves its purpose not only for someone with a visual impairment alone but also for someone with both visual and hearing impairments. As they would have a hearing impairment, it would be hard for them to respond to the buzzer. It would also be an inconvenience for everyone else when the buzzer goes off when pointed at every obstacle by the user in a quiet place such as a library or at night, when everyone is sleeping. Instead of the buzzer, we could make the alerts in the form of vibrations, so only the user knows about the obstacle and the device does not cause any noise. We could also keep both buzzer and vibrations and instead include a switch, so the buzzer work only when the switch is switched on, but the vibrations work all the time, even when the switch is not switched on.

REFERENCES

Banerjee, A., Saba, S. A., Rana, S., & Chakraborty, S. (2020, June). Bionic eye-A review. In *2020 8th International Conference on Reliability, Infocom Technologies and Optimization (Trends and Future Directions)(ICRITO)* (pp. 501–504). IEEE.

Disabled World. Disability benefits, facts, statistics, resources. https://www.disabled-world.com/disability/, Accessed on March 2022.

Junsheng, W. (2013, December). Improvement of Ir proximity sensor based on digital simulation mixed subtraction circuit. *Sensors & Transducers*, 160(12), 42–48.

Kasowski, J., & Beyeler, M. (2022). Immersive virtual reality simulations of bionic vision. *In Proceedings of the Augmented Humans 2022 (AHs '22)*. (pp. 82–93). New York: Association for Computing Machinery. https://doi.org/10.1145/3519391.3522752.

Komal, S., Abdul, B., & Shukla, V. K. (2021). Green Internet of Things (G-IoT) technologies, application, and future challenges. *Green Internet of Things and Machine Learning: Towards a Smart Sustainable World*, 317–348.

Nazim, S., Firdous, S., Pillai, S. R., & Shukla, V. K. (2022). Smart glasses: A visual assistant for the blind. In 2022 *International Mobile and Embedded Technology Conference (MECON)* (pp. 621–626). doi: 10.1109/MECON53876.2022.9751975.

Shukla, V. K., & Verma, A. (2019). Enhancing user navigation experience, object identification and surface depth detection for 'low vision' with proposed electronic cane. In *2019 Advances in Science and Engineering Technology International Conferences (ASET)* (pp. 1–5). doi: 10.1109/ICASET.2019.8714213.

Siraj, A., & Shukla, V. K. (2020). Framework for personalized car parking system using proximity sensor. In *2020 8th International Conference on Reliability, Infocom Technologies and Optimization (Trends and Future Directions) (ICRITO)* (pp. 198–202). doi: 10.1109/ICRITO48877.2020.9197853.

Smith, E. M., Gowran, R. J., Mannan, H., Donnelly, B., Alvarez, L., Bell, D., ... Wu, S. (2018). Enabling appropriate personnel skill-mix for progressive realization of equitable access to assistive technology. *Disability and Rehabilitation: Assistive Technology*, 13(5), 445–453.

Trayush, T., Bathla, R., Saini, S., & Shukla, V. K. (2021). IoT in healthcare: Challenges, benefits, applications, and opportunities. In *2021 International Conference on Advance Computing and Innovative Technologies in Engineering (ICACITE)* (pp. 107–111). doi: 10.1109/ICACITE51222.2021.9404583.

Treeratanaporn, T., Torat, T., & Kongtaworn, T. (2021). Usability evaluation of touch screen interface with various user groups. In *2021 25th International Computer Science and Engineering Conference (ICSEC)* (pp. 149–154). doi: 10.1109/ICSEC53205.2021.9684661.

UX Collective. Human computer interaction for the visually impaired. https://uxdesign.cc/human-computer-interaction-for-the-visually-impaired-a467ad61175b, Accessed on March 2022.

Vyas, S., & Bhargava, D. (2021). *Smart Health Systems: Emerging Trends*. Springer Singapore.

Vyas, S., Shukla, V. K., Gupta, S., & Prasad, A. (Eds.). (2022). *Blockchain Technology: Exploring Opportunities, Challenges, and Applications*. CRC Press

World Health Organization. Blindness and vision impairment. https://www.who.int/news-room/fact-sheets/detail/blindness-and-visual-impairment, Accessed on March 2022.

World Health Organization. Disability, and health. https://www.who.int/news-room/fact-sheets/detail/disability-and-health, Accessed on March 2022.

6 Contemporary role of edge-AI in IoT and IoE in healthcare and digital marketing

Shaurya Gupta, Sonali Vyas

CONTENTS

6.1 INTRODUCTION

The chief technological developments in the area of healthcare (McGrow 2019) include the surge in data accessibility, combined with greater computing power, and progress with respect to machine learning procedures, which have nurtured the expansion of AI-based applications, and which transform practically every facet of everyday life. Additionally, internet-associated sensors and smart devices plus wearable smart devices, associated with the Internet of Things (IoT), is augmenting the normal experience and improving the quality of life. In addition, increasing resistance to cloud-centered AI clarifications, in addition to the necessity for applications in terms of analysing the extraordinary capacity and rapid data streams in a real-time environment (Satyanarayanan et al. 2015; Nastic et al. 2017), has motivated hardware designers to create reduced AI accelerators, ensuring AI in delivering to edge computing. Edge computing (Garcia et al. 2015; Shi et al. 2016a; Satyanarayanan et al. 2013) imparts an important character to the integration of such developments. Cloud-based solutions deliver solutions to spotted data fields (Bouzefrane et al. 2014) but there are genuine concerns regarding confidentiality and privacy. In addition, remote AI programs will become progressively unified and collaboratively start to solve multifaceted jobs (Montes & Goertzel 2019). Although bootstrapping systems from the cloud is quite feasible, a dispersed model including Edge AI agents and practices is introduced. This new pattern of edge intelligence involves a cyber-physical entity that delivers raw data and acts on it efficiently, whereas edge computing is confronted with a few exceptional encounters from AI structures. There has been extraordinarily successful developments in the area of artificial intelligence, specifically in deep learning, which marked an observable innovation in terms of:

- Workstation image visualisation.
- Natural language processing.
- Well-being carefulness.
- Self-directed driving and surveillance.

AI technologies have extended from a central mode to a mobile or distributed mode, giving rise to a novel domain called edge-AI, with vivid developments which are markedly variable in terms of expertise, social behaviour, besides regimes. Edge AI couples intellect and investigation in terms of associated devices, organizations for information gathering and accumulating, in addition to dispensation (Shi et al. 2016). It permits an extensive variability of novel applications involving data gathering and exploration, combined together. For instance, billions of mobile phone owners are using numerous smartphone applications like translation services, digital supporters, as well as well-being observing services. Edge hardware device units generally have stringent device restraints, like restricted computing competences and memory capability in server environments. The proposal behind disposition for diverse, large-scale edge-AI methods necessitates considerable manufacturing energies as well as various multifaceted exploration challenges. Innovative design methods, as well as design computerisation gears, are essential for facing cumulative sets of edge-AI requests. Empowering design approaches are categorised under specialisation and co-design. Design specialisation judiciously acclimatises collective machineries for the circumstances of edge-AI applications, like prototype compression or devoted hardware accelerators. Co-design syndicates two or supplementary focused technologies in case of optimisation prospects.

Zhou et al. (2019), Wang et al. (2020), and Xu et al. (2020) graphed the important perceptions in addition to contemporary developments of edge-AI, including the foremost spheres of applications other than universal expertise. Artificial intelligence, machine learning, and edge computing (Deng et al. 2020) have also become an essential part of the innovative Internet of Things (IoT) or Internet of Everything (IoE) in terms of digital advertising environs (Nilsson 2014). AI is being used extensively in digital marketing nowadays. Edge computing licenses dispensation of definite data locally, near to the source, which has implications for processing (Meng et al. 2020). However, certain subtle information is not shared on the cloud (Janakiram 2019). Now, AI has been developed to be crucial in terms of edge computing acceptance, in addition to the fact that it has become the default terminus for positioning machine-learning models which are trained on the cloud platform. Applications in terms of digital marketing are increasing multi-fold over time and customers are using varied devices to accomplish it. Digital marketing in terms of the cloud has been an indispensable part of AI or ML operations (Stone et al. 2020), in addition edge-AI changes the healthcare environment. Apart from this, unusual safety and confidentiality concerns are raised which need to be minimised in order to defend user privacy data being used in digital marketing. User smart devices play a significant role in digital marketing and gather many forms of user data for aiding the marketing purpose. IoT or IoE hardware device units can work continuously, in addition to tracking numerous customer activities, including the delivery of valued modified amenities, with these being extremely useful in terms of digital marketing and in varied healthcare domains. As an example, hardware device activity and online tracing consist of customer procurements, whereabouts data, app commotion, acquaintances etc. Amassing dissimilar bases of information altogether helps in construction of customer digital outlines which become a robust basis of information for publicising aptitude and judgment making. Tracking data gathering increases the use in the future of IoT and IoE hardware devices, with respect to customers. AI has its applications in digital marketing which involves learning with the help of machines. Digital publicity involves not only promotion of products, but also wide-ranging areas like medicinal or wellbeing publicity. Digital marketing becomes quite crucial when considering the case of smart households, robots, and metropolises. Edge-AI is applied in varied facets of digital marketing for examples of the processing of information which exists locally without transferring customer data to the cloud in addition to allowing machine-learning algorithms to function locally on hardware device units (Sachdev 2020). Aggressors or attackers may amend business transactions by which the customer obtains a faulty product or where their private information goes under the attacker's control. Edge hardware devices may require networks which may encourage the local processing of data. Considering applications, data, and services all together (Caprolu et al. 2019) egde-AI provides good relations to customers and also processes information locally, which in turn significantly reduces the risks related to safety and confidentiality. Engaging edge-AI helps to personalise the consumer's understanding in addition to increasing the faith of the patrons (AI- and ML-based edge devices center the conclusions or some varied parameter which becomes a beneficial tool in terms of digital publishing. Edge hardware devices would ultimately turn out to be influential from their present state, apart from the model including the cloud, which would be part of general architecture (Hagan et al. 2019a). Edge-AI delivers a receptive outline in terms of digital marketing framework as a dynamic response centered on verdicts concluded via AI. Associated sensors and actuators concerning edge-AI hardware device units also deliver significant information for the purpose of digital marketing. Automatic marketplace re-segmentation, centered on dynamic info using edge-AI, is quite feasible because of local dispensation besides numerous facets of customer data which are accessible on-device. Taking into consideration the edge-AI model, dealers are quite capable of spontaneously helping in custom-made publicity of customers based on habits and actions of the consumers as well as through learned predictions based on customer partialities, though some information is gathered which may be personal for the customer in addition to being used in steering innumerable publicity analytics. A cloud model necessitates communication among smart devices and the cloud, of which a customer can be apprehensive at times, particularly if suitable procedures are not even being considered; edge-AI assists in moderating apprehensions of these kinds. These security concerns may cause damage to clients of digital publishing amenities; therefore, safety and confidentiality concerns must be addressed.

6.2   EDGE ESSENTIALS

The principal spheres of edge-AI are as follows:

- Edge reserving.
- Edge training.
- Edge extrapolation.
- Edge divesting

First, edge reserving refers to information gathering, grouping and storage in edge hardware devices and neighboring atmospheres in subsidiary edge applications (Hagan et al. 2019). Consumers information is produced by their smartphones, whereas ecological observing devices and sensors stock information in neighboring edge servers. Furthermore, edge training exploits the confined information plus computing power of the edge, minus high bandwidth necessities of transporting data firstly to the cloud. Edge training entails abridged bit-widths in order to keep up with the hardware device constraints. Considering a supplementary benefit, it preserves customer data confidentiality by circumventing the transporting of data offsite. Furthermore, edge extrapolation involves implementation of AI algorithms at the edge. Lastly, edge divesting deals with a dispersed computing pattern wherein hardware device units discharge application responsibilities to the cloud. Divesting escalates the computation competence of edge hardware devices, subject to inadequate resources.

6.3   EDGE DEVICES

These edge devices can be categorised based on computing class, namely:

- Central Processing Unit (CPU)-based.
- Field Programmable Gate Array (GA)-based.
- Graphics Processing Unit (GPU)-base.

6.3.1 CPU-BASED EDGE DEVICES

CPUs represent a critical component while considering dispensation, in addition to control systems. CPU-centered edge devices offer the benefits of adaptability, low power, low cost, multitasking, and effortless programming. They are considered for universal instruction sequences as they follow inadequate parallelism. Multi-core devices include the Nvidia Jetson group (Alvarado et al. 2020), the AMD Ryzen group (Naffziger et al. 2021), and the Arm Mali GPUs (Gronquist et al. 2018).

6.3.2 FPGA-BASED EDGE DEVICES

FPGAs (field-programmable gate arrays) are incorporated circuits constituted via an architecture focusing on improvement of parallelism, through CPU-centered hardware devices, which are good for enormous parallel computations. CPU-based edge devices include the Arm Cortex-M (Alkim et al. 2016), the Raspberry Pi series (Severance 2013), the Nano Pi series (Ma'anf et al. 2021), and the Speed MAIX series (Hao et al. 2021).

6.3.3 GPU-BASED EDGE DEVICES

GPUs were initially considered in terms of image dispensation, apart from computation in respect to a parallel structure, yet are now progressively being used in accelerating AI jobs which have immense computing requirements. High enactment is achieved via parallelism and programmability; entrenched GPUs are unambiguously designed to have low power and be low cost, apart from which they predominate in numerous edge devices involved in deep-learning errands. GPU-based edge devices are a group of programmable logic blocks, which are quite effective in terms of application flexibility, for example, subsidiary subjective bit-width and conventional numerical set-ups (Darvish et al. 2020). They can accomplish more sophisticated tasks than CPUs (Biookaghazadeh et al. 2018; Nurvitadhi et al. 2017; Cass 2019). FPGAs frequently outpace GPUs in terms of low-latency intentions specifically for time-limited jobs (Shi et al. 2020) plus require fewer commands than CPUs or GPUs while delivering similar throughput. FPGAs though, are limited in terms of on-chip memory, while also exhibiting from low programmability. ASICs (application-specific integrated circuits) can apparently outpace other processors, with a considerable sophisticated computational output in addition to lower power consumption. ASICs are aimed at savings in terms of offsetting with the implementation of quality design and substantiation costs. ASICs, which are restricted to edge-AI applications, include Google Edge TPU (Liang 2020) and Ascend 310 AI processor (Reuther et al. 2020).

6.4 KNOWLEDGE MARKET IN EDGE-AI-ENABLED IOT

Edge-AI units When considered with respect to the knowledge market, the assimilated information with equivalent yields is known as knowledge coins (KCs).

This is an innovative cryptographic coinage which is somewhat related to BTC and Ether, which are used in Bitcoin and Ethereum, respectively. The knowledge market consists of the following components.

6.4.1 TRUSTED AUTHORITY (TA)

A TA may be an administration subdivision, accountable for resetting the knowledge market, especially in terms of trading. It may create public constraints and cryptographic keys for marketplace applicants. Subsequently, after registration on a TA, edge-AI nodes besides Knowledge-Augmented Genertion (KAG) might be the authentic associates.

6.4.2 EDGE-AI NODES

Edge-AI nodes, when considered in the case of IoT, act accordingly to the role state, i.e., knowledge seller, buyer, or futile node. Apart from that, they act as seller after determining information from composed sensory information or after receiving information requests. Apart from that, they upload the encoded knowledge-to-knowledge administrators. Knowledge cannot be considered public in nature, as a knowledge buyer finds varied information benefits when considering a market scenario. As knowledge is assimilated, pertinent knowledge coins are paid for the purpose of generating economic revenues instantaneously. Futile nodes neither deliver nor procure knowledge coins in the market.

6.4.3 KNOWLEDGE AGGREGATORS

The density in cellular networks, when considering the case of 4G networks, is increasing quite rapidly and will reach the mark of 50 BS/km^2, at which point it will be transformed to 5G networks (Ge et al. 2016). Integrating multi-access edge computing into base station ultra-dense systems will involve the following developments (Guo et al. 2018). Every base station will be fortified with improved 3C, i.e., cache, calculation, and communication resources. Base stations are customarily linked via high-speed underwired linkages. Consequently, being edge-AI nodes, they also contribute as knowledge administrators in the marketplace and stock, accomplishing the uploading of encrypted KCs, in addition to recording the knowledge interchange information. Temporarily, they guarantee the safety and confidentiality of the knowledge marketplace.

6.5 SAFETY AND CONFIDENTIALITY CONCERNS FOR EDGE-AI IN DIGITAL ADVERTISING AND HEALTHCARE IN IOT/IOE ENVIRONMENTS

Consider a cloud-centered model which faces various safety and confidentiality concerns, which stands as an area of research involving many domains, like healthcare and digital advertising. Edge computing has many assistances concerning safety and confidentiality (Porambage et al. 2019), which are being increased by edge-AI in IoT and IoE environments. The edge-AI models have the capability of associating with a cloud model. Edge device confirmation (Lee et al. 2018) jeopardises some of the safety concerns if it is not executed successfully. Furthermore, edge device endorsement must not be extensive because it may lead to unlawful admittance to individual information in addition to amenities. Taking an instance, In terms of digital marketing situation, consider an example where individual information is warehoused then administered on edge devices to deliver greater modified explanations to customers and patients, as well as from medicinal practioners. It comprises of data involving individual favourites, and other clustered information of consumers. Open-source susceptibilities survive reason, being open and free access to open-source code (Hagan et al. 2019; Rauti et al. 2018). Customer information may be stolen or influenced in order to implement malevolent or aggressive advertising facilities by means of some of the tricking algorithms (Jones et al. 2019), which represents another serious concern (Rabinovici 2012). In addition to the security of devices and protection of data, safety has become a solemn fear among consumers, as well as varied companies with major concerns regarding confidentiality, which serves as a discerning aspect of an business (Zhang et al. 2020). One of the distinguishing features regarding edge information dispensation involves indulgence and broadcasting of information without internet or cloud connection (Lee et al. 2018). Customers retain varied IoT devices and depend on them for needs and goods purchase and varied other functions being marketed to them, apart from which the clients use the devices for making acquisitions, attaining endorsements, making enquiries, and making requirements for the purpose of computerized inclusion (Sachdev 2020). Moreover, client analytics and data positioning, which are being used to provide modified and local amenities and in cases of clients or patients the facility of data positioning helps in delivering medicinal supervision remotely or distantly. Additionally, retargeting and remarketing (Conick et al. 2016) stand as prime digital publicizing approaches wherein, taking an instance where any customer has searched for a specific item, he may again be targeted for buying the same merchandise with some offers or discounts. Edge-AI recommender structures (Su et al. 2019) are very much helpful in digital advertising perspectives in terms of generating merchandise and provision commendations. With the advancement of time, more and more research will be done in order to involve edge-AI in a much greater digital advertising recommendation framework. Nevertheless, this comparatively novel tactic may aid in terms of retaining data and realizing the overall resolution of providing recommendations that will help in enhancing safety and confidentiality.

6.6 CONCLUSION AND FUTURE SCOPE

In addition to confidentiality concerns, this chapter also discussed various key aspects regarding edge-AI in the field of IoT and IoE domains, particular in healthcare and the digital advertising framework. Apart from that, it discussed various verticals of edge-AI in the fields of digital advertising and medicine, in addition to heightened safety and confidentiality. Though it is obvious that, such a paradigm, while handling very large-scale applications in healthcare and digital marketing domains, requires the addressing of many safety issues in addition to confidentiality concerns. The chapter deliberated various safety and confidentiality issues, apart from numerous possible extenuations plus deliberations pertinent to digital advertising and healthcare conditions, as well as covering many related legal and commercial angles in today's context. As the volume of data is ever increasing, in the future it will be important as to in which way edge-AI is going to be employed on wide-ranging devices in any kind of digital advertising or the ever-growing healthcare sector, along with complying on the methodical level, assuring safety and confidentiality rules to be followed without compromise.

REFERENCES

Alkim, E., Jakubeit, P., & Schwabe, P. (2016, November). Newhope on arm cortex-m. In *Security, Privacy, and Applied Cryptography Engineering: 6th International Conference, SPACE 2016, Hyderabad, India, December 14-18, 2016, Proceedings* (pp. 332–349). Cham: Springer International Publishing.

Alvarado Rodriguez, O., Dave, D., Liu, W., & Su, B. (2020, November). A study of machine learning inference benchmarks. In *2020 4th International Conference on Advances in Image Processing* (pp. 167–171).

Biookaghazadeh, S., Zhao, M., & Ren, F. (2018). Are FPGAs suitable for edge computing? In *{USENIX} Workshop on Hot Topics in Edge Computing (HotEdge 18)*.

Bouzefrane, S., Mostefa, A. F. B., Houacine, F., & Cagnon, H. (2014, April). Cloudlets authentication in NFC-based mobile computing. In *2014 2nd IEEE International Conference on Mobile Cloud Computing, Services, and Engineering* (pp. 267–272). Oxford, UK: IEEE.

Caprolu, M., Di Pietro, R., Lombardi, F., & Raponi, S. (2019, July). Edge computing perspectives: Architectures, technologies, and open security issues. In *2019 IEEE International Conference on Edge Computing (EDGE)* (pp. 116–123). IEEE.

Cass, S. (2019). Taking AI to the edge: Google's TPU now comes in a maker-friendly package. *IEEE Spectrum, 56*(5), 16–17.

Conick, H. (2016). *10 Minutes with Kirthi Kalyanam*. Marketing Insights, p. 1–4.

Darvish Rouhani, B., Lo, D., Zhao, R., Liu, M., Fowers, J., Ovtcharov, K., … Burger, D. (2020). Pushing the limits of narrow precision inferencing at cloud scale with microsoft floating point. *Advances in neural information processing systems, 33,* 10271–10281.

Deng, S., Zhao, H., Fang, W., Yin, J., Dustdar, S., & Zomaya, A. Y. (2020). Edge intelligence: The confluence of edge computing and artificial intelligence. *IEEE Internet of Things Journal, 7*(8), 7457–7469.

Garcia Lopez, P., Montresor, A., Epema, D., Datta, A., Higashino, T., Iamnitchi, A., … Riviere, E. (2015). Edge-centric computing: Vision and challenges. *ACM SIGCOMM Computer Communication Review, 45*(5), 37–42.

Ge, X., Tu, S., Mao, G., Wang, C. X., & Han, T. (2016). 5G ultra-dense cellular networks. *IEEE Wireless Communications, 23*(1), 72–79.

Gronqvist, J., & Lokhmotov, A. (2018). Optimizing OpenCL Kernels for the ARM Mali-T600 GPUs. In *GPU Pro 360 Guide to Mobile Devices* (pp. 167–198). AK Peters/CRC Press.

Guo, H., Liu, J., Zhang, J., Sun, W., & Kato, N. (2018). Mobile-edge computation offloading for ultra-dense IoT networks. *IEEE Internet of Things Journal*, 5(6), 4977–4988.

Hagan, M., Siddiqui, F., & Sezer, S. (2019, August). Enhancing security and privacy of next-generation edge computing technologies. In *2019 17th International Conference on Privacy, Security and Trust (PST)* (pp. 1–5). IEEE.

Hao, C., Dotzel, J., Xiong, J., Benini, L., Zhang, Z., & Chen, D. (2021). Enabling design methodologies and future trends for edge AI: Specialization and co-design. *IEEE Design & Test*, 38(4), 7–26.

Janakiram, M. (2019, July 15). How AI accelerators are changing the face of edge computing. *Forbes*.

Jones, S. S., & Groom, F. M. (Eds.). (2019). *Artificial Intelligence and Machine Learning for Business for Non-engineers*. CRC Press.

Lee, Y. L., Tsung, P. K., & Wu, M. (2018, April). Techology trend of edge AI. In *2018 International Symposium on VLSI Design, Automation and Test (VLSI-DAT)* (pp. 1–2). IEEE.

Liang, X. (2020). *Ascend AI Processor Architecture and Programming: Principles and Applications of CANN*. Elsevier.

Ma'arif, F., Gao, Z., Li, F., & Ghifarsyam, H. U. (2021, July). The new analysis of discrete element method using ARM processor. In *IOP Conference Series: Earth and Environmental Science* (Vol. 832, No. 1, p. 012016). IOP Publishing.

McGrow, K. (2019). Artificial intelligence: Essentials for nursing. *Nursing*, 49(9), 46.

Meng, K., Cao, Y., Peng, X., Prybutok, V., & Youcef-Toumi, K. (2020). Smart recovery decision-making for end-of-life products in the context of ubiquitous information and computational intelligence. *Journal of Cleaner Production*, 272, 122804.

Montes, G. A., & Goertzel, B. (2019). Distributed, decentralized, and democratized artificial intelligence. *Technological Forecasting and Social Change*, 141, 354–358.

Naffziger, S., Beck, N., Burd, T., Lepak, K., Loh, G. H., Subramony, M., & White, S. (2021, June). Pioneering Chiplet technology and design for the AMD EPYC™ and Ryzen™ processor families: Industrial product. In *2021 ACM/IEEE 48th Annual International Symposium on Computer Architecture (ISCA)* (pp. 57–70). IEEE.

Nastic, S., Rausch, T., Scekic, O., Dustdar, S., Gusev, M., Koteska, B., & Prodan, R. (2017). A serverless real-time data analytics platform for edge computing. *IEEE Internet Computing*, 21(4), 64–71.

Nilsson, N. J. (2014). *Principles of Artificial Intelligence*. Morgan Kaufmann. https://stacks.stanford.edu/file/druid:zd294jv9941/zd294jv9941.pdf.

Nurvitadhi, E., Venkatesh, G., Sim, J., Marr, D., Huang, R., Ong Gee Hock, J., ... Boudoukh, G. (2017, February). Can FPGAs beat gpus in accelerating next-generation deep neural networks? In *Proceedings of the 2017 ACM/SIGDA International Symposium on Field-Programmable Gate Arrays* (pp. 5–14).

Porambage, P., Kumar, T., Liyanage, M., Partala, J., Lovén, L., Ylianttila, M., & Seppänen, T. (2019). Sec-EdgeAI: AI for edge security Vs security for edge AI. In *The 1st 6G Wireless Summit* (Levi, Finland).

Rabinovici, I. (2012). The right to be heard in the charter of fundamental rights of the European Union. *European Public Law*, 18(1), 149–173.

Rauti, S., Koivunen, L., Mäki, P., Hosseinzadeh, S., Laurén, S., Holvitie, J., & Leppänen, V. (2018). Internal interface diversification as a security measure in sensor networks. *Journal of Sensor and Actuator Networks*, 7(1), 12.

Reuther, A., Michaleas, P., Jones, M., Gadepally, V., Samsi, S., & Kepner, J. (2020, September). Survey of machine learning accelerators. In *2020 IEEE High Performance Extreme Computing Conference (HPEC)* (pp. 1–12). IEEE.

Sachdev, R. (2020, April). Towards security and privacy for edge AI in IoT/IoE based digital marketing environments. In *2020 Fifth International Conference on Fog and Mobile Edge Computing (FMEC)* (pp. 341–346). IEEE.

Satyanarayanan, M. (2013, June). Cloudlets: At the leading edge of cloud-mobile convergence. In *Proceedings of the 9th International ACM Sigsoft Conference on Quality of Software Architectures* (pp. 1–2).

Satyanarayanan, M., Simoens, P., Xiao, Y., Pillai, P., Chen, Z., Ha, K., & Amos, B. (2015). Edge analytics in the internet of things. *IEEE Pervasive Computing*, 14(2), 24–31.

Severance, C. (2013). Eben upton: Raspberry pi. *Computer*, 46(10), 14–16.

Shi, W., Cao, J., Zhang, Q., Li, Y., & Xu, L. (2016). Edge computing: Vision and challenges. *IEEE Internet of Things Journal*, 3(5), 637–646.

Shi, P., Gao, F., Liang, S., & Yu, S. (2020, December). Multi-model inference acceleration on embedded multi-core processors. In *2020 International Conference on Intelligent Computing and Human-Computer Interaction (ICHCI)* (pp. 400–403). IEEE.

Stone, M., Aravopoulou, E., Ekinci, Y., Evans, G., Hobbs, M., Labib, A., ... Machtynger, L. (2020). Artificial intelligence (AI) in strategic marketing decision-making: A research agenda. *The Bottom Line*, 33(2), 183–200.

Su, X., Sperlì, G., Moscato, V., Picariello, A., Esposito, C., & Choi, C. (2019). An edge intelligence empowered recommender system enabling cultural heritage applications. *IEEE Transactions on Industrial Informatics*, 15(7), 4266–4275.

Wang, X., Han, Y., Leung, V. C., Niyato, D., Yan, X., & Chen, X. (2020). Convergence of edge computing and deep learning: A comprehensive survey. *IEEE Communications Surveys & Tutorials*, 22(2), 869–904.

Xu, D., Li, T., Li, Y., Su, X., Tarkoma, S., Jiang, T., ... Hui, P. (2020). Edge intelligence: Architectures, challenges, and applications. *arXiv preprint arXiv:2003.12172*.

Zhang, J., Zhang, F., Huang, X., & Liu, X. (2020). Leakage-resilient authenticated key exchange for edge artificial intelligence. *IEEE Transactions on Dependable and Secure Computing*.

Zhou, Z., Chen, X., Li, E., Zeng, L., Luo, K., & Zhang, J. (2019). Edge intelligence: Paving the last mile of artificial intelligence with edge computing. *Proceedings of the IEEE*, 107(8), 1738–1762.

7 Authentication of edge-AI-based smart healthcare system
A review-based study

Akanksha Upadhyay, Bhajneet Kaur

CONTENTS

7.1 INTRODUCTION

Artificial intelligence (AI) uses expert systems that can mimic human intelligence without requiring human input. In order to solve challenging challenges, AI is used to learn from prior experiences (Gupta & Nagpal 2020; Han & Han 2021). Most Internet of Things (IoT) applications have relied on cloud computing for data processing and storage to handle the enormous amounts of data generated by IoT devices on a regular basis (Yassine et al. 2019). One practical option for enabling IoT systems turns out to be multi-access edge computing, which offers storage and processing resources at the edge networks for low-latency and real-world applications (Porambage et al. 2018). Furthermore, EoT, or Edge-of-Things, for smart healthcare systems, was produced by the union of multi-access edge computing (MEC) and IoT. It has been discovered that blockchain, as a new paradigm, is more reliable and secure in lowering the risk of user or patient data being compromised (Pan et al. 2019). Utilising emerging technologies like Blockchain Edge of Things (BEoT), EoT, and IoT, cloud computing offers patient data tracking, health monitoring, drug inventory and management, among other services (Mutlag et al. 2019). Another emerging technology is the IoT, where data are transferred from edge computers to cloud servers to enable safe and optimal resource utilisation (Li et al. 2020). Security and authentication in modern technologies are among the most challenging issues. These systems now have the capacity to make decisions, and a breach might cause tremendous harm. In the healthcare sector, privacy is also a key consideration.

DOI: 10.1201/9781003244592-7

The goal of the research described in this chapter is to undertake a thorough analysis of current studies that have used applications of cutting-edge technologies for data authentication. The work is divided into three main sections: Section 7.2 investigates prior research on data authentication, using new technology applications, notably in the healthcare industry. The purpose of Section 7.3's validation of the review, using word cloud analysis, is to confirm the literature's relevance to the current investigation. Finally, the Conclusion section (Section 7.4) provides a summary of the current study.

7.2   A DETAILED REVIEW: EDGE-AI-BASED SMART HEALTHCARE SYSTEM

Kamruzzaman et al. (2022) suggest that the use of edge-AI and the Internet of Medical Things (IoMT), two complex ideas, is increasingly widespread in Smart Cities healthcare. These technologies may be used to measure and manage networked healthcare, which may also be very helpful since it minimises the amount of human labour and increases management effectiveness. The researchers conducted a review-based study to investigate the challenges and opportunities with edge-AI for network-based healthcare in smart cities. The authors carefully considered various study modalities and divided them into two categories. Following a review of the studies, it was found that it is increasingly important for healthcare personnel to manage data, acknowledge difficulties or challenges, manage emergency cases, monitor patient histories, diagnose and treat diseases that manifest differently in patients, and treat illnesses that are spreading more widely and affecting a larger population. Instead, solutions like edge-AI, IoMT, 5G, fog computing, and cloud computing have been emphasised as means to address these expanding problems. But where the most recent technologies have been used, the outcomes have improved. The researchers also noted that these implementations produced favorable results from the standpoints of both patients and healthcare professionals. A detailed study also highlighted the need for further verification and application of the numerous models that have been proposed in various types of research to confirm their effectiveness and guarantee that they may be applied successfully in a variety of contexts (Rajasekar et al. 2021). A method for securely authenticating a distant user involves a remote server confirming a user's identity over a dependable communication network. Since then, several remote user authentication methods have been developed, but each has advantages and disadvantages of its own. The proposed authentication systems have a significant impact on the strengths and weaknesses of real-time applications such as e-health, telemedicine, the Internet of Things, the cloud, and multi-server apps. One of the weak systems that continues to provide access by unwanted parties to personal information is Transaction and Management Information Systems (TMISs). Meanwhile, remote user authentication, one of the strategies, has proven essential in accelerating IoT. Security is a major issue, even if the IoT provides secure access to remote services. Data are shared among many end users via cloud computing services and a multi-server architecture, which calls for a high level of security. In spite of extensive research and development into remote user authentication approaches for healthcare, IoT, multi-server, and cloud applications, the vast majority of these systems are either susceptible to security threats or lack crucial features. Numerous remote user authentication systems were subjected to an analytical and thorough evaluation by the researchers, who then classified them based on their intended use. One hundred of the most advanced remote user authentication methods have been looked at and rated on their benefits, key features, computing costs, storage costs, and transmission costs (Prabadevi et al. 2021). At the edge of things, blockchain technology is gaining traction in several technological fields as a workable and revolutionary technological solution. The Internet of Things and edge computing have combined to create the Edge of Things, a new technical solution. The blockchain-enabled Edge of Things, or BEoT, a new paradigm established by the combination of blockchain and the IoT, is essential for enabling potential quick response times and effective security systems and services. In order to enable industrial applications in a range of IoT use cases, including smart homes, smart healthcare, smart grid, and smart transportation, the authors have proposed a ground-breaking BEoT architecture, which will be supervised by blockchain on the edge network. In the suggested research, the authors also looked into the potential of BEoT in providing security services such as user authorisation, confidentiality, vulnerability detection, and information security. The authors made BEoT, a new solution based on MEC and blockchain that gives IoT-enabled applications high security at the edge of the network and low latency (Zhang et al. 2021). Edge-based AI complements cloud-based AI. It eliminates data streaming and cloud storage privacy issues. It provides real-time applications where every millisecond matters and brings AI to remote regions with poor networking infrastructures by enabling edge devices. Edge-enabled AI applications, like self-driving cars and intelligent healthcare, present security risks, according to the authors. Edge devices may analyse data and act, making them vulnerable to attack. The increased use of computationally limited devices in edge situations and the rise of leakage threats provide substantial security challenges. The authors propose improving edge-AI security by creating leakage-resistant authenticated key exchange (LRAKE) protocols. The proposed protocol can be readily implemented into security and communication standards. The research includes prototypes, implementation details, and a Bluetooth 5.0 use-case for the proposed protocol. The authors suggested that further theoretical and practical details will help deploy LRAKE protocols in edge-AI applications (Minahil et al. 2021). To cut costs and upgrade healthcare facilities, a larger volume of healthcare data has progressively begun to be stored and communicated. In this context, the growth of e-health clouds creates new opportunities for accessing medical data that are dispersed throughout the world. But this achievement also raises several new risks and issues, such as how to guarantee the integrity, security, and confidentiality of particularly susceptible healthcare data. A key issue among these is data authentication, which ensures that sensitive medical data stored in clouds is inaccessible to unauthorised users. Three methods of authentication – smart cards, passwords, and biometrics – meet the demand for strong security. The researchers have introduced many three-factor Elliptic Curve Cryptosystem (ECC)-based authentication techniques for use with e-health clouds. On the other hand, most of the protocols have serious security flaws and high computational and communication costs. As a result, the authors created a cutting-edge security system for the e-health cloud that guards against a range of dangers, such as password guessing, attacks on stolen smart cards, impersonation, and user anonymity. Additionally, the researchers have conducted a thorough security analysis of the protocol using the random oracle model (ROM). In comparison to current protocols, the researchers found that the suggested approach is more cost effective in terms of computing and communication. The proposed protocol was therefore claimed to be more efficient, trustworthy, and secure (Vimal et al. 2021). In this study, a fall detection method with increased accuracy was proposed. Three phases of data processing – convolution layer, pooling layer, and overall layer – have been developed to integrate data analysis and estimate fall detection-utilising feature detection. The testing revealed that the vision-based estimate was 98% accurate. The study employs a dataset of several photo collections to determine the Support Vector Machine (SVM)- and Artificial Neural Network (ANN)-based fall detection accuracy. By utilising IoT sensor data and data storage through fog-based retrieval, the Convolutional Neural Network (CNN) approach increases classification and accuracy rate of detection (Li et al. 2020). The accuracy of detection in rural areas is also included with WiFi that uses Long Range Radio (LoRA). The data provided was improved by data analysis employing edge gateway, and consequently, the system's forecasting performance has imprroved with time. The fall detection for clinical observation was reported using the raw data information that was obtained from the study and the investigation of online data analysis and sequencing (Li et al. 2020; Cui et al. 2021). One of the newest technologies, edge intelligence (EI) combines ideas from artificial intelligence with mobile edge computing techniques using 5G and beyond 5G (B5G) networks. There are more security and privacy issues when integrating EI with heterogeneous networks, like those that use wireless local area networks. In this study, the security aspects of EI-enabled, heterogeneous B5G networks were explored. These security aspects include authentication and reliability-based user equipment (UE) detection. There has been discussion of the technical issues. A unique, uniform authentication framework, that works with edge computing and authenticates UEs consistently across different networks while keeping their privacy, has been developed (Amin & Hossain 2021). Patients increasingly expect a complicated and intelligent healthcare system that is tailored to their own health needs. With 5G and cutting-edge IoT sensors, edge computing makes it possible for real-time and smart healthcare solutions that meet requirements for energy use and latency. Previous surveys on smart healthcare systems included topics that dealt with architectures based on technologies, such as cloud computing, fog computing, data authentication, security, and various sensors and devices used in edge computing frameworks. Other than this, the past studies didn't pay attention to the IoT applications for healthcare that were implemented in edge computing systems. To increase the significance of edge nodes, the Graphical Processing Unit (GPU) devices were embedded at the edge level. Additionally, the computational power of the model was dramatically improved by deploying GPU-powered nodes at the fog level. These GPU-powered nodes were also used at the fog level to boost the model's computational and data-processing capacities. Where training-based deep-learning (DL) models are still not viable at the fog and edge levels, workload distribution and deep network approaches have been identified as potential solutions in smart healthcare systems. The main purpose of the research was to look at existing and upcoming edge computing architectures and methodologies for smart healthcare, as well as to understand the expectations and constraints of various application scenarios. The authors investigated edge intelligence that uses state-of-the-art deep-learning algorithms to target health data categorisation with the tracking and recognition of vital signs. This research also includes a thorough examination of the use of cutting-edge artificial intelligence-based categorisation and prediction approaches to edge intelligence. Edge intelligence, although having numerous benefits, has hurdles in terms of computing complexity and security. To provide an improved quality of patient life, the study identified prospective recommendations based on the current research for developing edge computing services for healthcare. Furthermore, the research also provides a quick summary of how IoT-driven solutions are being used in edge-based platforms for healthcare treatments (Hayyolalam et al. 2021). This article shows how artificial intelligence techniques and cutting-edge technology are being applied to enhance smart healthcare systems. By processing locally, edge technology enables smart healthcare systems by reducing latency, network stress, and power consumption. AI also gives the machine greater intelligence. These two technologies undoubtedly increased the intelligence of the smart healthcare system's components and offered several advantages. The study offers a thorough framework for smart healthcare that uses edge technologies and AI concurrently to enhance healthcare systems. The suggested solution distributes processes from sensors to cloud servers. The time, complexity, and network load were decreased when various tasks were performed on sensors using a lightweight AI technique. Additionally, using a flexible AI technique to perform parallel computation on the edge layer lowers latency, enables quicker reaction and decision-making, and enables caregivers to receive real-time warnings – all of which are essential in smart healthcare. The proposed model takes into account the security and privacy requirements for the entire smart healthcare system, including delicate medical data, network links, and user authentication and permission. Although some of the drawbacks of earlier smart healthcare architectures are addressed by the proposed system architecture, other problems, such as data loss and autonomous network management, still need to be resolved (Shukla et al. 2021). Healthcare systems are digitising data. Smart contracts and other blockchain technologies are becoming increasingly important to process and monitor IoT data constantly. Healthcare IoT generates trustworthy patient health data. Large data volumes make user-device communication dangerous. This work addresses IoT-based healthcare data and device authentication. The researchers then offer a secure method for handling patient health data. The approach improves malicious node identification accuracy and reliability. The researchers' unique solution uses fog computing and blockchain. For authentication of healthcare Internet-of-Things devices and patient health data, this study introduces a three-layer framework, an applicable mathematical model and framework, and one of the encryption approaches, namely, an advanced signature-based encryption (ASE) method based on fog computing. For users of real-time services and IoT-based healthcare, the objective is to increase secure data transfer. At the edge, the proposed architecture and algorithm will be able to offer secure transaction and transmission services. ASE outperforms cloud-based and other frameworks and approaches. The novel ASE method is accurate for dependability, false node detection, and throughput. ASE in the fog computing (FC) environment detected fake nodes with 91% accuracy, whereas cloud accuracy was 83%. The ASE algorithm was 95% reliable in FC and 87% reliable in the cloud. The suggested technique is tested using iFogSim (Net-Beans) and SimBlock (Jan et al. 2021). Sensors, network-enabled devices (IoMT), and widespread data capture have pushed the healthcare industry to make diagnostics and remote monitoring easier for patients. Information authenticity and verification are challenging in such an environment, and no one can provide secure communication without overcoming these issues. Without a solid authentication process, you can't ensure data integrity, authorisation, nonrepudiation, user validity, or information verification. We used Wireless Multimedia Sensor Network (WMSN) to develop strong, lightweight authentication for IoMT. The proposed approach addresses all the literature flaws. ProVerif2.00 and BAN were used to test the protocol's resilience. The evaluation shows that the suggested approach is rapid and secure. Comparative investigation shows that the suggested approach is light and secure, unlike previous methods (Deepa et al. 2020). Information and Communication Technology (ICT) innovations have smartened many sectors of life. Smart apps and technologies have become necessary, yet their use has led to long-term health problems in modern environments. Diabetes affects all ages. The suggested work uses Ridge-Adaline Stochastic Gradient Descent Classifier (RASGD) to enhance an AI-based disease-prediction system. The suggested study uses Absolute shrinkage and selection operator and ridge regression to improve the classification model. RASGD uses a highly optimised model to reduce classifier costs. Using ridge regression with the ASGD Classifier improved its convergence speed. Finally, the recommended scheme's findings were compared to regression and SVM to validate the intelligent and agile system. The intelligent system has a 92% accuracy rate, greater than other classifiers (Wu et al. 2020). One of the best-known ICT innovations nowadays is the Internet of Things. On the other hand, developing a reliable and secure authentication system for IoT-based infrastructures is still challenging (Zargar et al. 2021). Another study showed that the techniques used by Amin et al. (2018) and Maitra et al. (2016) are susceptible to password-guessing attacks in offline mode, user tracking attacks, and other attacks (Zhou et al. 2019). The stated vulnerability led to the suggestion of a simple IoT authentication scheme. Along with crucial security features, like mutual authentication, user audit, and session-based security, the IoT-based authentication system also provides resistance to a range of assaults. Additionally, when the plan was analysed, problems were found. The researchers then put forward an enhanced scheme based on their method that satisfied the security specifications and was also immune to well-known threats. Anonymity and authenticity cannot be guaranteed while the authentication process is in progress. The researchers then created a new certification system to make up for the Zhou et al. (2019) system. The suggested method has user anonymity and mutual authentication properties and is resistant to common assaults. The researchers also added a new parameter to the first stage of the authentication process that may quickly determine whether the user-inputted identity and password are accurate. Improvements to IoT-based cloud computing authentication were also suggested, and performance evaluation results showed that the plan had a high degree of computation and solid security. The proposed authentication technique can therefore be applied to actual IoT devices (Li et al. 2020).

Edge computing is an architecture that successfully addresses a range of processing and calculation-related issues. Edge computing is one of the technologies that, by increasing the transmission speed and computational capability of IoT-enabled healthcare systems, offers efficient data services with no delay. The authors suggested a framework for an edge computing system based on software-defined networking that uses a lightweight authentication technique to authenticate IoT devices utilising the edge servers for IoT-based healthcare. The authentication-enabled gadget first stores the patient's data before collecting and transmitting it to the edge servers for additional processing. The efficiency of the suggested framework for IoT-driven healthcare systems was assessed using computer-based simulations. The authors created an experimental set-up, a simulation scenario, performance evaluation measures, and finally an analysis of the simulation findings before running the simulation on a variety of settings. For the proposed scheme, the performance evaluation metrics include the computation of average reaction time, packet delivery ratio, average delay, throughput, and control head. For both edge and cloud servers, average response time was measured and compared in terms of upload and download times, waiting times, and system load. Other parameters of performance evaluation metrics, i.e., packet delivery ratio, average delay, throughput, and control head was performed for traditional network, edge computing network, and software-defined networking-based edge computing networks. The authors indicated that, based on simulation outputs for three different situations, it has been validated that the proposed system is efficient, and that the proposed method can be improved to ensure patients' data privacy (Xu et al. 2020).

As a new computing paradigm that provides many solutions to the problems faced by traditional clouds, edge computing (EC) will greatly boost the expansion of the IoT industry and increase the variety of its application ecosystem. It is vital to apply privacy protection as well as those techniques that can enhance the security and dependability of EC for high-quality IoT services. This paper provided a survey of the application of AI and EC in IoT security. First, the basic concepts and vocabulary were presented. Then, EC was linked with the IoT service architecture. The evaluation of edge-based IoT's traditional and AI-driven privacy safeguards came next. The researchers also emphasised the use of AI and blockchain to enhance IoT security. The author also talked about problems with keeping IoT services safe in the EC and with open AI (Ansari et al. 2020).

Edge computing handles data at or around its source as IoT sensors and devices generate more data. Restricting data to the edge node reduces latency while ensuring data security and privacy. However, because of resource-constrained hardware and software heterogeneities, many edge computing systems are exposed to a variety of threats. Additionally, the expanding practice of incorporating intelligence into edge computing systems has given rise to a unique set of security flaws, such as data and model poisoning and evasion attempts. The researchers outlined the most significant threats to edge intelligence in the suggested system. The researchers also discussed the study's future objectives and noted that cutting-edge technologies like blockchain and deep reinforcement learning can be applied to improve the performance of current edge-based AI systems (Martínez-Peláez et al. 2019).

It's more critical now than ever to enhance authentication processes to reduce assaults and security vulnerabilities that limit application performance due to the rapid adoption of cloud computing and IoT. In this study, the researchers introduced a novel IoT-based cloud computing authentication technique. The authors contend that the scheme protocol developed by Zhou et al. (2019) is neither secure nor safe. They asserted that, after looking over the protocol, they found some security holes and other issues that made the system unstable. Researchers suggest a new version with three steps to increase security. The user must log in during the first step, after which mutual authentication will take place and key agreement will follow. Additionally, they added a sub-phase known as "proof of connection" attempt, which confirms user participation before the server participates. According to the research, the new technique is an upgrade over earlier attempts because it satisfies the security requirements and is effectively resistant to the majority of common and well-known assaults. Also, the performance research shows that the registration and login phases of the new system require less communication cost than older authentication protocols (Dhillon & Kalra 2019). Patients can now obtain healthcare services from home thanks to the development of cloud computing and the Internet of Things (IoT) technologies, which allow remote medical specialists to monitor patients in real time. In some cases, patient information is kept at a centralised healthcare facility where a doctor can access it on a regular basis. However, the public WiFi situation raises fundamental questions about patient privacy. Recently, several authentication methods for healthcare services have been reported in the literature. Nevertheless, most of these methods have been proven not to meet the security requirements. Additionally, it was stated that they failed to consider how a doctor might access information kept on a cloud server. In this research, researchers introduced a multi-factor authentication method based on the cryptographic elliptic curve approach that permits authorised medical professionals to access patient health data stored on a cloud server. The proposed methodology is confirmed to be secure against several attacks, including "replay" and "man-in-the-middle assaults", using the web-based AVISPA tool. A comparison of how well the system works and how well it protects against security risks shows that the system achieves session key agreement and protects effectively against security risks (Lee & Park 2019).

With the aid of intelligent systems and services, urban populations have evolved with behavioral patterns, flexible economics, systems engineering, and contemporary lifestyles, among other things. The report added that a broad range of traits, including management, adaptation, flexibility, decision-making, security, and user-friendliness, must be present for smart systems services to achieve their goals. AI is now known to be a type of technology that can help people act in a reasonable way, simulate cognitive and semantic operations, and represent data well (Hartmann et al. 2019).

An edge computing environment, combined with 5G speed and contemporary computing techniques, is one of the alternatives for enhancing performance and lowering power consumption for real-time data collection and analysis for healthcare (Vyas et al. 2022, 2023). Studies done in the past on healthcare have concentrated more on new fog architecture and sensors, ignoring the problem of best practices in computing utilised in on-device deployment in edge computing architecture. The primary goals of the study were to describe the device needs and concerns for various use cases, as well as to analyse current and new edge computing architectures and approaches for healthcare applications (Vyas et al. 2021, 2022). The suggested method views the detection of falls and the monitoring of physiological data as the two main focuses of the edge computing application. Other low-latency programs monitor illness symptoms, including the gait problems that Parkinson's sufferers have. This study also includes a thorough investigation of edge computing activities, such as transmission, security, verification, classification, compression, and forecasting (Abdellatif et al. 2019).

The successful improvement of the healthcare system is the top priority of every government on the globe. It can be difficult to offer flexible services to consumers at the most affordable price, however. The most promising possibilities for delivering smart healthcare are the future wireless technologies and edge computing, which can enable real-time and affordable patient remote monitoring. The authors have discussed their research perspectives for employing MEC for applications in smart health (Vyas & Gupta 2022). It was also said that it is quite achievable to meet the requirements for smart health by visualising a MEC-based architecture and outlining the benefits of putting in-network and context-aware processing. Additionally, the study revealed how to employ such an architecture to deliver multi-modal data reduction and edge-based feature extraction for event recognition. The former makes effective and inexpensive compression possible, but the latter offers great dependability and prompt response in an emergency. Lastly, we talk about the main problems and opportunities that edge computing may present, as well as possible directions for future research.

7.3 CONCLUSION

Mobility and intelligence have shaped internet interactions. As connectivity and communication speed improved, digital solutions shifted to the cloud and interconnected devices. Intelligent mobility will benefit individuals, businesses, and society even more. "Push and pull" have benefited every sector, including healthcare (Shnurenko et al. 2020). Healthcare has adopted AI for decision-making, suggestions, diagnostics, and more. To perform smart and automated tasks, the AI-driven healthcare system needs authorised data from authenticated users. Data authentication is a key research topic. The current chapter reviews earlier studies to determine researchers' focus and provide data security and verification systems. The evaluation found that studies focus more on data authentication than user authentication.

REFERENCES

Abdellatif, A., Mohamed, A., Chiasserini, C., Tlili, M., & Erbad, A. (2019). Edge computing for smart health: Context-aware approaches, opportunities, and challenges. *IEEE Network*, 33(3), 196–203.

Amin, R., Kumar, N., Biswas, G., Iqbal, R., & Chang, V. (2018). A lightweight authentication protocol for IoT-enabled devices in distributed cloud computing environment. *Future Generation Computer Systems*, 78, 1005–1019.

Amin, S., & Hossain, M. (2021). Edge intelligence and internet of things in healthcare: A survey. *IEEE Access*, 9, 45–59.

Ansari, M. S., Alsamhi, S. H., Qiao, Y., Ye, Y., & Lee, B. (2020). Security of distributed intelligence in edge computing: Threats and countermeasures. In *The Cloud-to-Thing Continuum* (pp. 95–122). Cham: Palgrave Macmillan.

Cui, Q., Zhu, Z., Ni, W., Tao, X., & Zhang, P. (2021). Edge-intelligence-empowered, unified authentication and trust evaluation for heterogeneous beyond 5G systems. *IEEE Wireless Communications*, 28(2), 78–85.

Deepa, N., Prabadevi, B., Maddikunta, P., Gadekallu, T., Baker, T., Khan, M., & Tariq, U. (2020). An AI-based intelligent system for healthcare analysis using ridge-adaline stochastic gradient descent classifier. *The Journal of Supercomputing*, 77(2), 1998–2017.

Dhillon, P., & Kalra, S. (2019). A secure multi-factor ECC based authentication scheme for Cloud-IoT based healthcare services. *Journal of Ambient Intelligence and Smart Environments*, 11(2), 149–164.

Gupta, I., & Nagpal, G. (2020). *Artificial Intelligence and Expert Systems*. Mercury Learning and Information.

Han, J., & Han, J. (2021). Evaluation of Artificial Intelligence Techniques Applied in Watson and AlphaGo. *Academic Journal of Computing & Information Science*, 4(8), 29–36.

Hartmann, M., Hashmi, U., & Imran, A. (2019). Edge computing in smart health care systems: Review, challenges, and research directions. *Transactions on Emerging Telecommunications Technologies*, 33(3), 1–25.

Hayyolalam, V., Aloqaily, M., Ozkasap, O., & Guizani, M. (2021). Edge intelligence for empowering IoT-based healthcare systems. *IEEE Wireless Communications*, 28(3), 6–14.

Jan, S., Ali, S., Abbasi, I., Mosleh, M., Alsanad, A., & Khattak, H. (2021). Secure patient authentication framework in the healthcare system using wireless medical sensor networks. *Journal of Healthcare Engineering*, (2021), 1–20.

Kamruzzaman, M., Alrashdi, I., & Alqazzaz, A. (2022). New opportunities, challenges, and applications of edge-AI for connected healthcare in internet of medical things for smart cities. *Journal of Healthcare Engineering*, 2022, 1–14.

Lee, D., & Park, J. H. (2019). Future trends of AI-based smart systems and services: Challenges, opportunities, and solutions. *Journal of Information Processing Systems*, 15(4), 717–723.

Li, J., Cai, J., Khan, F., Rehman, A. U., Balasubramaniam, V., Sun, J., & Venu, P. (2020). A secured framework for SDN-based edge computing in IOT-enabled healthcare system. *IEEE Access*, 8, 135479–135490.

Maitra, T., Islam, S., Amin, R., Giri, D., Khan, M., & Kumar, N. (2016). An enhanced multi-server authentication protocol using password and smart-card: Cryptanalysis and design. *Security and Communication Networks*, 9(17), 4615–4638.

Martínez-Peláez, R., Toral-Cruz, H., Parra-Michel, J., García, V., Mena, L., Félix, V., & Ochoa-Brust, A. (2019). An enhanced lightweight IoT-based authentication scheme in cloud computing circumstances. *Sensors*, 19(9), 2098.

Minahil, R., Ayub, M., Mahmood, K., Kumari, S., & Sangaiah, A. (2021). Lightweight authentication protocol for E-health clouds in IoT-based applications through 5G technology. *Digital Communications and Networks*, 7(2), 235–244.

Mutlag, A., Abd Ghani, M., Arunkumar, N., Mohammed, M., & Mohd, O. (2019). Enabling technologies for Fog computing in healthcare IoT systems. *Future Generation Computer Systems*, 90, 62–78.

Pan, J., Wang, J., Hester, A., Alqerm, I., Liu, Y., & Zhao, Y. (2019). EdgeChain: An Edge-IoT framework and prototype based on blockchain and smart contracts. *IEEE Internet of Things Journal*, 6(3), 4719–4732.

Porambage, P., Okwuibe, J., Liyanage, M., Ylianttila, M., & Taleb, T. (2018). Survey on multi-access edge computing for internet of things realization. *IEEE Communications Surveys & Tutorials*, 20(4), 2961–2991.

Rajasekar, V., Jayapaul, P., Krishnamoorthi, S., & Saračević, M. (2021). Secure remote user authentication scheme on health care, IoT and cloud applications: A multilayer systematic survey. *Acta Polytechnica Hungarica*, 18(3), 87–106.

Shnurenko, I., Murovana, T., & Kushchu, I. (2020). *Artificial Intelligence: Media and Information Literacy. Human Rights and Freedom of Expression*. Moscow, Hove: UNESCO Institute for Information Technologies in Education, TheNextMinds.

Shukla, S., Thakur, S., Hussain, S., Breslin, J., & Jameel, S. (2021). Identification and authentication in healthcare internet-of-things using integrated Fog computing based blockchain model. *Internet of Things*, 15, 100422.

Vimal, S., Robinson, Y. H., Kadry, S., Long, H. V., & Nam, Y. (2021). IoT based smart health monitoring with CNN using edge computing. *Journal of Internet Technology*, 22(1), 173–185.

Vyas, S. (2023). Extended reality and edge AI for healthcare 4.0: Systematic study. In *Extended Reality for Healthcare Systems* (pp. 229–240). Academic Press.

Vyas, S., & Bhargava, D. (2021). *Smart Health Systems: Emerging Trends*. Singapore: Springer.

Vyas, S., & Gupta, S. (2022). Case study on state-of-the-art wellness and health tracker devices. In *Handbook of Research on Lifestyle Sustainability and Management Solutions Using AI, Big Data Analytics, and Visualization* (pp. 325–337). IGI Global.

Vyas, S., Gupta, S., Bhargava, D., & Boddu, R. (2022). Fuzzy logic system implementation on the performance parameters of health data management frameworks. *Journal of Healthcare Engineering*, 2022, Article ID 9382322, 11 pages.

Wu, H., Chang, C., Zheng, Y., Chen, L., & Chen, C. (2020). A secure IoT-based authentication system in cloud computing environment. *Sensors*, 20(19), 5604. doi: 10.3390/s20195604.

Xu, Z., Liu, W., Huang, J., Yang, C., Lu, J., & Tan, H. (2020). Artificial intelligence for securing IoT services in edge computing: A survey. *Security and Communication Networks*, 2020, 1–13.

Yassine, A., Singh, S., Hossain, M. S., & Muhammad, G. (2019). IoT big data analytics for smart homes with Fog and cloud computing. *Future Generation Computer Systems*, 91, 563–573.

Zargar, S., Shahidinejad, A., & Ghobaei-Arani, M. (2021). A lightweight authentication protocol for IoT-based cloud environment. *International Journal of Communication Systems*, 34(11), e4849.

Zhang, J., Zhang, F., Huang, X., & Liu, X. (2021). Leakage-resilient authenticated key exchange for edge artificial intelligence. *IEEE Transactions on Dependable and Secure Computing*, 18(6), 2835–2847.

Zhou, L., Li, X., Yeh, K.-H., Su, C., & Chiu, W. (2019). Lightweight IoT-based authentication scheme in cloud computing circumstance. *Future Generation Computer Systems*, 91, 244–251.

8 Automated Wheelchair for the Physically Challenged with AIoT Modules

Priyanka Mishra, Sanatan Shrivastava

CONTENTS

DOI: 10.1201/9781003244592-8

8.1 INTRODUCTION

Disability is a state in which a person's capacity to do daily tasks is significantly hampered. Due to a variety of circumstances, people with disabilities have impaired bodily functioning. Nearly 1 billion people worldwide could be considered impaired. According to Figure 8.1, approximately 15% of the world's population, or nearly 1.2 billion individuals, experience severe functioning impairments, necessitating the use of healthcare services. As the population ages and chronic health issues become more common, there are more people living with disabilities. Disabilities can take on a variety of forms and dimensions. Whereas some health issues associated with disabilities are associated with poor health and high levels of healthcare consumption, others are not. On the other hand, people with disabilities are in need of mainstream healthcare services because they suffer from the same general healthcare needs as the general population. The right to the finest healthcare accessible without discrimination is guaranteed by Article 25 of the United Nations Convention on the Rights of Persons with Disabilities. In spite of this, few nations offer people with disabilities adequate help. Only a small number of nations gather data in the health field that enables handicap disaggregation. This was notably clear during the COVID-19 pandemic, when authorities neglected to consider handicaps when deciding the response to the pandemic. In addition to experiencing worse health situations during and after the pandemic, individuals with disabilities are now three times more likely than the general public to contract COVID-19, experience severe COVID-19 symptoms, or die because of the sickness.

8.2 IMPLICATIONS OF COVID-19 ON DIFFERENTLY ABLED INDIVIDUALS

We are continually learning more about COVID-19, a novel disease, including who is more prone to contract it. Most people who have disabilities are more likely to catch COVID-19 or become seriously ill from it. People with significant underlying chronic medical conditions, such as chronic lung disease, a serious cardiac condition, or a compromised immune system, tend to be more susceptible to becoming unwell from COVID-19. According to Figure 8.1, official estimates indicate that

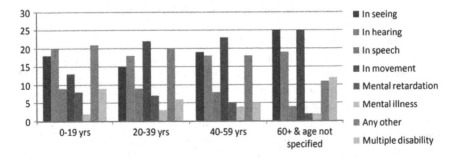

FIGURE 8.1 Distribution of individuals with different disabilities. (Source: 2016 Social Statistics Profile, Ministry of Statistics and Programme Implementation, Govt. of India).

approximately 2.5% of the population of India is disabled. According to the World Health Organization, 80% of the global population with disabilities live in middle- and low-income nations, although this percentage is likely overestimated. People with disabilities need access to primary healthcare just like everyone else. In addition, some disabilities are linked to underlying medical conditions where, should patients contract COVID-19, symptoms would be worse. People with disabilities are more likely to get inadequate medical attention, given their poorer access to facilities, capital constraints, and poorer access to transportation in low- and middle-income countries (Disability and Health 2020). Furthermore, because they depend on direct physical contact for support and lack access to essential public health information, people with disabilities find it difficult to employ preventative measures like social distancing that try to stop the coronavirus from spreading.

8.2.1 OBSTACLES FACED DURING THE PANDEMIC TO FACILITATE DISABLED

Reports have noted difficulties suffered by the disabled in terms of acquiring food, necessities, and life-saving medical procedures during the lockdown, in addition to the difficulty accessing information and helplines. Furthermore, the organisations that maintain the response during these health crises have made varied and tenacious efforts. However, the difficulties that health officials faced involved some of the following situations.

- Ensuring information is available, ensuring that lockout restrictions should not apply to caregivers, and employees with certain disabilities should not be allowed to perform essential service-related work.
- Offering disabled people in quarantine necessary services, giving precedence in treatment to those with disabilities. One of the most difficult tasks the administration has been striving to do is immunization of the residents of rural and village areas.
- Teaching emergency response professionals about, among other things, the needs of people with disabilities.

These recommendations are optional, thus there hasn't been much progress in putting them into practice. People are more conscious of social protection's importance in fostering resilience and healing because of the epidemic. In India, the National Social Assistance Program (NSAP) offers a monthly pension to those with severe and numerous impairments who are living below the poverty level, according to the NSAP. The COVID-19 epidemic offers a chance for social institutions to change and heal as well as for formerly divided communities to come together. People with impairments, for instance, have long looked for flexible and work-from-home choices, but have largely been unsuccessful. If we want to build environments that are more friendly to everyone, it is crucial that we comprehend the significance of workplace accommodations.

8.2.1.1 Barriers faced by people with disabilities

There is an extremely complex web of interconnected factors, related not only to the individual but to the individual's environment and social/political structures.

These factors are thought to limit the daily activities of people with disabilities (Disabled Population in India: Data and Facts 2021). According to the social concept of disability, people with disabilities face social, physical, or mental barriers (Singh & Nizamie 2009). When seeking medical care, people with impairments must overcome several obstacles, such as the following:

- *Exorbitant expenditure.* In low-income counties, two factors, namely the prices of healthcare services and transportation, are largely responsible for the lack of much-needed healthcare for people with disabilities. Just over one-half of people with disabilities cannot afford healthcare, compared to about one-third of people without disabilities.
- *Physical impediments.* Due to uneven access to buildings (hospitals, health centers), inaccessible medical equipment, inadequate restroom facilities, difficult parking spaces, narrow doorways, internal steps, and poor signage, there are barriers in healthcare facilities for the disabled. Because mammography equipment only supports women who can stand and examination tables are not height adjustable, these factors prevent many women with mobility issues from receiving cervical and breast cancer screenings.
- *Availability of limited services.* There is a lack of suitable services for people with disabilities. Numerous studies have demonstrated that, particularly in rural and isolated areas, people with disabilities have enormous unmet healthcare needs.
- *Insufficient skills.* People with physical impairments were more than four times more likely to receive poor care, almost twice as likely to be denied care, and nearly three times more likely to claim that the medical staff's abilities weren't sufficient to meet their needs.

Social impediments play an important role in affecting a person's ability to function and on the environment in which they were born, raised, educated, and employed. The following are a few instances of social barriers. In the US, 22.3% of people with disabilities and 7.3% of those without disabilities earn less than $15,000 a year (World Health Organization 2001; Houtenville & Boege 2019; Centers for Disease Control and Prevention 2019). Non-disabled children are four times less likely to be the victims of violence than children with any type of disability (Houtenville & Boege 2019). Figure 8.2 provides more details on these numbers. In contrast to 22.3% of people without disabilities who are high-school graduates, only 10.1% of people with a disability are high-school graduates.

8.2.1.2 Impact of barriers, especially during pandemics, on people with disabilities

Today, it is acknowledged that disabilities are a human rights issue. People are rendered physically disabled as well as socially disabled. These barriers can be removed if non-governmental organisations, governments, professionals, people

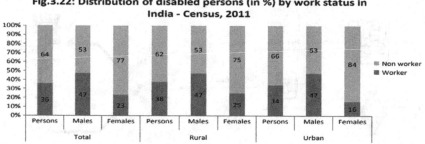

FIGURE 8.2 Percentages of working and non-working physically challenged individuals. (Source: Centre for Disease Control and Prevention).

with disabilities and their families collaborate (Quinn & Degener 2002). People with disabilities face considerable challenges because of COVID-19 and other pandemics, including growing barriers to healthcare, information, and crucially important support networks (World Health Organization 2021). People with disabilities experience a unique mix of pressures and challenges that may worsen their mental health. Access to essential medical supplies is more challenging for people with impairments, according to research, and this difficulty might increase when resources are scarce. The distance between them could make them feel more alone. Loneliness and social isolation, according to the National Academies of Science, Engineering, and Medicine, increase the risk of acquiring heart disease, dementia, and other illnesses. If they contract the virus, it may be more difficult for persons with disabilities to practice social distancing and take preventive measures because they may be more likely to experience effects associated with their impairment. The widely held belief that handicapped individuals must be looked after and confined in restricted settings for their "protection" robs them of fundamental dignity and the chance to discover and understand who they are. However, in these challenging circumstances, people with disabilities run the risk of being drawn even further from their communities. People with physical disabilities have been prevented from achieving economic security and independence due to a variety of cultural presumptions about their ability which consistently improve requirements of professionals.

8.3   TECHNOLOGY IN ASSISTING THE PHYSICALLY CHALLENGED

8.3.1   AAROGYA SETU

The Indian government created a technological miracle with the Arogya Setu app. The program helps the Indian government locate hotspots and stop COVID-19 from spreading by doing so. The more users it has, the more effective the app will be in halting the spread of the virus. By identifying and reducing the danger

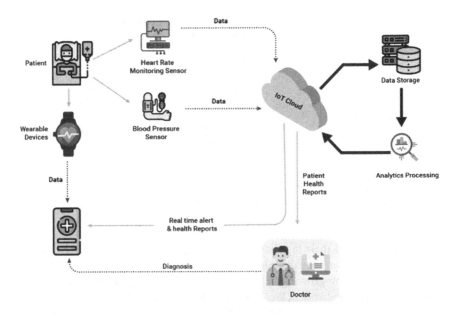

FIGURE 8.3 AIoT has a significant impact on the overall healthcare industry. (Courtesy of Embedded Computing Design (www.embeddedcomputing.com)).

of infection in both you and others, Aarogya Setu enhances the safety of persons in your immediate vicinity (Gupta et al. 2020).

8.3.2 WORKING OF AAROGYA SETU

Aarogya Setu uses the technique of contact tracing as you go about your everyday activities to keep tabs on the persons you have or might have meet. Figure 8.3 shows the Aarogya Setu App's quick operation. You will be informed right away and will be given access to preventative medical care if any of your contacts subsequently test positive for COVID-19. Aarogya Setu will alert you and arrange for immediate medical attention if you have first- or second-degree contact with a COVID-19-infected person. The self-assessment test can also be used to determine infection risks.

8.3.3 CHALLENGES FACED BY AAROGYA SETU TO ASSIST QUADRIPLEGICS

To aid customers in better managing their own health, large numbers of mobile health (mHealth) apps have been developed during the past ten years. But very few of these mHealth apps were created with the disabled group in mind, and even fewer have had their accessibility for people with disabilities tested. Because of this, it might be challenging for those with impairments to use many of these mHealth apps (Zhou et al. 2020). Unfortunately, those who are blind or deaf cannot use Aarogya Setu because the necessary COVID-19 adjustments were not made available. This can eventually lead us to the conclusion that the extreme public health emergency, lockdown, and recovery efforts have harmed people with disabilities disproportionately. During times of upheaval and crisis, people with disabilities are among those most vulnerable to abuse and exclusion. As a result, it is possible to argue that today's state of mHealth development underrepresents especially disabled people (Jones et al. 2018).

8.4 IMPORTANCE OF ARTIFICIAL INTELLIGENCE OF THINGS (AIOT) IN HEALTHCARE

The term "everyone, everywhere, at any time, using any service, on any network" refers to the Artificial Internet of Things (AIoT). The Internet of Things is a huge phenomenon in forthcoming technologies with an immense potential to have a large impact across numerous industries. It involves connecting individually identifiable smart devices and objects to the current internet infrastructure, with additional advantages as indicated in Figure 8.3.

One of the benefits is enhanced device, system, and service connectivity that goes beyond machine-to-machine (M2M) scenarios. As a result, automation can be advantageous in almost any industry (Islam et al. 2015).

8.5 REVOLUTIONIZING HEALTHCARE USING THE ARTIFICIAL INTELLIGENCE OF THINGS (AIOT)

The field of medicine and healthcare is one of the most intriguing IoT application areas. The IoT may enable a variety of medical applications, including senior care, exercise programs, chronic illness management, and remote health monitoring. Assuring patient and medical professional adherence to therapy and medicines at home is another significant potential application (Ometov et al. 2021). As a result, IoT smart devices or objects can include medical equipment, sensors, and imaging and diagnostic tools. By enabling remote provisioning, healthcare practitioners may experience less device downtime, thanks to the Internet of Things. To keep various devices running smoothly and continuously, the Internet of Things can also precisely determine when to replace their supplies (Ometov et al. 2021). When considering several practical factors, academics have concentrated their endeavors recently on investigating the potential of the IoT in the healthcare sector, including challenges faced by the disabled. As a result, numerous apps, services, and prototypes are developed specifically for this problem. A large number of network topologies and platforms, new services and applications, interoperability, and security are developed by IoT-based health care centers. In addition, a few nations and organizations have produced guidelines and standards for using IoT in the medical industry (Mulla 2019). On the other hand, the adoption of the Internet of Things in the healthcare industry is still in its infancy.

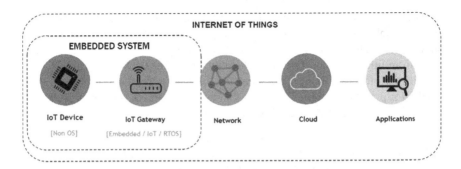

FIGURE 8.4 Internet of Things and embedded systems: A relationship. (Courtesy of SR University Educational Society, Hyderabad, Telangana).

8.6   DICHOTOMY BETWEEN THE INTERNET OF THINGS (IOT) AND EMBEDDED SYSTEMS

The Internet of Things should not be mistaken for embedded systems, as clearly seen in Figure 8.4. One may be confused at first appearance of the two domains but, after careful consideration, it becomes clear that they are completely different.

8.6.1   EMBEDDED SYSTEMS

With real-time processing limitations in some circumstances, embedded systems are controllers that serve a single operation as a part of a bigger mechanical or electrical system. Embedded systems are typically found as a component of a larger device that involves both physical and mechanical parts, as well as software and hardware implementation. Figure 8.5 shows the relationship between embedded systems and the Internet of Things. Many contemporary devices are under the control of embedded systems. Embedded systems employ more than 90% of the microprocessors that have been created. Microcontrollers, which are microprocessors with built-in memory and peripheral interfaces, are more frequently employed in contemporary embedded systems than are ordinary microprocessors, which need peripheral interface circuits and external memories (Noorpuri 2015).

8.6.2   THE INTERNET OF THINGS (IOT)

IoT, which stands for the Internet of Things, represents embedded technology (ET), network technology (NT), and information technology (IT). All that is required is the installation of NT and IT infrastructure to convert your embedded device into an IoT system. Your smart air conditioning system will have an embedded system called an ES (embedded system) that uses a WiFi module to transmit temperature data to the cloud (the internet) from a sensor. You need an embedded system like this. The WiFi network and the cloud are the two components of your

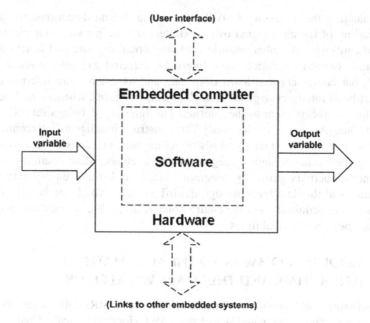

(User interface)

Embedded computer

Input
variable

Software

Output
variable

Hardware

(Links to other embedded systems)

FIGURE 8.5 The embedded systems whitebox perspective (Sun et al. 2021).

network technology. Information technology involves a program which will be installed on your phone, which receives the data. In accordance with the information, it receives your GPS coordinates and the app will start the air conditioning. A simple IT infrastructure serves as the basis for mobile apps.

$$\text{Internet of Thing} = \text{IT} + \text{ET} + \text{NT}$$

For example, consider that, in your house, you have a smart air conditioning unit that is connected to the internet. This "object" is internet-connected. Imagine that you have just returned from work on a scorching summer day. When you enter your home, you want it to be cool enough. As a result, you might utilise a mobile device to switch on your home's air conditioning when you return home from work. Additionally, when you leave the office, your phone will send a notification to your home's air conditioner. This scenario is plausible, given that your phone can track your GPS locations, detect your movement, and control the air conditioning based on the temperature outdoors. You will receive an alert on your phone only when the air conditioning is on.

8.7 FUTURE OF INDUSTRY 4.0: SMART WHEELCHAIR WITH AIOT

The development of a low-cost smart wheelchair seeks to combine a health-monitoring system powered by a microcontroller with a standard wheelchair, implementing the necessary COVID-19 safeguards and detections, including the sending of the alert signal over a wireless mobile network and the detection of cardiovascular abnormalities utilising breathing rate and heart rate to determine oxygen saturation level. Internet-connected gadgets are referred to as IoT, but computers that learn from data and experience are referred to as AI. Artificial intelligence gives "dumb" objects a "brain", whereas the Internet of Things connects them to the internet. The Internet of Things serves as the "brain", and AI serves as the "body", to construct intelligent, interconnected systems. The decision-making skills of AI are advantageous for IoT systems because they enhance data management and analysis, while resulting in significant productivity gains. By integrating tactile and strain sensory data from the sensors at the data level through the IoT module, which can be utilised to evaluate data acquired from the chair (Rofer et al. 2009), we may attain more complex perception capabilities.

8.8 MODULES COMMON TO THE AUTOMATED WHEELCHAIR AND THE SMART WHEELCHAIR

The Department of Scientific and Industrial Research (DSIR) of the Government of India approved the "Automated Wheelchair (AWC) for the Physically Challenged" project, which is what gave rise to the "Smart Wheelchair" study. Following the COVID-19 outbreak, the Ministry of Social Justice and Empowerment published regulations on 27 March 2020to prevent the infection of individuals with disabilities. Despite this, the lockdown was extremely difficult for persons with disabilities. There have been several examples encountered during the COVID-19 lockdown that served as inspiration for the design of the Smart Wheelchair. This project aims to keep disabled individuals in the public eye and aid them in their fight against COVID-19. Smart Wheelchair concentrates on offering aid and assistance particularly to disabled people suffering from COVID-19 or any pandemic in general, in contrast to AWC (Automated Wheelchair), which is made for general use by the disabled. The approved AWC project helps quadriplegics become independent. People who are quadriplegics are unable to move all four limbs. Automated Wheelchair (AWC) is the basic tenet upon which Smart Wheelchairs are built. Several typical modules include:

1) Global Positioning System (GPS) and Bluetooth
2) GPS-based real-time positioning
3) Accelerometer for a wiper motor
4) Module for head motion recognition
5) Module for detecting obstacles
6) Sensor-based module

The modules mentioned above are present in both SWC and AWC. To accumulate the smart features that can make the SWC useful in aiding the disabled, several AIoT-related modules are also overlaid on the device.

8.9   SMART WHEELCHAIR (SWC) MODULES

It is vital to remember that the goal of the Smart Wheelchair (SWC) is to protect disabled persons, especially quadriplegics, from COVID-19 by integrating three additional modules into the AWC. These modules are the Alexa Assistant Module, the Robotic Arm Module (Saponara et al. 2021), integrated with smart phone handsets, and the Module for Maintaining Social Distancing (Kim et al. 2021).

8.9.1   Social distancing module

Because preserving social isolation is one of the most crucial components of remaining safe during pandemics, this built-in module is crucial. The World Health Organisation states that keeping a predefined distance between two individuals is one method for preventing physical contact with potential COVID-19 carriers. The influenza virus and SARS-CoV-2 propagate similarly to other respiratory viruses. It is believed that avoiding contact with people may help prevent the spread of common respiratory infections. Therefore, long-term social exclusion may be one of the most successful methods to stop a respiratory virus pandemic (Al-barrak et al. 2017). Passive infrared (PIR) sensors, which are specifically made for motion sensing, have a wide range of applications. The OCTIOT PIR sensor is recommended in this paper (Chi et al. 2017) because of its efficiency, simplicity of use, and remote controllable capabilities. In Figure 8.6, a typical OCTIOT PIT sensor is illustrated. Utilising OCTi-Sense Technology, OCTIOT sensor systems enable precise motion detection, as well as being energy efficient during installation (Chi et al. 2017).

FIGURE 8.6   OSOYOO UNO board and connecting wires in a PIR sensor.

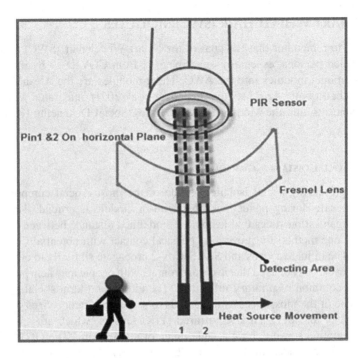

FIGURE 8.7 Working principle of PIR motion in social distancing. (Courtesy of ELPROCUS).

Some features of OCTIOT sensors make it possible to use them in the featured wheelchair. The OCTIOT sensor is made of materials of high quality, demonstrating both its safety feature and the ongoing dedication to providing reliable service and a worthwhile product. This makes the device more resilient to rough treatment and heavy use (Chi et al. 2017). The sensor is lightweight and small, making installation easier. The ability of OCTIOT sensors to be easily installed is also quite helpful. According to this, the wheelchair's maneuverability and smoothness of action are maintained. The range of this sensor makes it even more suitable. A common IoT sensor has a range of 5–8 meters (Chi et al. 2017). This goes a long way toward maintaining social distance in a crowded setting. The typical range for the OCTIOT sensor's power consumption is 0.4–0.7 W. The overall system efficiency is maintained when the sensor is attached to the wheelchair.

The PIR sensor on the OCTIOT keeps the handicapped person at a social distance from anyone nearby. Figure 8.7 shows how PIR sensors can identify human movement within a specific range. They function by using the parameters listed for the sensor. The majority of PIR sensors use a binary Yes/No technique to generate findings and are employed to identify the presence of people, animals, and other objects. In essence, we can use PIR sensors to detect the presence of any living being near the wheelchair and to calculate the distance between people who are present nearby. Instead of actively emitting energy into the environment, the sensor passively absorbs it by detecting infrared light. The pyroelectric device sends out a warning when the infrared radiation of any living object (or a hot particle) impacts on the optical system. The OCTIOT microwave (MW) sensor can be employed in these types of situations. This sensor can identify human presence over a small space to preserve social distance. Security is one of the main applications for the PIR system. PIR sensors detect the presence of people and animals via bodily heat radiation. This might be utilised for activities like recording video or unlocking doors, among others. PIR sensors are frequently utilised because of how little electricity they use. Because of all its advantages, the OCTIOT sensor is a very practical and reliable option for adding to the Smart Wheelchair.

8.9.2   EERG HEADSETS AND ROBOTIC ARM MODULE

The need for a brain-controlled wheelchair is necessary for those who are incapable of utilising a motorised wheelchair because of various cognitive shortcomings, i.e., motor issues, sensory issues, etc. For accurate recording of readings and signal interpretation, conductive gel must be applied to the skin around the electrodes of electroencephalography (EEG) sensors. EEG is an example of a technique for measuring brain activity. EEG is a tool used to capture the electrical activity generated by brain neurons firing along the scalp. With the aid of several electrodes on the head, EEG is the recording of the electrical activity of the brain over a short period of time. Additionally, the program has access to these data on the cloud (Huang et al. 2012). The creation of EEG is a function of the neurons. When the potential generated by neurons travels through nerve fibers, neurotransmitters are formed. The benefit of using a portable EEG brainwave headset is that it uses dry active sensor technology to read brain electric activity.

An electroencephalogram is a visual representation of brain activity. Since EEG signals are a mirror of person-dependent inner mental activity, they are private and difficult to mimic. The information generated is highly confidential since brain activity is closely associated with a person's stress and mood (Abiyev et al. 2016). The EEG signal serves as a representation of the number of signals that the brain outputs (Mtshali & Khubisa 2019). It is possible to take a non-invasive measurement using scalp electrodes. Such electrical activities originate from neurons when they work as a part of the nervous system. These four impulses can be retrieved by the EEG and processed later. A wheelchair, with an EEG installed on top, is shown in Figure 8.8. Figure 8.9 illustrates the functioning of the brain–computer interface (BCI). The signal processing and the process of extracting features from the BCI after signal acquisition work to detect movement direction. Once a direction has been selected, the control actions are engaged, ordering the robotic arm to move in one of four directions, i.e., right, left, up, or down, enabling it to grab real-world tangible objects.

FIGURE 8.8 Smart Wheelchair (SWC) with robotic arm mounted with electroencephalogram (Zgallai et al. 2019).

8.9.3 ALEXA ASSISTANT MODULE

Quadriplegics can be greatly benefited by sensors, smart phones, smart s appliances, cloud computing, and virtual assistants (Pawlaszczyk et al. 2019). The Smart Wheelchair will have a capability to speed up movement, thanks to Alexa assistant's integration. As part of smart home automation, the patient will be able to manage Smart Wheelchairs by speaking simple verbal commands that Amazon's Alexa built-in voice recognition system will interpret. These users' commands are detected for instructions (Gebrosky et al. 2020). Either an embedded system design or an Internet of Things can be used to deploy the module (Artificial Internet of Things). The most recent generation of the Amazon Echo Dot is an excellent smart device. It is Amazon's two-way loudspeaker product line and was introduced in the market at the end of 2018 (Vyas & Gupta 2022). To allow voice control and identification, it uses elements from Alexa. A WiFi connection and a consistent power source are necessary to use the Alexa Voice Service. The slim and portable design of the Echo Dot, according to Amazon,

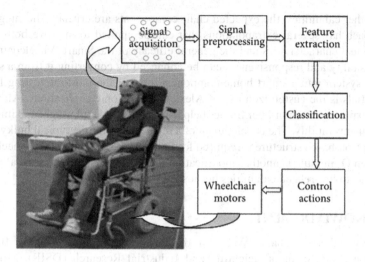

FIGURE 8.9   Working of the chair-mounted portable EEG (Ajay et al. 2021).

makes it feasible for any environment. This enables us to add it to our wheelchair without modifying it. Using the voice recognition feature, you can make transactions or conduct online orders. Alexa can also be installed off the wheelchair for situations where the wheelchair cannot be focused, such as when visiting a doctor. When a person's temperature or other vital signs exceed a predetermined threshold, Alexa can help by monitoring temperature readings and providing alarms. It uses very little electricity and is incredibly energy efficient when it comes to hauling. It can be plugged back into the Smart Wheelchair to continue charging in wired or wireless modes after it has been charged for up to 2–2.5 hours.

8.10   CONCLUSION AND FUTURE WORK

The Smart Wheelchair is a practical response to the requirement of society for sophisticated and intelligent Assistive Technology that is both useful in general and specific circumstances, such as pandemics. It made use of infrared sensors during the pandemic emergency to carry out social seclusion and obstacle avoidance techniques. If the wheelchair user's temperature and heart rate rise beyond a set normal threshold, an alert message is transmitted to the selected people. The AIoT enables these processes to be performed with the least possible latency. Smart Wheelchairs can be employed inside now that access to drop-off areas is more constrained. The first usable Smart Wheelchair will be marketed as a tool that can function on its own inside but needs assistance outside or in unmodified interior situations. More areas will be accessible to Smart Wheelchairs as sensor technology develops. Therefore, it makes sense to consider usability, mobility, and affordability as key components for future developments in Smart Wheelchairs. The Internet of Things has helped to tackle many issues, and new AIoT innovations are expected to boost Smart Wheelchair technology and help the disabled during emergencies, like pandemics. To support the disabled during pandemics and other calamities, the expected chair components are crucial. The suggested approach has several extrapolations that can be applied to improve both some individual characteristics and the general efficacy of the Smart Wheelchair. The accessibility and responsiveness can be enhanced by converting it from a stand-alone system into a smart home component. One of the most interesting future potentials is the customized use of Alexa/Google Home applications. Although very expensive, carbon-fiber frames help to reduce the overall weight and improve its maneuverability. The development of a replacement for the typical bulky plastic- or iron-based structure is required for future scope. Equipping the wheelchair with an O_2 module is another modification. Disabled persons are especially susceptible to fire-related calamities because of their immobility.

ACKNOWLEDGMENT

"Automated Wheelchair (AWC) for the Physically Challenged" was funded by The Department of Scientific and Industrial Research (DSIR), Ministry of Science and Technology, Government of India under the PRISM initiative DSIR/PRISM/119/2016-17. We appreciate DSIR giving us the tools we required to conduct this investigation. Additionally, we would like to thank the authors of the articles reviewed for assisting us in gathering crucial information for this chapter.

REFERENCES

Abiyev, R. H., Akkaya, N., Aytac, E., Günsel, I., & Çağman, A. (2016). Brain-computer interface for control of wheelchair using fuzzy neural networks. *BioMed Research International*, 2016, Article ID 9359868, 9. https://doi.org/10.1155/2016/9359868

Ajay, M., Srinivas, P., & Netam, L. (2021, April 15). *Smart Wheelchair*. A. K. Dubey, A. Kumar, S. R. Kumar, N. Gayathri, & P. Das (Eds.). https://doi.org/10.1002/9781119711230.ch16

Al-barrak, L., Kanjo, E., & Younis, E. M. G. (2017). NeuroPlace: Categorizing urban places according to mental states. *PLoS One*, 12(9), e0183890. https://doi.org/10.1371/journal.pone.0183890

Centers for Disease Control and Prevention, National Center on Birth Defects and Developmental Disabilities, Division of Human Development and Disability. Disability and Health Data System (DHDS) data [online]. Accessed on 6 August 2019.

Chi, M., Yao, Y., Liu, Y., Teng, Y., & Zhong, M. (2017). Learning motion primitives from demonstration. *Advances in Mechanical Engineering*, 9, 168781401773726. https://doi.org/10.1177/1687814017737260

Disability and health. https://www.who.int/news-room/fact-sheets/detail/disability-and-health, Accessed on 1 December 2020.

Disabled population in India: Data and facts. *Wecapable.com*. Web. September 6, 2021. https://wecapable.com/disabled-population-india-data/

Gebrosky, B., Grindle, G., Cooper, R., & Cooper, R. (2020). Comparison of carbon fibre and aluminium materials in the construction of ultralight wheelchairs. *Disability and Rehabilitation Assistive Technology*, 15, 432–441. https://doi.org/10.1080/17483107.2019.1587018

Gupta, R., Bedi, M., Goyal, P., Wadhera, S., & Verma, V. (2020). Analysis of COVID-19 tracking tool in India: Case study of *Aarogya Setu* mobile application. *Digital Government: Research and Practice*, 1(4), Article 28 (December 2020), 1–8. https://doi.org/10.1145/3416088

Houtenville, A., & Boege, S. (2019). *Annual Report on People with Disabilities in America: 2018.* Durham, NH: University of New Hampshire, Institute on Disability.

Huang, X., Altahat, S., Tran, D., & Sharma, D. (2012). Human identification with electroencephalogram (EEG) signal processing. In *2012 International Symposium on Communications and Information Technologies (ISCIT)* (pp. 1021–1026). https://doi.org/10.1109/ISCIT.2012.6380841

Islam, S. M. R., Kwak, D., Kabir, M. H., Hossain, M., & Kwak, K. (2015). The internet of things for health care: A comprehensive survey. *IEEE Access*, 3, 678–708. https://doi.org/10.1109/ACCESS.2015.2437951

Jones, M. L., Morris, J. T., & DeRuyter, F. (2018). Mobile healthcare and people with disabilities: Current state and future needs. *International Journal of Environmental Research and Public Health*, Sharon Shea; machine-to-machine (M2M); Tech target; IoT Agenda; Updated August 2019, https://internetofthingsagenda.techtarget.com/definition/machine-to-machine-M2M

Kim, M.-C., Kweon, O. J., Lim, Y. K., Choi, S.-H., Chung, J.-W., & Lee, M.-K. (2021). Impact of social distancing on the spread of common respiratory viruses during the coronavirus disease outbreak. *PLoS One*, 16(6), e0252963. https://doi.org/10.1371/journal.pone.0252963; https://octiot.com/sensor-solutions.php

Mtshali, P., & Khubisa, F. (2019). A smart home appliance control system for physically disabled people. In *2019 Conference on Information Communications Technology and Society (ICTAS)* (pp. 1–5). https://doi.org/10.1109/ICTAS.2019.8703637

Mulla, I. A. (2019). Comprehensive study on embedded system and IoT. *International Advanced Research Journal in Science, Engineering and Technology*, 6(8), 74. Copyright to IARJSET. https://doi.org/10.17148/IARJSET.2019.6813

Noorpuri, M. (2015). *Exploring Microcontroller Technology, Programming, Interfacing & Implementation.* https://doi.org/10.13140/RG.2.1.3066.8969

Ometov, A., Shubina, V., Klus, L., Skibińska, J., Saafi, S., Pascacio, P., … Lohan, E. S. (2021). A survey on wearable technology: History, state-of-the-art and current challenges. *Computer Networks*, 193, 108074. ISSN 1389-1286. https://doi.org/10.1016/j.comnet.2021.108074

Pawlaszczyk, D., Friese, J., & Hummert, C. (2019). 'Alexa, tell me …' – A forensic examination of the Amazon Echo Dot 3rd Generation. *International Journal of Computer Sciences and Engineering*, 7(11), 20–29. Accessed on 1 October 2021.

Quinn, G., & Degener, T. (2002). *The Current Use and Future Potential of United Nations Human Rights Instruments in the Context of Disability*, Geneva: United Nations.

Rofer, T., Mandel, C., & Laue, T. (2009, June). Controlling an automated wheelchair via joystick/head-joystick supported by smart driving assistance. In *2009 IEEE International Conference on Rehabilitation Robotics* (pp. 743–748). IEEE.

Rolling updates on coronavirus disease (COVID-19). World Health Organization. https://www.who.int/emergencies/diseases/novel-coronavirus-2019/events-as-they-happen, Accessed on 31 July 2021.

Saponara, S., Elhanashi, A., & Gagliardi, A. (2021). Implementing a real-time, AI-based, people detection and social distancing measuring system for Covid-19. *Journal of Real-Time Image Processing*. https://doi.org/10.1007/s11554-021-01070-6

Singh, A., & Nizamie, S. H. (2004). Disability: The concept and related Indian legislations. *Mental Health Reviews*. http://www.psyplexus.com/mhr/disability_india.html, Accessed on 24 December 2009.

Sun, Z., Zhu, M., Zhang, Z., Chen, Z., Shi, Q., Shan, X., … Lee, C. (2021). Artificial Intelligence of Things (AIoT) enabled virtual shop applications using self-powered sensor enhanced soft robotic manipulator. *Advanced Science*, 8, 2100230. https://doi .org/10.1002/advs.202100230

Vyas, S., & Gupta, S. (2022). Case study on state-of-the-art wellness and health tracker devices. In *Handbook of Research on Lifestyle Sustainability and Management Solutions Using AI, Big Data Analytics, and Visualization* (pp. 325–337). IGI Global.

World Health Organization. (2001). *International Classification of Functioning, Disability and Health* (p. 214). Geneva: WHO.

World Health Organization. https://www.who.int/mediacentre/news/notes/2012/child _disabilities_violence_20120712/en/externalicon

Zgallai, W., et al. (2019). Deep learning AI application to an EEG driven BCI smart wheel-chair. In *2019 Advances in Science and Engineering Technology International Conferences (ASET)* (pp. 1–5). https://doi.org/10.1109/ICASET.2019.8714373

Zhou, L., Saptono, A., Setiawan, I. M. A., & Parmanto, B. (2020). Making self-management mobile health apps accessible to people with disabilities: Qualitative single-subject study. *JMIR Mhealth Uhealth*, 8(1), e15060. https://doi.org/10.2196/15060

9 Comparison of machine-learning and deep-learning algorithms for stroke prediction

Mayank Singhal, Manan Pruthi, Nivedita Singhal, Preeti Nagrath, Rachna Jain, Ashish Kumar

CONTENTS

9.1 INTRODUCTION

Stroke is a great burden in the World today. It is the second greatest cause of death. According to a study done by the WHO, almost 15 million people suffer a stroke globally every year. Europe has a mean of approximately 650,000 stroke deaths each year. Many population-based studies for the stroke disorder have been conducted over the past years to determine the types and the fatality rates (Anbuselvan 2020). The risk of stroke increases with heart disease and stroke-related deaths

DOI: 10.1201/9781003244592-9

are predicted to increase to 5 million in upcoming years, compared with 3 million in 1998. Causes of mortality from stroke are an outcome of comorbidities and/ or complications. The onset of stroke and the following first month after it is the most crucial time for survival of a patient, with a large number of deaths in the very first week. Hypertension, fever, urinary tract infection, hypotension, cerebral edema, aspiration pneumonia, herniation, hyperglycemia, and hypoglycemia are some of the complications of stroke (Wolf et al. 1991). If a patient is able to survive the first week, even then death can happen due to various complications that result from relative immobility like sepsis, pneumonia, and pulmonary embolism. Stroke doesn't differentiate between people on the basis of race, gender, or age, though it will be right to say that the probability of getting a stroke increases manifold for a patient with certain risk factors that may cause a stroke. It becomes extremely important for a person to protect themself and others also by realising personal risk and how it needs to be managed (Lee et al. 2018). It is scientifically proven that 80% of strokes can be prevented by following this method. There are some factors that can cause strokes which represent bad habits such as smoking, drinking alcohol, and physical inactivity. These factors can be reduced by changing the lifestyle itself, i.e., by adopting good habits like early to bed and early to rise, going for a morning walk, doing physical exercises on a regular basis, eating healthy food, etc. On the other hand, some factors can usually be cured only by appropriate treatment. A study showed that there are a total of ten factors that are related to 90% of stroke risk and approximately half of these can be modified. On the other hand, though, non-modifiable risk factors cannot be controlled (Rajora et al. 2021). These days, machine learning has made a place for itself among the most demanding fields in modern technology. A machine-learning model can easily predict the outcomes with minimal human intervention, thereby reducing human effort and increasing the accuracy of prediction. It is a form of the domain known as artificial intelligence. Stroke prediction can also be done by using several machine-learning techniques. The factors present in the dataset used for stroke prediction include age, gender, heart disease, work type, BMI, smoking status, etc. (Flueckiger et al. 2018). The proposed model uses different algorithms such as logistic regression, KNN, random forest, decision tree, SVM, Naïve Bayes, XGBoost, MLP Classifier, CNN, and LSTM to predict stroke among individuals based on the above-mentioned input factors present in the dataset on which different algorithms are applied. Furthermore, all these algorithms are compared with each other and the algorithm with the greatest accuracy is identified.

The upcoming section (Section 9.2) provides the problem statement of the proposed model. The next section (Section 9.3) gives a background on the previous research done in similar domains. Furthermore, details about the proposed model (Section 9.4) have been discussed followed by some of the classification algorithms (Section 9.5) that have been used in the proposed model. The later sections contain the basic idea about integration of Internet of Things (IoT) (Section 9.6) with the proposed model along with the experimental setup and analysis of results (Section 9.7) obtained after applying various machine and deep learning algorithms. The last two sections consist of the conclusion (Section 9.8) that was drawn after studying the results thoroughly followed by discussions on the future scope of the project (Section 9.9).

9.2   PROBLEM STATEMENT

Nowadays, stroke has emerged as one of the major causes of death globally. It has basically two categories of risk factors associated with it, namely modifiable and non-modifiable risk factors. Stress, heart diseases, smoking, drinking alcohol, and high cholesterol are some of the examples of modifiable risk factors. The central goal of our project is to fabricate a model to predict stroke accurately based on patient risk variables that may be modified with the help of various machine-learning and deep-learning techniques over a dataset taken from the Kaggle website.

9.3   LITERATURE SURVEY

To gain the required knowledge regarding the various concepts which are related to the present research, the existing literature was studied thoroughly. Following are some of the key conclusions that were drawn from them.

In Rakshit and Shrestha (2021), the proposed model evaluated the most efficient algorithm for stroke prediction by comparing the accuracy scores of various machine-learning models. Among all the algorithms tested, the decision tree algorithm emerged victorious with an accuracy score of 100%.

In Shashank et al. (2020), the model proposed here made use of several prediction algorithms such as neural network, Naïve Bayes, and decision tree. Therefore, this project helps to predict the risk of stroke using prediction models, and provides personalised warnings, along with lifestyle correction messages with the help of a web application.

In Wolf et al. (1991), stroke prediction was achieved by developing a health risk appraisal function using the Framingham Heart Study cohort.

In Limbitote et al. (2020), the research paper consists of a survey on the different machine- learning algorithms that can predict heart diseases. The authors have drawn a summary of the various algorithms and further found the most efficient algorithm by analyzing their different features.

In Rajdhan et al. (2020), the authors of the paper have used Naïve Bayes and genetic algorithms to predict heart diseases. A UCI dataset has been used here to train the model with attributes that include age, gender, old peak, blood pressure, cholesterol level, etc. Also, a web-based machine-learning application has been deployed for the user to input his/her medical details, using purely these factors for predicting the presence of a heart disease.

In Lee et al. (2018), the authors calculated the probability of stroke prediction for a data of ten years and then divided the individual probabilities of users suffering a stroke into five different categories.

In Sudha et al. (2012), neural network, Naïve Bayes, and decision tree algorithms have been used for detection of patients suffering from stroke disease.

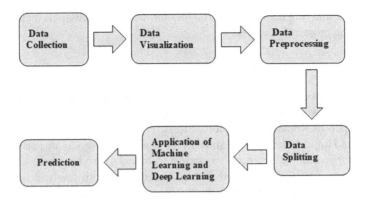

FIGURE 9.1 Workflow of the model.

The observations proved that neural networks have greater accuracy, as compared with the other two classification methods.

In Rajora et al. (2021), heart stroke prediction has been analyzed by implementing different machine-learning algorithms. Also, the receiver operating characteristic (ROC) curve is plotted for every algorithm. To implement it, Apache Spark is used. Gradient Boosting Algorithm showed the maximum score on the ROC scale, i.e., 0.90, when compared with other algorithms.

In Anbuselvan (2020), various classification algorithms have been studied and the model with the greatest accuracy has been obtained to predict heart disease in the patient. Random forest and XGBoost turned out to be the best-performing algorithm, whereas KNN turned out to be the least successful of all those algorithms considered.

9.4   PROPOSED MODEL

In this work, a model that predicts stroke based on the patient's input parameters – such as age, smoking status, BMI, average blood glucose level, etc. – has been established. The Kaggle website is where the dataset for stroke prediction was taken. The workflow of the model proposed is depicted in Figure 9.1. First, data collection and data visualisation has been done, after which data preprocessing is carried out to obtain a clean dataset with no missing values. Second, the clean dataset has been divided into training and testing data and different algorithms are applied on it to obtain the prediction (Schwaab et al. 2008). Accuracy of each algorithm is obtained as a percentage and analysed to identify the best algorithm for use to predict the risk of stroke.

9.4.1   DATASET DESCRIPTION

The dataset used in stroke prediction has been extracted from a popular website named Kaggle. Extracted dataset contains 12 attributes and 5,110 rows. Some of these attributes include gender, work type, age, average glucose level, BMI,

	id	gender	age	hypertension	heart_disease	ever_married	work_type	Residence_type	avg_glucose_level	bmi	smoking_status	stroke
0	9046	Male	67.0	0	1	Yes	Private	Urban	228.69	36.6	formerly smoked	1
1	51676	Female	61.0	0	0	Yes	Self-employed	Rural	202.21	NaN	never smoked	1
2	31112	Male	80.0	0	1	Yes	Private	Rural	105.92	32.5	never smoked	1
3	60182	Female	49.0	0	0	Yes	Private	Urban	171.23	34.4	smokes	1
4	1665	Female	79.0	1	0	Yes	Self-employed	Rural	174.12	24.0	never smoked	1
...	...	...	...	...	...	...	...	...	...	...	...	...
5105	18234	Female	80.0	1	0	Yes	Private	Urban	83.75	NaN	never smoked	0
5106	44873	Female	81.0	0	0	Yes	Self-employed	Urban	125.20	40.0	never smoked	0
5107	19723	Female	35.0	0	0	Yes	Self-employed	Rural	82.99	30.6	never smoked	0
5108	37544	Male	51.0	0	0	Yes	Private	Rural	166.29	25.6	formerly smoked	0
5109	44679	Female	44.0	0	0	Yes	Govt_job	Urban	85.28	26.2	Unknown	0

5110 rows × 12 columns

FIGURE 9.2   The dataset.

previous strokes, to name but a few. Stroke is the outcome here. Other than the identity, residence type, and gender, all other features have been used to train the model. The X variables are used to store the independent attributes whereas the Y variable is used to store the dependent attribute, which is stroke. Figure 9.2 shows the dataset that has been used.

9.4.2 DATA PREPROCESSING

The stroke prediction dataset that has been taken from Kaggle consists of 201 missing values in the column named 'bmi' that have to be filled. If missing values are available in the dataset, it may ultimately lead to a decrease in the accuracy of our model. The values missing for the bmi attribute are filled with the mean of bmi. Also, label encoding is carried out to transform the categorical values into numerical values as training can only be done on the numerical value attributes. Normalisation of the dataset is also done using Standard Scaler (Brochu et al. 2010). The dataset obtained after data preprocessing is displayed in Figure 9.3.

	gender	age	hypertension	heart_disease	ever_married	work_type	Residence_type	avg_glucose_level	bmi	smoking_status	stroke
0	1	67.0	0	1	1	2	1	228.69	36.600000	1	1
1	0	61.0	0	0	1	3	0	202.21	28.893237	2	1
2	1	80.0	0	1	1	2	0	105.92	32.500000	2	1
3	0	49.0	0	0	1	2	1	171.23	34.400000	3	1
4	0	79.0	1	0	1	3	0	174.12	24.000000	2	1
...	...	...	...	...	...	...	...	...	...	...	...
5105	0	80.0	1	0	1	2	1	83.75	28.893237	2	0
5106	0	81.0	0	0	1	3	1	125.20	40.000000	2	0
5107	0	35.0	0	0	1	3	0	82.99	30.600000	2	0
5108	1	51.0	0	0	1	2	0	166.29	25.600000	1	0
5109	0	44.0	0	0	1	0	1	85.28	26.200000	0	0

5110 rows × 11 columns

FIGURE 9.3   Dataset after data preprocessing.

9.4.3 Data visualisation

Data visualisation is conducted to gain insights into the dataset, and it makes interpretation of data easier, using different types of graph. Heatmaps are drawn to present the correlation between different parameters of the extracted dataset, as shown in Figure 9.4. A pie chart has been plotted to present the percentage of stroke patients and non-stroke patients, as shown in Figure 9.5. A count plot (Ng 2004) is plotted to obtain the number of stroke and no-stroke events in males and females, as shown in Figure 9.6, while a scatter plot to evaluate the relationship between BMI and average glucose level is shown in Figure 9.7.

9.4.4 Data splitting

Using the train test split function, imported from 'sklearn' in Python, the retrieved dataset after data preprocessing was divided into training and testing data. The dataset was split into ratios of 80% and 20% for training and testing, respectively. Feature selection was performed to obtain the most-contributory and the least-contributory features (Hippisley-Cox et al. 2017; Singh & Choudhary 2017) The least-contributory features were gender and residence type, so these two features were excluded from the dataset. Age, BMI, average glucose level, smoking status, cardiac disease, and other characteristics represent the independent features, whereas the dependent feature is simply stroke.

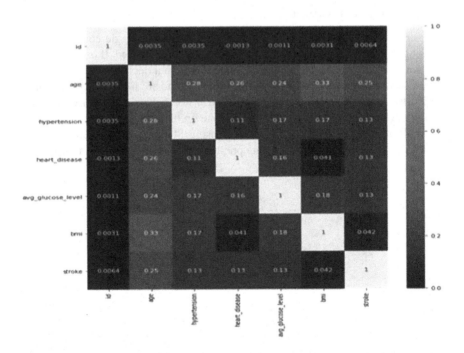

FIGURE 9.4   Correlation between different attributes of the extracted dataset.

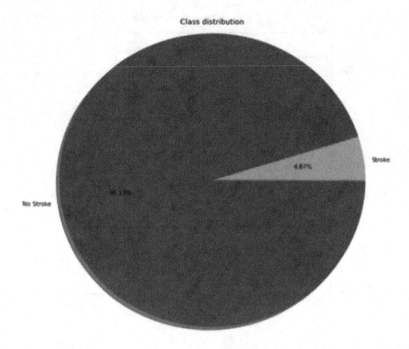

FIGURE 9.5 Percentage of stroke patiens and non-stroke patients.

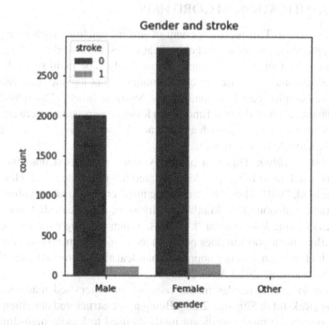

FIGURE 9.6 Count of stroke and no stroke in males and females.

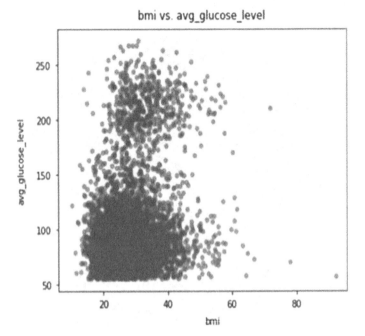

FIGURE 9.7   BMI and average glucose level.

9.5   CLASSIFICATION ALGORITHMS

Logistic regression. This is a component of several machine-learning algorithms that are employed in the solution of classification issues. It works on the principles of the famous mathematical concept of probability. The main point that distinguishes a linear and a logistic regression model is that logistic regression model uses a more complex cost function, i.e., the 'sigmoid function'. According to the hypothesis, the result of the cost function in logistic regression is between 0 and 1. It provides various measures, such as accuracy, F1 score, precision, recall, confusion matrix, etc. (Anbuselvan 2020).

K-nearest neighbor. This is a part of various supervised machine-learning algorithms used in solving problems related to regression and classification (Limbitote et al. 2020). Here, 'K' means the number of nearest neighbors. In this, mathematical equations like Manhattan distance, Euclidean distance, etc., are used for calculating least-distant 'k' points. When training data are supplied to this algorithm, the algorithm does not train itself at all. It memorises the training dataset, which is a much better approach than learning a function from the training data (Kumar et al. 2020; Vyas 2023).

Decision tree. This resides in the category of supervised machine-learning algorithms (Rakshit & Shrestha 2021). Being a tree-structured classifier, decision trees are among the most significant methods used to handle high-dimensional data (Sudha et al. 2012). It is used to build a training model which can evaluate the target variable accurately just by learning some easy rules achieved using the training data (Shah & Bharti 2020; Sudha et al. 2012).

Random forest classifier. This comes under the classification of a supervised machine-learning algorithm. Being a combination of numerous decision trees, it is used in solving regression and classification problems. Bagging is used to train the forest produced by the random forest algorithm. Bagging is basically an ensemble meta-algorithm that is used for increasing the accuracy of algorithms. This algorithm predicts by taking the mean of the output from various decision trees. The accuracy varies in accordance with the number of decision trees: the more decision trees, the greater the accuracy (D'Agostino et al. 2008).

Naïve Bayes. Naïve Bayes classifiers are grouped under the classification of machine-learning algorithms. It is based on the well-known Bayes' Theorem; all these algorithms work under the same philosophy that each set of features that is being sorted doesn't depend on the others (Rajdhan et al. 2020; Sudha et al. 2012)

Support vector machine. This belongs to the category of algorithms for supervised machine learning. Its primary usage lies in solving regression problems. The main idea behind using this algorithm is plotting a decision boundary so that the n-dimensional space can be separated into classes. Such a boundary is referred to as a hyperplane. The algorithm basically selects the extreme points (support vectors) which assist in making the hyperplane. This is the reason the algorithm has been termed the support vector Machine (Kumar et al. 2020; Lumley et al. 2002).

XGBoost. Extreme gradient boosting, also known as XGBoost, falls under the category of ensemble machine-learning techniques. Using the decision tree as a foundation, it performs particularly well with small- to medium-sized tabular data. It's frequently used in solving problems related to regression, classification, ranking, and user-defined prediction (Horn & Horn 1986).

MLP Classifier. Multilayer perceptron (MLP) is an addition to the feed-forward neural network (Sudha et al. 2012). It comprises three layers. The first one is the input layer which absorbs the input signal for its processing. The second is the output layer which performs activities such as classification and prediction. The third is the hidden layer that controls the movement of data in a forward direction (data flow from input to output layer) (Bergstra et al. 2011). The neurons present in the MLP are trained by the help of an algorithm, named the "Back-propagation learning algorithm". Pattern recognition, prediction, classification, and approximation are its main uses.

Convolutional neural network (CNN). This is a type of artificial neural network that is used to process images. CNN comprises three major types of layers, namely the pooling layers, convolutional layers, and the fully connected layers. Stacking all these layers forms a CNN architecture, using a special technique known as convolution (Oh et al. 2019; Katz et al. 1963).

Long short-term memory. It is a type of recurrent neural network. It is used to process single data points (such as images) in addition to full sequences of data (such as videos). There are four main components of an LSTM unit. The first one is the cell that remembers values over inconsistent time frames (Zheng et al. 2003). In addition to the cell, there are three gate components (input, output, and forget gates). Such gates can manage data transfer into as well as out of the cell.

9.6   SMARTWATCH BASED ON IOT

Our proposed model has the full potential of being integrated with the power of IoT and hence can be used for more practical purposes. A smartwatch or any similar wearable device can be used which can take values like age, gender, smoking status, marital status, and BMI as inputs from the user, to calculate other parameters, such as the presence of heart disease, hypertension, and average glucose level of its user by itself. Furthermore, all these data can be stored in an IoT cloud. The smart watch can even be connected to a mobile application, using Bluetooth (Pu et al. 2016). The data on the cloud can then be stored on a database and our machine and deep-learning algorithms can be used on it to predict whether the user is prone to suffer a stroke or not. The decision tree has achieved the highest accuracy of 96.10 % of all the algorithms tested and this can be used for prediction. This prediction can then be fed onto the cloud from where it can be put up as a notification on the mobile application of the user (Cho et al. 2020). Furthermore, an alarm can be buzzed on the users' smartwatch through Bluetooth. Figure 9.8 represents the workflow of our proposed IoT model.

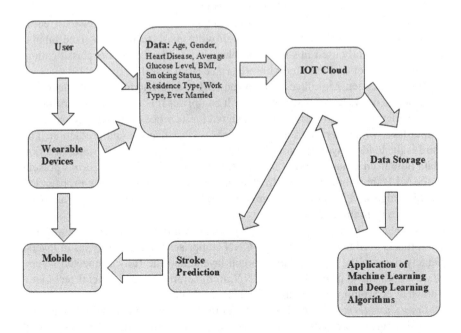

FIGURE 9.8   Workflow of proposed model.

9.7   EXPERIMENTAL SET-UP

To perform this study, we used Google Colab, which is a Jupyter Notebook environment that runs on the cloud. This enabled all our team members to work on the project at the same time. We used different algorithms to predict stroke, and, to compare these algorithms, we calculated different parameters such as precision, accuracy, F1-Score and recall (Chilamkurthy et al. 2018; Freire & de Arruda 2016). In essence, accuracy can be defined as the ratio of the number of accurate forecasts to the total number of predictions made. Precision is a phrase used to describe the ratio of positive samples that have been correctly classified to all positive samples, regardless of whether the classification was accurate or not. Recall is the proportion of positive samples that were correctly identified as positive to all available positive samples. The precision and recall measurements are combined to form the F1 score. The F1 score performs reasonably well on uneven data.

9.7.1   RESULT ANALYSIS

The results obtained after applying different algorithms are shown in Table 9.1. Among the machine-learning algorithms used, decision tree came up with the highest accuracy of 96.1%, whereas MLP classifier gave us the best accuracy of 96.08% among the deep-learning algorithms. Overall, decision tree emerged as the best algorithm of all the various algorithms tested, with the highest accuracy of 96.1%.

TABLE 9.1
Results obtained after applying different algorithms

Algorithm	Accuracy	Precision	Recall	F1-score
Logistic regression	96.08	0.92	0.96	0.94
KNN	95.89	0.92	0.96	0.94
Decision tree	96.10	0.92	0.96	0.94
Random forest	95.98	0.92	0.96	0.94
Gaussian Naïve Bayes	92.27	0.93	0.91	0.92
Bernoulli Naïve Bayes	95.00	0.92	0.96	0.94
Multinomial Naïve Bayes	91.09	0.93	0.91	0.92
SVM	96.08	0.92	0.96	0.94
XGBoost	96.08	0.92	0.96	0.94
MLP Classifier	96.08	0.92	0.96	0.94
CNN	95.10	0.93	0.95	0.94
LSTM	92.17	0.93	0.92	0.93

Abbreviations: KNN: K-Nearest Neighbor, SVM: Support Vector Machine, MLP: Multilayer
          Perceptron, CNN: Convolutional Neural Network, LSTM: Long Short-Term Memory.

9.8 CONCLUSION

The number of strokes is rising rapidly worldwide, so there is an urgent need to propose an effective system which will predict stroke accurately beforehand, in order that patients can seek a medical consultation from a doctor. Our proposed model has been successful in predicting strokes and decision tree has achieved a maximum accuracy of 96.1 % among all the algorithms tested.

9.9 FUTURE SCOPE

This project aims to predict the risk of stroke through a prediction model for all people who are vulnerable to the risk factors. The accuracy of the model can further be increased and the risk of stroke can be predicted even more accurately. The research can be improved by web deployment of the proposed model (Rajdhan et al. 2020). In future, this project could be further extended to produce the stroke percentage with the help of the output from the current project (Shashank et al. 2020).

REFERENCES

Anbuselvan, P. (2020). Heart disease prediction using machine learning techniques. *International Journal of Engineering Research & Technology*, 9, 515–518.

Bergstra, J., Bardenet, R., Kégl, B., & Bengio, Y. (2011, December). Implementations of algorithms for hyper-parameter optimization. In *NIPS Workshop on Bayesian Optimization* (Vol. 29).

Brochu, E., Cora, V. M., & De Freitas, N. (2010). A tutorial on Bayesian optimization of expensive cost functions, with application to active user modeling and hierarchical reinforcement learning. arXiv preprint arXiv:1012.2599.

Chilamkurthy, S., Ghosh, R., Tanamala, S., Biviji, M., Campeau, N. G., Venugopal, V. K., ... Warier, P. (2018). Deep learning algorithms for detection of critical findings in head CT scans: A retrospective study. *The Lancet*, 392(10162), 2388–2396.

Cho, H., Kim, Y., Lee, E., Choi, D., Lee, Y., & Rhee, W. (2020). Basic enhancement strategies when using Bayesian optimization for hyperparameter tuning of deep neural networks. *IEEE Access*, 8, 52588–52608.

D'Agostino Sr, R. B., Vasan, R. S., Pencina, M. J., Wolf, P. A., Cobain, M., Massaro, J. M., & Kannel, W. B. (2008). General cardiovascular risk profile for use in primary care: The Framingham Heart Study. *Circulation*, 117(6), 743–753.

Flueckiger, P., Longstreth, W., Herrington, D., & Yeboah, J. (2018). Revised Framingham stroke risk score, nontraditional risk markers, and incident stroke in a multiethnic cohort. *Stroke*, 49(2), 363–369.

Freire, V. A., & de Arruda, L. V. R. (2016, November). Identification of residential load patterns based on neural networks and PCA. In *2016 12th IEEE International Conference on Industry Applications (INDUSCON)* (pp. 1–6). IEEE.

Hippisley-Cox, J., Coupland, C., & Brindle, P. (2017). Development and validation of QRISK3 risk prediction algorithms to estimate future risk of cardiovascular disease: Prospective cohort study. *BMJ*, 357.

Horn, S. D., & Horn, R. A. (1986). The computerized severity index. *Journal of Medical Systems*, 10(1), 73–78.

Katz, S., Ford, A. B., Moskowitz, R. W., Jackson, B. A., & Jaffe, M. W. (1963). Studies of illness in the aged: The index of ADL: A standardized measure of biological and psychosocial function. *JAMA*, 185(12), 914–919.

Kumar, N. K., Sindhu, G. S., Prashanthi, D. K., & Sulthana, A. S. (2020, March). Analysis and prediction of cardio vascular disease using machine learning classifiers. In *2020 6th International Conference on Advanced Computing and Communication Systems (ICACCS)* (pp. 15–21). IEEE.

Lee, J. W., Lim, H. S., Kim, D. W., Shin, S. A., Kim, J., Yoo, B., & Cho, K. H. (2018). The development and implementation of stroke risk prediction model in National Health Insurance Service's personal health record. *Computer Methods and Programs in Biomedicine*, 153, 253–257.

Limbitote, M., Damkondwar, K., Mahajan, D., & Patil, P. (2020). A survey on prediction techniques of heart disease using machine learning. *International Journal of Engineering Research & Technology (IJERT)*, 9(6), 2278–0181.

Lumley, T., Kronmal, R. A., Cushman, M., Manolio, T. A., & Goldstein, S. (2002). A stroke prediction score in the elderly: Validation and web-based application. *Journal of Clinical Epidemiology*, 55(2), 129–136.

Ng, A. Y. (2004, July). Feature selection, L 1 vs. L 2 regularization, and rotational invariance. In *Proceedings of the Twenty-first International Conference on Machine Learning* (p. 78).

Oh, C., Tomczak, J., Gavves, E., & Welling, M. (2019). Combinatorial bayesian optimization using the graph cartesian product. *Advances in Neural Information Processing Systems*, 32.

Pu, L., Zhang, X., Wei, S., Fan, X., & Xiong, Z. (2016, October). Target recognition of 3-d synthetic aperture radar images via deep belief network. In *2016 CIE International Conference on Radar (RADAR)* (pp. 1–5). IEEE.

Rajdhan, A., Agarwal, A., Sai, M., Ravi, D., & Ghuli, P. (2020). Heart disease prediction using machine learning. *International Journal of Research and Technology*, 9(4), 659–662.

Rajora, M., Rathod, M., & Naik, N. S. (2021, January). Stroke prediction using machine learning in a distributed environment. In *International Conference on Distributed Computing and Internet Technology* (pp. 238–252). Cham: Springer.

Rakshit, T., & Shrestha, A. (2021). Comparative analysis and implementation of heart stroke prediction using various machine learning techniques. *International Journal of Engineering Research and Technology (IJERT)*, 10.

Schwaab, M., Biscaia Jr, E. C., Monteiro, J. L., & Pinto, J. C. (2008). Nonlinear parameter estimation through particle swarm optimization. *Chemical Engineering Science*, 63(6), 1542–1552.

Shah, D., & Bharti, S. K. (2020). Heart disease prediction using machine learning techniques. *SN Computer Science*, 1, 1–6.

Shashank, H. N., Srikanth, S., & Thejas, A. M. (2020). *Prediction of Stroke Using Machine Learning*. Doctoral dissertation, CMR Institute of Technology, Bangalore.

Singh, M. S., & Choudhary, P. (2017, August). Stroke prediction using artificial intelligence. In *2017 8th Annual Industrial Automation and Electromechanical Engineering Conference (IEMECON)* (pp. 158–161). IEEE.

Sudha, A., Gayathri, P., & Jaisankar, N. (2012). Effective analysis and predictive model of stroke disease using classification methods. *International Journal of Computer Applications*, 43(14), 26–31.

Vyas, S. (2023). Extended reality and edge AI for healthcare 4.0: Systematic study. In *Extended Reality for Healthcare Systems* (pp. 229–240). Academic Press.

Wolf, P. A., D'Agostino, R. B., Belanger, A. J., & Kannel, W. B. (1991). Probability of stroke: A risk profile from the Framingham Study. *Stroke*, 22(3), 312–318.

Zheng, Y. L., Ma, L. H., Zhang, L. Y., & Qian, J. X. (2003, November). On the convergence analysis and parameter selection in particle swarm optimization. In *Proceedings of the 2003 International Conference on Machine Learning and Cybernetics* (IEEE Cat. No. 03EX693) (Vol. 3, pp. 1802–1807). IEEE.

10 Edge computing-based containerized deep-learning approach for intrusion detection in healthcare IoT

S. Prabavathy

CONTENTS

10.1 INTRODUCTION

The digitization era empowers the healthcare systems to use the breakthroughs of the technology revolution. Digitisation in healthcare systems are focused toward harnessing medical data, enhancing patient-care service, and minimising the cost of medical service (Velthoven et al. 2019). The technologies involved in digital healthcare include the Internet of Things (IoT), artificial intelligence, cloud computing, and edge computing. These pioneering technologies have also brought about multifaceted changes in healthcare applications and modified the medical application pattern from disease-focused to patient-focused application. It has also moved the focus from treatment of diseases toward preventive healthcare (Jayaratne et al. 2019). These technologies have also made remarkable changes by focusing on regional-level personalised data management along with general

DOI: 10.1201/9781003244592-10

clinical data management (Hassanalieragh et al. 2015). The changes made by these technologies at all levels of healthcare applications has improved the quality and efficacy of healthcare systems to a more advanced level.

The Internet of Things (IoT) is playing a key role in digitising healthcare systems by deploying intelligent sensors and communicating through the Internet Protocol (IP) to provide a pervasive environment. Vast amounts of research are being conducted in IoT for healthcare applications (Farahani et al. 2020; Negash et al. 2018; Strielkina et al.2018). The integration of IoT has accelerated the transformation of the healthcare system and improved people's standard of living, toward a healthy life.

The IoT facilitates real-time remote patient monitoring using IoT devices worn by patients to support physicians to achieve effective treatment. A wide variety of body sensors and IoT healthcare devices have been invented and used for various healthcare applications, such as remote patient monitoring (Archip et al. 2016), smart pills (Goffredo et al. 2015), wearable IoT devices (), disease diagnostics and treatment using robots (Cianchetti et al. 2017), etc. A complete contextual analysis and detailed insights are provided about patients' health by the data harnessed from the healthcare IoT devices which help the physicians in terms of treatment and support for medical research. The major application of IoT in healthcare is remote patient monitoring which provides real-time personalised healthcare with reduced costs and time (Kumar 2017). The wearable devices, such as heart rate monitoring devices, fitness bands, sleep analysers, blood pressure measuring devices, glucometers, etc., are used to monitor patients in real time (Khan et al. 2016). It is useful in predicting risks in advance by tracking the health and well-being of elderly people.

The data harnessed from IoT medical devices and sensors have great potential in healthcare. The patient data are available to the doctors at all times when needed, facilitating faster diagnostics and treatment. Using the clinical insights from the data, precise dosages of drugs can be provided by the doctor. These data allow the identification of risks and benefits of various combinations of drugs. The data support physicians and healthcare professionals to make fast and reliable decisions and actions. Governments uses healthcare system data to predict the spread of disease, to prioritise medical research, and to direct funding for health services.

The major challenge faced by healthcare systems in integrating IoT is data privacy and security. Real-time patient data are collected, processed, and stored using the IoT-based medical devices which are vulnerable to security and privacy threats (Chacko et al. 2018). Security and privacy must be ensured in the collection and management of patient data because attacks on healthcare IoT devices may be catastrophic (Devi et al. 2016). Cybercriminals may compromise IoT healthcare devices to take control of the device or use the patient data for fraudulent activities. Any modification in the patient data can lead to false diagnostics, delays in treatment, or sometimes lead to causalities under emergency conditions (Gopalan et al. 2020). IoT healthcare devices involve heterogeneous technologies which are growing but not completely standardised, in potential privacy and security threats. Increasing the number of connected healthcare IoT devices involved in critical tasks leads to more potential vulnerabilities than ever (Hathaliya et al. 2020). The integration of heterogeneous IoT devices in decentralised architecture with insufficient security designs leads to many security problems in healthcare IoT. Hence, healthcare IoT needs a widely distributed security mechanism with a collaborative security process between different IoT healthcare devices (Mutlag et al. 2019). Various intrusion detection systems (IDS) have been designed for IoT (Prabavathy et al. 2018; Ge et al. 2019; Almiani et al. 2020) but very few IDS are specifically available for healthcare IoT (Thamilarasu et al. 2020). The state-of-the-art IDS for healthcare IoT are based on cloud technology. These IDS suffer from latency and are unsuited for the healthcare sector which involves heterogeneous devices generating huge volumes of real-time data from a dynamic environment and requiring a timely response (Khattak et al. 2015). To satisfy this requirement, IDS should be implemented near to the physical system, so that the data from the IoT devices are collected, processed, and stored at the edge. Implementing IDS at the edge network analyses the data quickly, identifies the threats and attacks, and makes actionable decisions at a faster rate. Edge computing provides a distributed service for computational offloading in IDS but healthcare IoT need an intelligent IDS for detecting threats and attacks from large numbers of heterogeneous medical IoT devices. The traditional machine-learning algorithms are not efficient for IDS in healthcare IoT. The traditional machine-learning algorithms involve shallow learning and cannot detect unforeseen attacks in high-dimensional massive data from healthcare IoT devices. Healthcare IoT needs an intelligent IDS which has the powerful learning ability of artificial intelligence and which can analyse enormous volumes of data from heterogeneous devices to detect the attacks more accurately and efficiently (Pande et al. 2021). To meet this requirement of healthcare IoT, deep-learning algorithms can be used in IDS for healthcare IoT. Deep learning has the ability to process and analyse vast amounts of IoT data to identify the potential vulnerabilities and cyber-attacks in IoT applications. Unfortunately, deep-learning algorithms are computationally intensive and require more resources. Most of the edge nodes are resource-constrained devices which are inadequate to implement deep-learning algorithms. Container-based virtualization can be used to implement deep-learning-based IDS at the edge nodes. Container-based virtualisation is a lightweight implementation of the hypervisor-based virtualisation of cloud computing. In container-based virtualisation, the process is isolated at the operating system level of the host machine (Roberto et al. 2016). A software containerisation platform like Docker (Boettiger et al. 2015) Kubernets (Burns et al. 2016) can be used to containerise the deep-learning-based IDS. The objective of the proposed work is to develop a containerised intrusion detection system using a deep-learning algorithm at the edge nodes to detect attacks on healthcare IoT.

10.2   BACKGROUND

10.2.1   EDGE COMPUTING

Edge computing allows computation and data storage near to the source of the data with the architecture of distributed computing technology. An edge node refers to any computing or networking resource in the track from IoT devices at

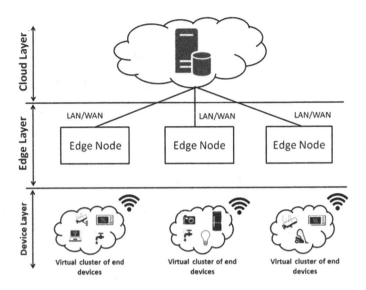

FIGURE 10.1   Edge computing architecture

the end to the cloud data centers. It processes the upstream data for IoT devices and processes downstream data for cloud services. For example, a network gateway device act as an edge node in smart home applications between the home appliances and the cloud (Shi et al. 2016). Edge computing processes the data near to the source, hence it reduces the amount of data transmitted and the transmission latency for streaming the data up to the cloud for processing. The computing is close to the data sources in edge computing so that the analysis and processing are done quickly and cost effectively by reducing the data streaming cost in the cloud. In addition, edge computing supports IoT applications by providing location awareness to IoT devices, handling the heterogeneity issues by enabling interoperability and flexibility, using uniform programmable interfaces by virtualisation (Hassan et al. 2018). Its distributed paradigm provides high availability and greater scalability for large-scale IoT applications. The architecture of edge computing is shown in Figure 10.1.

10.2.2   Deep Learning for IoT

Deep learning is a subset of machine learning that allows computers to learn from experience. It is also an advanced artificial neural network. It is the advancement of artificial neural networks that can imitate human cognition (Pouyanfar et al. 2018). Simple artificial neural networks (ANN) were limited by computing power and lacked accuracy. In order to improve the accuracy, the number of layers in ANN were increased and this led to deep neural network. Since it has more layers of connected networks, it can extract complex patterns from multiple simple features with minimal knowledge. This increase in accuracy made many

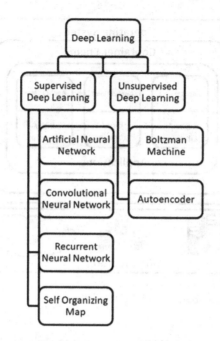

FIGURE 10.2   Deep-learning classification

safety-critical IoT applications to meet its expectations. In order to produce accurate results, deep learning systems need a high computation resource and large amounts of data for training the model. The deep neural networks are able to classify data from the output obtained from a series of "true or false" questions, involving complex mathematical calculations. Deep-learning algorithms are categorised into supervised learning and unsupervised learning, as shown in Figure 10.2. Supervised deep learning includes artificial neural network (ANN), convolutional neural network (CNN), recurrent neural network (RNN), and self-organising map (SOM). Unsupervised deep learning includes the Boltzmann machine and the autoencoder. The major applications of deep learning are driverless cars, Chabot, medical imaging diagnosis, facial recognition in social media, etc.

10.2.3   CONTAINERISATION

Containerisation is a software development approach which packs an application, along with its dependencies and environment, as an image and deploys it on a host-operating system. A container is a portable operating environment with the required resources to run an application. A container runs the application in an isolated manner without using the resources of other containers, like a separate physical computer or a virtual machine. The container technology is different from virtual machine technology; containers hold the application and its dependencies, but the operating system is shared whereas a virtual machine holds

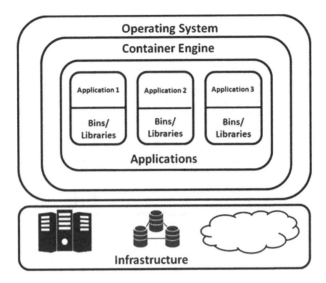

FIGURE 10.3   Containerisation of applications

the application and its dependencies along with the full guest-operating system. Hence, containers need fewer resources than virtual machines. In container-based virtualisation, the hardware infrastructure is divided into unique virtual divisions and the operating system is shared by multiple containers (Bhardwaj et al. 2021). The major advantage of containers is that they enable fast scale-up of applications by instancing new containers quickly and avoid the inconsistency problems in environmental set-up during deployment. The major concepts of containerisation are container host, container image, container, and container repository. The container host is the physical machine or virtual machine which will run the containers. The container image is a lightweight executable package of software required to execute an application, including code, libraries, system tools, and settings. The container is a runtime instance of container image. The container repository stores the image and its dependencies when a container is created. It can be made as a public or private registry. Figure 10.3 represents the application of containerisation.

10.3   RELATED WORK

A vast number of studies have shown the importance of privacy and security requirements in healthcare IoT (Awotunde et al. 2021; Karunarathne et al. 2021; Velthoven et al. 2019; Jayaratne et al. 2019; Hassanalieragh et al. 2015). Some attacks on healthcare IoT, such as inducing errors in diagnostic inferences will lead to physical injuries or sometimes death (Xie et al. 2021; Farahani et al. 2020). Another important attack on healthcare IoT is routing attacks on wireless body area network to drop the critical information or eavesdrop the data (Hajar et al. 2021; Negash et al. 2018; Strielkina et al. 2018). Various research studies have been carried out to provide security to healthcare IoT (Ullah et al. 2021; Archip et al. 2016; Goffredo et al. 2015; Cianchetti & Menciassi 2017) but research on intrusion detection systems for healthcare IoT is still in its infancy. Most of the existing IDS for IoT uses traditional machine-learning algorithms such as K-nearest neighbor, random forest, support vector machine, and others (Ahmad et al. 2021; Kumar 2017). These IDS were not effective because the IDS for healthcare IoT should build security instincts by analysing vast amounts of heterogeneous data from healthcare IoT devices (Manhas et al. 2021; Khan et al. 2016). This requirement can be satisfied by using deep-learning algorithms for IDS which can overcome the difficulties of IDS in feature selection and representation with limited labeled datasets (Thakkar et al. 2021; Chacko & Hayajneh 2018). A network IDS called self-taught learning was designed using autoencoder with softmax regression (Sekhar 2021; Devi & Muthuselvi 2016). This system was tested in a Network Security Laboratory-Knowledge Discovery in Databases (NSL-KDD) dataset. A flow-based anomaly detection system was implemented using a deep neural network in software defined network (SDN) (Alzahrani et al. 2021; Gopalan et al. 2021). The results of these deep- learning approaches outperformed traditional machine methods but, in these, deep learning is used only for pre-training but not for classification.

A deep neural network (DNN) was proposed to identify advanced persistent threats, was evaluated using a KDD dataset, and claimed RNN and (Long Short-Term Memory (LSTM) are required to improve the future defenses (Do Xuan et al. 2021; Hathaliya & Tanwar 2020). A deep neural network with three hidden layers, containing autoencoder and softmax regression, was proposed and the results were not accurate on some classes because of the fewer layers (Potluri et al. 2021; Mutlag et al. 2019). An unsupervised deep belief network which is used to train parameters was proposed, resulting in fewer errors in classification (Kang & Kang 2016; Prabavathy et al. 2018). A comprehensive survey on notable Network-based Intrusion Detection System (NIDS) approaches, that use deep and shallow learning, was carried out which concluded that deep learning outperforms shallow learning in detection accuracy (Hodo et al. 2017). The majority of the existing security solutions for IoT applications involves cloud technologies which are constrained by the number of devices, latency, and bandwidth (Alam et al. 2021; Zhou et al. 2017; Ge et al. 2019; Almiani et al. 2020). The number of devices in the healthcare environment is increasing exponentially and security is a major problem in cloud-based IoT applications. Edge computing can be an effective replacement for handling security issues in cloud-based IoT applications (Hassan et al. 2018; He et al. 2019). An IDS using edge computing for detecting selective forwarding attack on a mobile wireless sensor network was proposed by Yaseen et al. (2018) but this IDS can detect only selective forwarding attacks (Yaseen et al. 2018; Thamilarasu et al. 2020). Extreme Learning Machine (ELM)-based IDS was designed on the edge network for IoT applications in which training the model is performed at edge nodes, which are inappropriate for resource-constrained devices (Khattak et al. 2015; Prabavathy et al. 2018). In edge computing, the edge devices are heterogeneous in terms of computational capacities, power specifications, and operating system (Ozcan, M.O., Odaci, F. and Ari, I., 2019; Pande et al. 2021). To overcome this issue in implementing

IDS at edge node, containerisation can be used. Containers at edge devices are used to manage the applications without difficulty. Containerisation is applied in edge computing for various applications like smart homes (Ozcan, M.O., Odaci, F. and Ari, I.,; Morabito 2016), vehicular networks (Sami et al. 2020; Boettiger 2015), and industrial IoT (Okwuibe et al. 2020; Burns et al. 2016), but not applied in intrusion detection systems at edge nodes. Containerisation of security systems at fog node networks was proposed for a software defined network (SDN) (Prabavathy & Supriya 2021), but this system is specific to SDN and it performs behavior analysis for anomaly detection.

The proposed IDS is novel as it implements intrusion detection for healthcare IoT using deep-learning algorithms which are containerised and executed at the edge nodes to rapidly detect attacks from a vast amount of data from healthcare IoT devices.

10.4 PROPOSED EDGE COMPUTING-BASED IDS FOR HEALTHCARE IOT

The proposed IDS for healthcare IoT involves two major parts: 1. Building a deep-learning-based IDS at the cloud system; and 2. Containerizing the built model at the edge, as depicted in Figure 10.4.

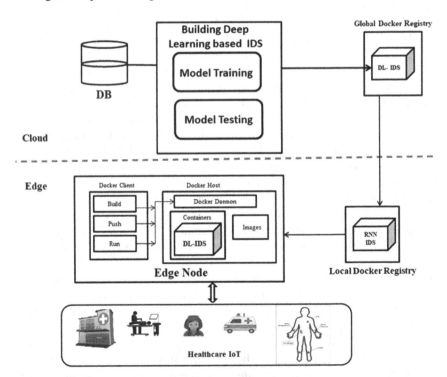

FIGURE 10.4   Proposed containerised edge-based IDS architecture

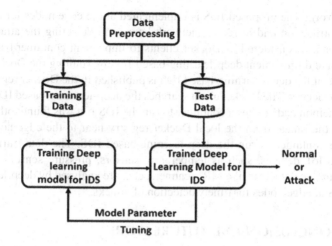

FIGURE 10.5 Deep-learning-based IDS

10.4.1 BUILDING DEEP-LEARNING-BASED IDS AT THE CLOUD SYSTEM

The distributed nature of healthcare IoT requires a distributed intrusion detection system for timely detection of attacks closer to the end devices. To achieve this goal, IDSs are placed at the edge nodes. Deep learning is used in developing the IDS for healthcare IoT. The deep-learning models will critically analyse the data to provide clear insights into the data, which is greatly needed in real-time critical applications like the healthcare sector. Building a deep-learning model needs more resource which can be provided by the cloud system. In the proposed system, the deep-learning-based IDS will be developed at the cloud and then it will be containerised to use at the edge nodes. The initial step in building the deep-learning model is to identify the suitable model and model parameters. Once the model is identified, the model is trained using healthcare IoT data. The data from various IoT healthcare devices are collected and preprocessed at the cloud storage system. The preprocessed data will be classified into training data and test data. The deep-learning model for detecting attacks on healthcare IoT are trained using these preprocessed training data at the cloud. The trained model is tested using the test data to check the accuracy of the developed model, and the model parameters are adjusted to reach the maximum accuracy. The deep-learning model with fine-tuned model parameters of maximum accuracy are containerized to be implemented at the edge nodes. Figure 10.5 shows an IDS based on deep learning.

10.4.2 CONTAINERISING THE BUILT MODEL AT EDGE NODES

Any device which possesses computing capability can be modeled as edge nodes, such as routers, switches, access points, servers, etc. Based on the computing and communication requirements, edge nodes can be added to or removed from the IoT network. The edge nodes connect the healthcare IoT devices to the cloud network. The proposed IDS is implemented at the edge nodes for efficient resource utilisation and to reduce network latency in detecting the attack. The edge nodes are considered as Docker clients to implement container-based virtualisation and implement deep-learning-based IDS by running the Docker host. The image of the deep-learning-based IDS is published in the Docker registry for the edge to access. The Docker client searches the deep-learning-based IDS in the Docker daemon and creates a container to run the IDS if it was found; otherwise, it obtains the image from the local Docker registry near to the edge nodes and builds the container to run the deep-learning-based IDS. The data traffic from healthcare IoT devices, such as temperature sensors, pressure sensors, etc., to high-end medical devices like MRI scanners, etc., are analysed by deep-learning-based IDS at edge nodes for timely detection of attacks.

10.5 CONCLUSION AND FUTURE WORK

In this chapter, edge-computing-based-containerised IDS, using deep-learning models, was proposed for healthcare IoT. The deep-learning model critically analyses the healthcare data to provide clear insights into the attacks on healthcare IoT. The containerisation allows the high-resource-consuming deep-learning-based IDS to be virtualised at the resource-constrained edge nodes. The implementation of IDS at the edges provides intelligence to edge nodes to learn and detect the cyber-attacks quickly and with greater accuracy. The proposed system can detect the attack quickly with high accuracy nearer to the source of attack, which is essential for critical applications like healthcare IoT. Future work will be to implement and evaluate the proposed system in a real-time healthcare environment and to identify the attackers' plan in advance to protect the healthcare IoT proactively

REFERENCES

Ahmad, R., & Alsmadi, I. (2021). Machine learning approaches to IoT security: A systematic literature review. *Internet of Things*, 14, 100365.
Alam, T. (2021). Cloud-based IoT applications and their roles in smart cities. *Smart Cities*, 4(3), 1196–1219.
Almiani, M., AbuGhazleh, A., Al-Rahayfeh, A., Atiewi, S., & Razaque, A. (2020). Deep recurrent neural network for IoT intrusion detection system. *Simulation Modelling Practice and Theory*, 101, 102031.
Alzahrani, A. O., & Alenazi, M. J. F. (2021). Designing a network intrusion detection system based on machine learning for software defined networks. *Future Internet*, 13(5), 111.
Archip, A., Botezatu, N., Şerban, E., Herghelegiu, P. C., & Zală, A. (2016, May). An IoT based system for remote patient monitoring. In *2016 17th International Carpathian Control Conference (ICCC)* (pp. 1–6). IEEE.
Awotunde, J. B., Jimoh, R. G., Folorunso, S. O., Adeniyi, E. A., Abiodun, K. M., & Banjo, O. O. (2021). Privacy and security concerns in IoT-based healthcare systems. In *The Fusion of Internet of Things, Artificial Intelligence, and Cloud Computing in Health Care* (pp. 105–134). Cham: Springer International Publishing. .

Bhardwaj, A., & Krishna, C. R. (2021). Virtualization in cloud computing: Moving from hypervisor to containerization—A survey. *Arabian Journal for Science and Engineering*, 46(9), 8585–8601.

Boettiger, C. (2015). An introduction to Docker for reproducible research. *ACM SIGOPS Operating Systems Review*, 49(1), 71–79.

Burns, B., et al. (2016). Borg, Omega, and Kubernetes: Lessons learned from three container-management systems over a decade. *Queue*, 14(1), 70–93.

Chacko, A., & Hayajneh, T. (2018). Security and privacy issues with IoT in healthcare. *EAI Endorsed Transactions on Pervasive Health and Technology*, 4(14).

Cianchetti, M., & Menciassi, A. (2017). Soft robots in surgery. In *Soft Robotics: Trends, Applications and Challenges: Proceedings of the Soft Robotics Week, April 25-30, 2016, Livorno, Italy* (pp. 75–85). Cham: Springer International Publishing..

Devi, K. N., & Muthuselvi, R. (2016, January). Parallel processing of IoT health care applications. In *2016 10th International Conference on Intelligent Systems and Control (ISCO)* (pp. 1–6). IEEE.

Do Xuan, C., & Dao, M. H. (2021). A novel approach for APT attack detection based on combined deep learning model. *Neural Computing and Applications*, 33(20), 13251–13264.

Farahani, B., Firouzi, F., & Chakrabarty, K. (2020). *"Healthcare IoT." Intelligent Internet of Things* (pp. 515–545). Cham: Springer.

Ge, M., Fu, X., Syed, N., Baig, Z., Teo, G., & Robles-Kelly, A. (2019). Deep learning-based intrusion detection for IoT networks. In *2019 IEEE 24th Pacific Rim International Symposium on Dependable Computing (PRDC)* (pp. 256–25609). IEEE.

Goffredo, R., Accoto, D., & Guglielmelli, E. (2015). Swallowable smart pills for local drug delivery: Present status and future perspectives. *Expert Review of Medical Devices*, 12(5), 585–599.

Gopalan, S. S., Raza, A., & Almobaideen, W. (2021). IoT security in healthcare using AI: A survey. In *2020 International Conference on Communications, Signal Processing, and their Applications (ICCSPA)*. IEEE.

Hajar, M. S., Al-Kadri, M. O., & Kalutarage, H. K. (2021). A survey on wireless body area networks: Architecture, security challenges and research opportunities. *Computers & Security*, 104, 102211.

Hassan, N., Gillani, S., Ahmed, E., Yaqoob, I., & Imran, M. (2018). The role of edge computing in internet of things. *IEEE Communications Magazine*, 56(11), 110–115.

Hassanalieragh, M., Page, A., Soyata, T., Sharma, G., Aktas, M., Mateos, G., Kantarci, B., & Andreescu, S. (2015, June). Health monitoring and management using Internet-of-Things (IoT) sensing with cloud-based processing: Opportunities and challenges. In *2015 IEEE International Conference on Services Computing* (pp. 285–292). IEEE.

Hathaliya, J. J., & Tanwar, S. (2020). An exhaustive survey on security and privacy issues in healthcare 4.0. *Computer Communications*, 153, 311–335.

He, D., et al. (2019). Intrusion detection based on stacked autoencoder for connected healthcare systems. *IEEE Network*, 33(6), 64–69.

Hodo, E., Bellekens, X., Hamilton, A., Tachtatzis, C., & Atkinson, R. (2017). Shallow and deep networks intrusion detection system: A taxonomy and survey. arXiv preprint arXiv:1701.02145.

Jayaratne, M., Nallaperuma, D., De Silva, D., Alahakoon, D., Devitt, B., Webster, K. E., & Chilamkurti, N. (2019). A data integration platform for patient-centered e-healthcare and clinical decision support. *Future Generation Computer Systems*, 92, 996–1008.

Kang, M.-J., & Kang, J.-W. (2016). Intrusion detection system using deep neural network for in-vehicle network security. *PloS One*, 11(6).

Karunarathne, S. M., Saxena, N., & Khan, M. K. (2021). Security and privacy in IoT smart healthcare. *IEEE Internet Computing*, 25(4), 37–48.

Khan, Y., Ostfeld, A. E., Lochner, C. M., Pierre, A., & Arias, A. C. (2016). Monitoring of vital signs with flexible and wearable medical devices. *Advanced Materials*, 28(22), 4373–4395.

Khattak, H. A. K., Abbass, H., Naeem, A., Saleem, K., & Iqbal, W. (2015, October). Security concerns of cloud-based healthcare systems: A perspective of moving from single-cloud to a multi-cloud infrastructure. In *2015 17th International Conference on E-health Networking, Application & Services (HealthCom)* (pp. 61–67). IEEE.

Kumar, N. (2017, August). IoT architecture and system design for healthcare systems. In *2017 International Conference on Smart Technologies for Smart Nation (SmartTechCon)* (pp. 1118–1123). IEEE.

Manhas, J., & Kotwal, S. (2021). Implementation of intrusion detection system for internet of things using machine learning techniques. *Multimedia Security: Algorithm Development, Analysis and Applications*, 217–237.

Morabito, R. (2016). *A Performance Evaluation of Container Technologies on Internet of Things Devices*. In *2016 IEEE Conference on Computer Communications Workshops (INFOCOM WKSHPS)*.(pp. 999–1000) IEEE.

Mutlag, A. A., et al. (2019). Enabling technologies for fog computing in healthcare IoT systems. *Future Generation Computer Systems*, 90, 62–78.

Negash, B., et al. (2018). *"Leveraging Fog Computing for Healthcare IoT."* *Fog Computing in the Internet of Things* (pp. 145–169). Cham: Springer.

Okwuibe, J., Haavisto, J., Harjula, E., Ahmad, I., & Ylianttila, M. (2020). SDN enhanced resource orchestration of containerized edge applications for industrial IoT. *IEEE Access*, 8, 229117–229131.

Ozcan, M. O., Odaci, F., & Ari, I. (2019, July). Remote debugging for containerized applications in edge computing environments. In *2019 IEEE International Conference on Edge Computing (EDGE)* (pp. 30–32). IEEE.

Pande, S., Khamparia, A., & Gupta, D. (2021). An intrusion detection system for healthcare system using machine and deep learning. *World Journal of Engineering*, 19(2), 166–174.

Potluri, S. (2021). *Efficient Deep Learning Algorithms for Securing Industrial Control Systems from Cyberattacks*. http://dx.doi.org/10.25673/36528.

Pouyanfar, S., et al. (2018). A survey on deep learning: Algorithms, techniques, and applications. *ACM Computing Surveys (CSUR)*, 51(5), 1–36.

Prabavathy, S., & Supriya, V. (2021). SDN based cognitive security system for large-scale internet of things using Fog computing. In *2021 International Conference on Emerging Techniques in Computational Intelligence (ICETCI)* (pp. 129–134). IEEE.

Prabavathy, S., Sundarakantham, K., & Shalinie, S. M. (2018). Design of cognitive fog computing for intrusion detection in Internet of Things. *Journal of Communications and Networks*, 20(3), 291–298.

Sami, H., Mourad, A., & El-Hajj, W. (2020). Vehicular-obus-as-on-demand-fogs: Resource and context aware deployment of containerized micro-services. *IEEE/ACM Transactions On Networking*, 28(2), 778–790.

Sekhar, C. H. (2021). Deep learning algorithms for intrusion detection systems: Extensive comparison analysis. *Turkish Journal of Computer and Mathematics Education (TURCOMAT)*, 12(11), 2990–3000.

Shi, W., et al. (2016). Edge computing: Vision and challenges. *IEEE Internet of Things Journal*, 3(5), 637–646.

Strielkina, A., Kharchenko, V., & Uzun, D. (2018). Availability models for healthcare IoT systems: Classification and research considering attacks on vulnerabilities. In *2018 IEEE 9th International Conference on Dependable Systems, Services and Technologies (DESSERT)* (pp. 58–62). IEEE.

Thakkar, A., & Lohiya, R. (2021). A review on machine learning and deep learning perspectives of IDS for IoT: Recent updates, security issues, and challenges. *Archives of Computational Methods in Engineering*, 28(4), 3211–3243.

Thamilarasu, G., Odesile, A., & Hoang, A. (2020). An intrusion detection system for internet of medical things. *IEEE Access*, 8, 181560–181576.

Ullah, A., Azeem, M., Ashraf, H., Alaboudi, A. A., Humayun, M., & Jhanjhi, N. Z. (2021). Secure healthcare data aggregation and transmission in IoT—A survey. *IEEE Access*, 9, 16849–16865.

Velthoven, M. H., Cordon, C., & Challagalla, G. (2019). Digitization of healthcare organizations: The digital health landscape and information theory. *International Journal of Medical Informatics*, 124, 49–57.

Xie, B., Xiang, T., Liao, X., & Wu, J. (2021). Achieving privacy-preserving online diagnosis with outsourced SVM in internet of medical things environment. *IEEE Transactions on Dependable and Secure Computing*, 19(6), 4113–4126.

Yaseen, Q., AlBalas, F., Jararweh, Y., & Al-Ayyoub, M. (2016). A fog computing based system for selective forwarding detection in mobile wireless sensor networks. In *2016 IEEE 1st International Workshops on Foundations and Applications of Self* W)* (pp. 256–262). IEEE.

Zhou, J., Cao, Z., Dong, X., & Vasilakos, A. V. (2017). Security and privacy for cloud-based IoT: Challenges. *IEEE Communications Magazine*, 55(1), 26–33.

11 Human mental experience through chatbots
A thematical analysis of human engagement with evidence-based cognitive-behavioral techniques

Nisha Solanki, Nidhi Singh, Disha Garg

CONTENTS

11.1 INTRODUCTION

As the cases of COVID-19 are rising tremendously worldwide, governments are taking the necessary steps to mitigate the pandemic's impact, such as asking people to self-isolate if they are experiencing any symptoms. Numerous apps help people with their health management, remote monitoring, and overall

DOI: 10.1201/9781003244592-11

health maintenance. These apps relieve the burden on the National Health Service (NHS) during peak demand times, but they also help the participants protect themselves and other people from any unnecessary risk (Vaidyam et al. 2019). Many AI chatbots use evidence-based cognitive-behavioral techniques (CBT) to make people feel understood (Abd-Alrazaq et al. 2020). When these chatbots are combined with professional human support, they provide high-quality mental health support 24/7. Multiple chatbots are offering early mental well-being assistance by elevating human mental connections with them. Many AI systems also integrate natural language understanding with clinical assurance for assisting everyone to develop skills that can be used to manage their mental health in the time of the new normal (Dosovitsky et al. 2020). By combining the science and art of an effective therapy within a portfolio of digital therapeutics (Daley et al. 2020), tools and applications that automate both the process and content of the therapy also create a technology that can establish trusting relationships with the people to fill the gaps in their entire healthcare journey from symptom monitoring to episode management. The study identifies and analyses four global themes (epidemiology characteristic of mental health, types of chatbots. benefits of using chatbots, future implications) and ten organising themes (characteristic, impact, symptoms, prevention, types of chatbots and sources, feasibility, ease of use, solving complex problems, trust, future implications).

This research paper is divided into six sections: Section 11.2 presents a review of the subject's literature, Section 11.3 illustrates the research objectives and methodologies, and Section 11.4 provides analysis and discussion, whereas Section 11.5 contains findings and recommendations and Section 11.6 contains conclusions and implications.

11.2 LITERATURE REVIEW

After an initial overview of related work, the researcher examined the available literature and found many studies had been done related to artificial intelligence (AI), chatbots, and machine learning (ML), related to tourism, education, online shopping, and other sectors. According to the latest study in 2021, healthcare during the pandemic also utilised this technology to maintain the vaccination records that would have taken longer without it (Srivastava 2021). At this time, chatbots were also used by the healthcare sector for various other purposes, including the maintenance of the mental health of participants by keeping them interactive and engaged (Romanovskyi et al. 2021). Artificial intelligence is not limited to the economic and professional setup but also makes the daily life of individuals easy and more convenient with the help of smart gadgets like Alexa and Siri (Tariq et al. 2021; Tariq & Abonamah 2021; Maher et al. 2020). This adoption of the technology for daily life was termed "easy artificial intelligence" by Tariq et al. (2021), whereas professionally used artificial intelligence technology was considered a problematic framework. AI helped in many aspects and made the transactions of major stakeholders (customers) very easy and convenient, and hence, the significant contribution of chatbots was found in booking flights, rail reservations, and hotels (Suanpang et al. 2021). All the previous studies had proven the successful communication between the chatbot and users' perception, but it failed to handle the sentimental and complicated elements. This gap was found due to machine-learning technology's lack of natural language, the second stage of chatbot conversation (Suta et al. 2020). In a variety of industries, eBay used ShopBot and Taco Bell's use of the chatbot "Tacobot" to take orders from the menu. Construction company Keyes used Roof.ai Chatbot to ask questions; in travel sectors, there are many chatbots like Expedia, Facebook and Messenger chatbots; Skyscanner, Facebook, and Messenger chatbots and many others have gained popularity in healthcare (in general) and mental health (in particular) over the past five years, in addition to the previously stated industries (Vyas & Gupta 2022). The earlier research was more related to the participant-friendly and convenient nature of chatbots for timely response to customers (Sahaja et al. 2019). The chatbots were also found to be effective in extracting information, like the search engines that also helped chatbots in effective conversations (Suresh et al. 2020; Maher et al. 2020). The technology of chatbots has evolved to that level with the aid of deep learning so that they can mimic the person to develop greater human feeling and more convenient ways like Google Maps and Siri to give a human voice (Verma et al. 2019; Jwala et al. 2019; Um et al. 2020; Ukpabi et al. 2019). However, in the same industry, technological advances aside, the primary negative effect of traditional agent services was observed, which hinders customers' intention to adopt and grow chatbot backend services (Pillai, R., & Sivathanu, B. (2020). This trust for the agent and adherence to the traditional process also affects the willingness of customers to adopt the technology in the tourism industry. In the e-commerce industry, sales decreased due to replacing human–human interaction with human–computer interaction, backed with customers' perception that machines cannot respond like a human (Xueming Luo et al. 2019). This problem was separated from the benefit of having more purchase options based on customers' choices that can ease customers' shopping (Hidayatullah et al. 2019). Chatbot technology lacks machine language and works on natural language, and the new technology, called "verbot", could be developed to work on the computer language (Gaikwad 2018). In the healthcare sector, these chatbots, with the help of AI, perform various functions, including entertainment and providing directions to other departments. The participant can easily and quickly access the status of their appointment and reports, which helps save on customer service costs (Athota et al. 2020). The healthcare professionals also developed a particular chatbot for pandemic situations that was proven to be effective in managing the mental shock of participants during and after quarantine by providing a communication platform for updating the status of pandemic risk and recovery (Ouerhani et al. 2020). Patient engagement is beneficial for keeping the patient mentally positive (Battineni et al. 2020), but the avoidance behavior of participants toward AI-supported chatbots can challenge the practice of patient engagement, and that may cause deterioration of the system by which mental healthcare professionals keep the patient stress free and occupied in some interactions (Athota et al. 2020). The traditional viewholders and participants with poor technical knowledge were also studied as the significant receptors to accepting chatbots in hospitals and other health facilities (Battineni et al. 2020). The emergence of chatbots and AI in the healthcare sector was initiated in combination with yoga, meditation, weight-loss solutions, the latter guiding the diet plans through regular interactions via the online system and chatbots (Verma et al. 2019). Over time, AI was utilised to delight the participant, with timely appointments and reminders of upcoming medical tests to help them schedule their visits accordingly (Suresh et al. 2020). The major players of the healthcare industry were also found to be effective at managing the vast customer base with the help of system-led services through AI-backed chatbots (Pillai et al. 2020). The pandemic has proved to be an opportunity for chatbots in the healthcare industry, especially in departments of mental health, as teams of psychiatrists in India found its usage to be effective at balancing the mental health of suffering participants at the time of treatment and quarantine (Huang et al. 2019). Chatbots were also suggested as the better tool for controlling infections at the time of pandemic through virtual assistance by registered doctors and healthcare professionals and maintenance of psychological balance at the time of a hostile and depressive environment (Battineni et al. 2020). There are many factors that can increase the acceptance of chatbots in the healthcare sector. However, some critical factors, like trust in the doctors in virtual mode, acceptability of technology-driven assistance, in-human interface for human interaction, are suggested to be studied for increasing the effectiveness of artificial intelligence in the healthcare sector (Athota et al. 2020; Vyas & Bhargava 2021). Mental health is found to be more critical for the young generation due to various life factors, demanding regular interaction and sharing of thoughts through human interactions (Oh et al. 2017). These aspects of AI-led chatbot adoption are found with a broader scope to study the acceptance and adaptability of chatbots in the healthcare sector. We know that the demand of the healthcare industry is increasing rapidly nowadays, especially after the COVID-19 pandemic (Vyas 2023).

11.3   RESEARCH PROBLEM AND AIM

The adoption of the chatbot for mental health issues depends upon human engagement with AI-enabled chatbots. Previous research (Abd-Alrazaq et al. 2020; Lucas et al. 2017; Anthes 2016) investigated only users' adoption and perceptions, but the user experience with chatbot was neglected. The literature offers no clear methodology to study the user experience with the chatbot, and this is an area that requires further exploration. Therefore, in the current study, the qualitative approach was utilised to determine the themes of user experience, so, in the future, a conceptual model can be constructed, where the main research objective is to identify the global themes of user experience.

11.4   RESEARCH METHODOLOGY

11.4.1   RESEARCH DESIGN

In this study, validated methods were used to identify the chatbots using understanding of natural language with clinical assurance for helping humans improve their mental health; through thematical analysis, researchers could identify the themes of current human sharing with chatbots. When it comes to identifying the theme, thematical analysis involves identifying, analysing, and finding patterns in data (Brawn et al. 2006). Qualitative research is required to study human behavior, attitude, beliefs, and opinions toward some objects and preferences and choices. On the contrary note, the purpose of quantitative methods is to have statistical values like ratios, averages, percentages of the sample population which the researcher want to study. Even when the researcher aimes to study the relationship between the attitude and behavior between two variables (Beeson et al. 2011). For the current study, a qualitative approach was selected to study how chatbots could help humans improve their mental health.

11.4.2 SAMPLE INSTRUMENT

This study is focused on how humans interact with chatbots which understand natural language in order to improve mental health conditions. For collecting qualitative data, unstructured, open-ended interviews were taken to identify different types of chatbots used by humans to resolve mental health issues and currently identify themes in a trend that humans are sharing with chatbots.

11.4.3 SAMPLE

The sample populations were the clients who came for consulting to the Department of Psychology of SGT University, Gurugram, India,. Purposive sampling techniques were used to select the sample population. A total of 15 samples of clients were taken for the current study.

11.4.4 DATA COLLECTION METHOD

For the current study, qualitative interviews were conducted to collect the data to identify the different types of chatbots used and identify themes in a trend that humans are sharing with chatbots. The phenomenological interview technique (Cypress 2018) was adapted to collect participants' personal experiences while using chatbots and how it was different from human interaction. To conduct the qualitative interview, telephone, WhatsApp, and Skype were used as the medium.

11.4.5 DATA ANALYSIS

For data analysis, NVivo software was used to identify themes and patterns. NVivo offers many advantages and significantly improves study quality (Hilal et al. 2013; Hilal & Alabri 2013). Qualitative data analysis has become more accessible and more professional than before. The program minimises handling responsibilities considerably and offers the researcher more time to detect trends, identify issues, and draw conclusions. Altogether, it is highly recommended that the qualitative researcher follows this software's processes to alleviate the confused, untimely, and time-consuming duty (). A qualitative approach is intended to develop in line with rapid progress in computer-assisted/quality data analysis (CAQDAS).

11.5   DATA ANALYSIS AND INTERPRETATION

The thematical analysis process can be divided into six broader subcategories. All six steps were necessary because a colossal amount of text was generated during qualitative data collection, and processing texts for analysis was complex. In the current study, ten organizing themes and 51 basic themes were identified based on (a) mental health condition, its symptoms and how the patient identified the mental health, and (b) how the chatbot helped in improving mental health. The 15 transcripts were collected from the 15 participants who were contacted for counseling in the SGT University Department of Psychology. The entire study consisted of a 55-minute unstructured interview for each participant. These were then transcribed verbatim. The study investigated how participants interpret feedback and how they use it. The discussions focused on how participants felt about their mental health they had survived COVID-19: how they found the symptoms, to what degree participants had taken precautionary steps, and whether they had used chatbots. Everyone who took part in an interview from which the extracted information was collected, agreed that the transcript extract could be used in the analysis. It was of interest to notice that participants reported their experiences and points of view. An essential component of the research is data collection and analysis, and the corresponding top-down or theoretical thematic analysis (Braun, V., & Clarke, V. (2006)), driven by the specific research question(s) and the analyst's focus, is distinguished from bottom-up or inductive analysis, which is driven more by the data. The study's primary goal was to come up with a clear and simple example that could be utilized as a reference for assessing qualitative data. The qualitative material's thematic network analysis has six-phase guidance (Braun, V., & Clarke, V. (2006)), a highly effective foundation for undertaking this type of study. The analytic method offered makes use of well-established and well-known methodologies. It suggests that topic analysis can be helped and presented more effectively using thematic networks. Thematic networks are a web-like structure that summarises texts into significant themes (Attride-Stirling 2001). The first stage is to understand the participant's mental health issues, symptoms, and assessment steps. All fifteen transcripts were read to understand the text and correctly interpret the result (Braun, V., & Clarke, V. (2006)). The result of the sample work is given in Table 11.1, and potential words were identified from the transcripts.

Interesting patterns emerged when examining all transcripts, such as re-occurring words, ideas, symptoms, chatbot importance, and future implication (). All the texts were read carefully and coded accordingly. Each subsequent transcript reading brought new insight into how chatbots helping to reduce mental health issues and how participants found chatbots in communication.

Initially, 51 codes were identified from the transcript, so no critical information was missed during the final analysis. All codes were consolidated into basic

TABLE 11.1

Extractions from written text to create code text

Extract from Transcripts	Coding
Initially, I chose to ignore the symptoms under the expectation that they would go away after a time of rest and recuperation. Nonetheless, after about a month, I began to experience melancholy, and the severity of my anxiety was growing more with each passing day. I was suffering big mood swings as a result.	a) Anxiety b) Mood Swings c) Melancholy
Hmm, you can say that, while sitting alone at home, I became self-critical. I can never do anything. A kind of feeling often came inside my mind. I feel a kind of loneliness. Negative self-talk.	a) Self-criticize b) Loneliness c) Negative self-talk
You could say that, while sitting alone at home, I became self-critical, with thoughts such as "I'll never be able to do anything" and "I'll never be able to do anything" frequently entering my thoughts. I'm experiencing a sense of loneliness. Self-deprecating self-talk.	a) Loneliness b) Self-deprecating self-talk c) Self-critical

themes in the third phase by accumulating codes with similar meanings (). In the fourth phase, several new themes were identified and scanned carefully, modified, and developed into the preliminary themes. NVivo was used to organise the data according to their respective codes. Based on organising themes, a color code was assigned. The fifth phase defined a few critical themes related to the subject of this research, like what themes were saying and how sub-themes were related. It is vital to introduce further definitions and basic concepts related to mental health, what participants discussed, and how much information they liked to share with chatbots. In the final phase, visual tools were used to describe, explore, and analyse empirical evidence in a straightforward and easy-to-understand manner after identifying the global topic and placing it at the center of the thematic network.

As seen in Figure 11.1 above, interpretation shows three separate layers of topics based on thematic network analysis. The first outermost layer is called the Basic Theme, which we identify based on textual data interpretation. Based on the identified basic theme, we further refine and cluster the related terminologies having semantic linkages. These are now high-order functional terminologies and define overall the context of basic themes. Since the basic themes are clustered together semantically, this second layer is also known as Organising Theme.

We now go further to a higher order, where these organising themes are further grouped and thematically linked further. The set thus created by using a group of organising themes is called the Global Theme. The global theme tells the overall context of the whole thematical analysis. It has a ripple effect of becoming a summary of central themes and helps identify and analyse the texts' context. Based on preliminary findings, it appears that usage of a mental health

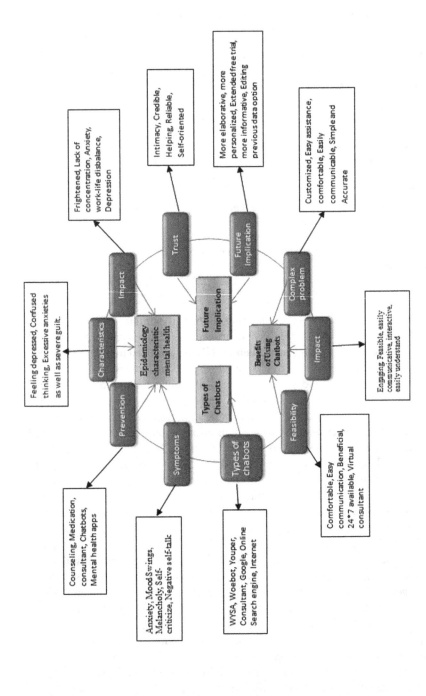

FIGURE 11.1   Structure of a thematic network.

TABLE 11.2
Basic to organising to global themes

Basic Themes	Organising Themes	Global Themes
• Feeling depressed • Confused thinking • Excessive anxieties • Severe guilt	Characteristic	Epidemiology characteristic of mental health
• Frightened • Lack of concentration • Work–life imbalance • Depression	Impact	
• Anxiety • Mood swings • Melancholy • Self-criticise • Negative self-talk	Symptoms	
• Counseling • Medication • Consultant • Chatbots	Prevention	
• WYSA • Woebot • Youper • Consultant • Google • Online Search engine • Internet	Types of chatbots and sources	Types of chatbots
• Comfortable • Easy communication • Beneficial • 24/7 availability • Virtual consultant	Feasibility	Benefits of using chatbots
• Engaging • Feasible • Easily communicative • Interactive • Easily understood	Ease of use	
• Customised • Easy assistance • Comfortable • Easily communicable • Simple and accurate	Solving complex problems	
• Intimacy • Credible • Helping • Reliable • Self-oriented	Trust	Future implication
• More elaborative • More personalised • Extended free trial • More informative	Future implications	

chatbot (Fitzpatrik et al. 2017) among the sample population was engaging while also dramatically reducing the prodrome (an early symptom) of anxiety, stress, and depression. Our current study found that when participants communicate their problems with a chatbot, it decreases their anxiety and depressive symptoms. Through thematic analysis, three chatbots found in India were identified as Wysa, Woebot, and Youper. They were designed to help combat depression. Wysa and Woebot suppressed symptoms of depression in participants who self-reportedly suffer from depression or anxiety (Huang et al. 2017). Only a few studies in India (Inkster et al. 2018; Vijayarani & Balamurugan 2019; Mishra et al. 2019: Prakash & Das 2020) have employed a mental health chatbot, and the results are promising. Baseline levels of anxiety and depression in the current study's participants were substantially more significant than would be expected in the general Indian population, according to previous research and studies. The word "cloud" in Figure 11.2 displays the essential takeaway messages from the interview participants.

The results obtained here may have implications for understanding whether chatbots feature what healthcare practitioners cannot provide over time. In some studies, virtual agents incorporated in chatbots have been proven to assist and to inspire users to use chatbots. In the 15 transcripts, the usefulness and convenience of use of chatbots were evaluated. Chatbots are straightforward to learn about and understand, according to participants in nine studies. Participants in six studies struggled to use the chatbot because they didn't know when or how to respond. Participants often rate the utility of mental health chatbots as good. Chatbots may be more realistic if they have an embodied virtual agent and can

FIGURE 11.2   Word cloud.

communicate verbally. A total of ten studies assessed participants' perception of how accurate the chatbots were in verbal and nonverbal responses. Even though chatbots are thought to be beneficial and straightforward to use, five participants found some limitations: dialogues are thought to be shallow, confused, or too short. This highlights an essential issue that should be addressed in creating future mental health chatbots. There is scope for further enhancement of the quality of the dialogue. Chatbot quality, in terms of responsiveness and response diversity, is crucial in this situation. Currently, systems have limited responses, which could be attributed to the fact that many chatbots are still in the early stages of development. Another crucial factor to be considered is the quality of the material presented and its agreement with the recommendations of the treating physicians. The fact that users went out of their way to find a mental health tool is not surprising, but it suggests that the chatbot can successfully reach its target demographic and could be a helpful way to engage people who are experiencing high levels of stress or mental health symptoms. This finding follows the idea that people actively seeking treatment or online consulting are more aware of AI-powered chatbots than people looking for face-to-face encounters or in a clinical setting. It suggests that the chatbot could be a useful tool for increasing access and identifying the most vulnerable people, allowing for faster access to appropriate expert treatment.

Another study compared AI chatbots that replied to the user with verbal and nonverbal empathic reactions with those with an embodied virtual agent (text-based chatbot). Participants regarded the AI chatbot as more usable and attentive than the online and offline consultations. The participants' trust in a chatbot is the subject of this theme. Participants in eight studies believed chatbots were trustworthy.

11.6   LIMITATIONS AND FUTURE SCOPE

The focus of this review was on chatbots that can only be utilised with stand-alone software and a web browser. This review was restricted to a chatbot that human operators do not control. As a result, patients' perceptions and views regarding chatbots and chatbots with various delivery modalities may differ from their perceptions and opinions about chatbots found in this review. Patients in different sections or regions of India may have varied perspectives and opinions about mental health chatbots, so the findings of this review may not be generalisable in every part of India. The researchers have conducted the study in the Delhi-National Capital Region, and, due to a lack of time, other states were not included. The current study has included some identified themes of people's behavior towards chatbots, and the rest were excluded. The principle of generalisation adds to the limitation of the study that describes the variation of results on different samples, and the findings of this study cannot be generalised for the entire population. The study has reflected various experiences of people toward chatbots during COVID-19, but the results at some other time in different situations may also vary. To be perceived as inspiring and engaging, a mental health chatbot must be sympathetic and create a relationship with the user. This could be accomplished by providing details on the secondary uses of the data obtained and data storage and processing protocols. In traditional healthcare settings, the patient–doctor or patient–therapist relationship is marked by trust and loyalty. Physicians must be convinced of the value of chatbot systems to encourage participant acceptability of chatbot use. Through the growth of AI and competition, chatbots were proven to be good resources for facilitating the customers with better and more timely responses. The limitations of the current study can be overcome in future work. This study may also be conducted to understand the human experience through chatbots in other industries as well, and the comparative studies of various generations with respect to chatbot experience and in different industries may also be studied. The extension of the current study to an increased population may also extract more relevant results for consideration. These studies may add to the quality of customer services by various players in the market and may also facilitate the development of an effective tool for handling the increased competition. The competencies of mental health chatbots must be improved. It is necessary to improve their ability to comprehend and respond effectively to human input. Methods for slightly altering or reformulating responses from the knowledge base could help deal with this problem. The most challenging part is deciding on a suitable response once an emergency has been recognised. The sentiment analysis technology, which has been used successfully to evaluate social media postings about suicide and self-harm, might be applied to health chatbot training. If it does not respond to individual user demands, the present way of constructing a knowledge base for a mental health chatbot is insufficient. Methods must contain patient-specific information that can be gleaned from medical records.

11.7   CONCLUSION

This study was used to identify different types of chatbots and identify the current themes of humans sharing with chatbots. The study was based on the qualitative approach, and a phenomenological unstructured, open-ended questionnaire technique was used to study the phenomenon. Thematical analysis was done to identify the themes and patterns for the study. The resulting sample identified seven themes, and four different chatbots which participants used to chat and discuss mental health.

DATA AVAILABILITY STATEMENT

It is vital to highlight that the following licenses and restrictions apply to the data used in this study. Due to the secret or commercially sensitive nature of certain data sets, access is allowed only upon request. The data have been anonymised and must be used strictly for research purposes. Upon request, access to these datasets is available from SGT University's Department of Psychology in Gurugram, Haryana, India.

REFERENCES

Abd-Alrazaq, A. A., Rababeh, A., Alajlani, M., Bewick, B. M., & Househ, M. (2020). Effectiveness and safety of using chatbots to improve mental health: Systematic review and meta-analysis. *Journal of Medical Internet Research*, 22(7), e16021.

Anthes, E. (2016). Mental health: There's an app for that. *Nature*, 532(7597), 20–23. https://doi.org/10.1038/532020a [Medline: 27078548]

Athota, L., Shukla, V. K., Pandey, N., et al. (2020). Chatbot for healthcare system using artificial intelligence. In *ICRITO 2020 – IEEE 8th International Conference on Reliability, Infocom Technologies and Optimization (Trends and Future Directions)*, 5(9), 619–622. https://doi.org/10.1109/ICRITO48877.2020.9197833

Attride-Stirling, J. (2001). Thematic networks: An analytic tool for qualitative research. *Qualitative Research*, 1(3), 385–405.

Battineni, G., Chintalapudi, N., & Amenta, F. (2020). Ai chatbot design during an epidemic like the novel coronavirus. *Healthcare (Switzerland)*, 8(2). https://doi.org/10.3390/healthcare8020154

Braun, V., & Clarke, V. (2006). Using thematic analysis in psychology. *Qualitative Research in Psychology*, 3(2), 77–101.

Cypress, B. (2018). Qualitative research methods: A phenomenological focus. *Dimensions of Critical Care Nursing*, 37(6), 302–309.

Daley, K., Hungerbuehler, I., Cavanagh, K., Claro, H. G., et al. (2020). Preliminary evaluation of the engagement and effectiveness of a mental health chatbot. *Frontiers in Digital Health*, 2, 41.

Dosovitsky, G., Pineda, B. S., Jacobson, N. C., et al. (2020). Artificial intelligence chatbot for depression: Descriptive study of usage. *JMIR Formative Research*, 4(11), e17065.

Fitzpatrick, K. K., Darcy, A., & Vierhile, M. (2017). Delivering cognitive behavior therapy to young adults with symptoms of depression and anxiety using a fully automated conversational agent (Woebot): A randomized controlled trial. *JMIR Mental Health*, 4(2), e19.

Gaikwad, T. (2018). Artificial intelligence based chat-bot. *International Journal for Research in Applied Science and Engineering Technology*, 6(4), 2305–2306. https://doi.org/10.22214/ijraset.2018.4393

Hidayatullah, A. F., Kurniawan, W., & Ratnasari, C. I. (2019). Topic modeling on Indonesian online shop chat. In *ACM International Conference Proceeding Series* (pp. 121–126). https://doi.org/10.1145/3342827.3342831

Hilal, A. H., & Alabri, S. S. (2013). Using NVivo for data analysis in qualitative research. *International Interdisciplinary Journal of Education*, 2(2), 181–186.

Huang, H. Y., & Bashir, M. (2017). Users' adoption of mental health apps: Examining the impact of information cues. *JMIR mHealth and uHealth*, 5(6), e83.

Huang, C. Y., Yang, M. C., Chen, Y. J., et al. (2019, December). A chatbot-supported smart wireless interactive healthcare system for weight control and health promotion. In *IEEE International Conference on Industrial Engineering and Engineering Management* (pp. 1791–1795). https://doi.org/10.1109/IEEM.2018.8607399

Inkster, B., Sarda, S., & Subramanian, V. (2018). An empathy-driven, conversational artificial intelligence agent (wysa) for digital mental well-being: Real-world data evaluation mixed-methods study. *JMIR Mhealth Uhealth*, 6(11), e12106. https://doi.org/10.2196/12106 [Medline: 30470676]

Jwala, K., Sirisha, G. N. V. G., & Padma Raju, G. V. (2019). Developing a chatbot using machine learning. *International Journal of Recent Technology and Engineering*, 8(1), 89–92.

Lucas, G. M., Rizzo, A., Gratch, J., et al. (2017). Reporting mental health symptoms: Breaking down barriers to care with virtual human interviewers. *Frontiers in Robotics and AI*, 4. https://doi.org/10.3389/frobt.2017.00051

Luo, X., Tong, S., Fang, Z., & Qu, Z. (2019, June). Machines versus humans: The impact of AI chatbot disclosure on customer purchases. *Luo, X, Tong S, Fang Z, Qu*, 20–33.

Maher, S., Kayte, S., & Nimbhore, S. (2020). Chatbots & Its techniques using AI: An review. *International Journal for Research in Applied Science and Engineering Technology*, 8(12), 503–508.

Mishra, A., Sapre, S., Shinde, S., et al. (2019). Intelligent chatbot for guided navigation of repository contend. *International Journal of Advanced Research in Computer and Communication Engineering*, 8(5), 25–28.

Oh, K. J., Lee, D., Ko, B., et al. (2017). A chatbot for psychiatric counseling in mental healthcare service based on emotional dialogue analysis and sentence generation. In *Proceedings – 18th IEEE International Conference on Mobile Data Management. MDM* (pp. 371–376). https://doi.org/10.1109/MDM.2017.64

Ouerhani, N., Maalel, A., Ghézala, H., et al. (2020). Smart ubiquitous chatbot for COVID-19 assistance with deep learning sentiment analysis model during and after quarantine, 1–9. https://doi.org/10.21203/rs.3.rs-33343/v1

Pillai, R., & Sivathanu, B. (2020). Adoption of AI-based chatbots for hospitality and tourism. *International Journal of Contemporary Hospitality Management*, 32(10), 3199–3226. https://doi.org/10.1108/IJCHM-04-2020-0259

Prakash, A. V., & Das, S. (2020). Intelligent conversational agents in mental healthcare services: A thematic analysis of user perceptions. *Pacific Asia Journal of the Association for Information Systems*, 12(2), 1.

Romanovskyi, O., Pidbutska, N., & Knysh, A. (2021). Elomia chatbot: The effectiveness of artificial intelligence in the fight for mental health. *CEUR Workshop Proceedings*, 2870, 1215–1224.

Sahaja, G., Priyanka, V., Anisha, M. P. R., et al. (2019). *JASC: Journal of Applied Science and Computations ISSN NO : 1076-5131 Chatbot-A Variety of Lifestyles*, VI(I), 367–378.

Srivastava, B. (2021). Did chatbots miss their "Apollo moment"? A survey of the potential, gaps and lessons from using collaboration assistants during COVID-19. *Patterns*, 2(8), 100308. https://doi.org/10.1016/j.patter.2021.100308

Suanpang, P., & Jamjuntr, P. (2021). A Chatbot prototype by deep learning supporting tourism. *Psychology and Education Journal*, 58, 1902–1911.

Suresh, P., Ravikumar, O., Hari Krishna Mahesh, K., et al. (2020). Content extraction through chatbots with artificial intelligence techniques. *International Journal of Scientific and Technology Research*, 9(2), 1960–1963.

Suta, P., Lan, X., Wu, B., et al. (2020). An overview of machine learning in chatbots. *International Journal of Mechanical Engineering and Robotics Research*, 9(4), 502–510. https://doi.org/10.18178/ijmerr.9.4.502-510

Tariq, M. U., & Abonamah, A. A. (2021). Proposed strategic framework for effective artificial intelligence adoption in UAE. *Academy of Strategic Management Journal*, 20(2), 1–14.

Ukpabi, D. C., Aslam, B., & Karjaluoto, H. (2019). Chatbot adoption in tourism services: A conceptual exploration. In *Robots, Artificial Intelligence and Service Automation in Travel, Tourism and Hospitality* (pp. 105–121). https://doi.org/10.1108/978-1-78756-687-320191006

Um, T., Kim, T., & Chung, N. (2020). How does an intelligence chatbot affect customers compared with self-service technology for sustainable services? *Sustainability*, 12(12). https://doi.org/10.3390/su12125119

Vaidyam, A. N., Wisniewski, H., Halamka, J. D., et al. (2019). Chatbots and conversational agents in mental health: A review of the psychiatric landscape. *The Canadian Journal of Psychiatry*, 64(7), 456–464.

Verma, P., & Jyoti, K. (2019). Chatbots employing deep learning for big data. *International Journal of Innovative Technology and Exploring Engineering*, 8(11), 1005–1010. https://doi.org/10.35940/ijitee.I8017.0981119

Vijayarani, M., & Balamurugan, G. (2019). Chatbot in mental health care. *Indian Journal of Psychiatric Nursing*, 16(2), 126.

Vyas, S. (2023). Extended reality and edge AI for healthcare 4.0: Systematic study. In *Extended Reality for Healthcare Systems* (pp. 229–240). Academic Press.

Vyas, S., & Bhargava, D. (2021). *Smart Health Systems: Emerging Trends*.

Vyas, S., & Gupta, S. (2022). Case study on state-of-the-art wellness and health tracker devices. In *Handbook of Research on Lifestyle Sustainability and Management Solutions using AI, Big Data Analytics, and Visualization* (pp. 325–337). IGI Global.

12 An early diagnosis of cardiac disease using feature-optimization-based deep neural network

Manaswini Pradhan

CONTENTS

12.1 INTRODUCTION

Heart disease describes a range of condition that affects the heart. The term "cardiac disease" is regularly used with cardiovascular disease (CVD). The blood to the heart is supplied by coronary supply routes and narrowing of coronary arteries is the major cause of heart failure. In the data analysis, assessing cardiovascular

DOI: 10.1201/9781003244592-12

disease risk is a significant task. The major cause of heart attack in United States is coronary artery disease. Cardiac disorder is more frequent among males than females. A survey carried out by the World Health Organization (WHO) estimated that 24% of deaths in India were due to cardiac disorder (WHO 2017). In 2015, over 30% of global deaths were due to CVD, leading to over 17 million deaths worldwide, a global health burden. Of those deaths, over 7 million were caused by heart disease, and greater than 75% of deaths due to CVD were in developing countries. In the United States alone, 25% of deaths were attributed to heart disease, killing over 630,000 Americans annually. Among heart disease conditions, coronary heart disease is the most common, causing over 360,000 American deaths as a result of heart attacks in 2015. Many people who die of a heart attack experienced symptoms that were previously undiscovered or simply ignored. It is time to predict heart disease before its actual occurrence, as suggested by Hajar (2017). There are several main factor risks of heart disease, including high cholesterol level, high blood pressure, smoking, use of alcoholic drinks, high sugar, lack of physical activities, CVD, and a hypertensive heart (Ali et al. 2019).

Feature extraction and selection are important steps for heart disease prediction. An optimum feature set should have effective and discriminating features, while mostly reducing the redundancy of features to avoid the "curse of dimensionality" problem as explained by Gu et al. (2018). Feature selection strategies are often used to explore the effect of irrelevant features on the performance of classifier systems (Suganya et al. 2016; Liu & Tang 2013). In this phase, an optimal subset of features, that are necessary and sufficient for solving the problem, is selected. Feature selection improves the accuracy of algorithms in reducing the dimensionality and removing irrelevant features, as discussed by Shen et al. (2012) and Singh et al. (2015). The orientation of the histogram feature provides the orientation of edges in the image, as demonstrated by Jeong et al. (2012). Textures are one of the most important features used in many applications. Texture features have been widely used in heart disease classification. The texture features are the ability to distinguish between abnormal and normal cases, as illustrated by Shen et al. (2012). Texture measures are two types: first order and second order. In the first order, texture measure is statistically calculated from an individual pixel. In the second order, the texture measure takes into account the relationship between neighbors, as shown by Pham et al. (2020) and Esteva et al. (2019). Texture features have been extracted and used as parameters to enhance the classification result.

Many predictive approaches are used for heart disease classification system, namely decision tree, K-nearest neighbor (KNN), support vector machine (SVM), Naïve Bayes (NB), and artificial neural network (ANN) approaches, and it also deploys more clustering techniques (Javier et al. 2019; Vivan et al. 2019; Rajakumar & George 2013; Pradhan & Bhuiyan 2023) to achieve effective prediction. Nowadays, deep-learning (DL) algorithms are mainly used for classification problems. Some of the main research areas into DL in the field of healthcare are the detection of phenotypic patterns from serum uric acid concentration, determination of physiologic patterns, and predicting the severity level of various diseases (Esteva et al. 2019; Pham et al. 2020; Pradhan 2023).

The main objective of this approach is to achieve cardiac image-based automatic heart disease diagnosis, using DNN with LPSO. The proposed research mainly consists of four stages, namely preprocessing, feature extraction, feature selection, and classification. Here, the feature extraction is done using a median filter. After feature extraction, the GLCM features are extracted from each cardiac image. To reduce the complexity and increase the classification accuracy, the important features are selected using the LPSO algorithm. After that, the selected features are provided to the classifier to classify an image as either normal or abnormal. The characteristics of the research are listed below:

- Initially, to remove the noise present in the image, a median filter is utilised.
- Then, the GLCM features are extracted from each image.
- To reduce the complexity and increase the accuracy, the important features are selected using the lion particle swarm optimisation (LPSO) algorithm. The LPSO is a combination of the lion optimisation algorithm (LOA) and the particle swarm optimisation (PSO) algorithm.
- Then, the selected features are given to the input of a deep neural network (DNN) classifier to classify an image as either normal or abnormal.
- The performance of the proposed approach is analysed in terms of different metrics, namely accuracy, sensitivity, and specificity.

The rest of this chapter is organised as follows; the literature review is presented in Section 12.2 and the proposed heart disease prediction system is explained in Section 12.3. The experimental results are analysed in Section 12.4 and the conclusion is presented in Section 12.5.

12.2 LITERATURE SURVEY

Many researchers have developed heart disease prediction systems, using cardiac images. Among them, some of the studies are analysed here. Rojas-Albarracin et al. (2019) developed a heart attack detection system with color images, using convolution neural network (CNN). Initially, they collect the images for training, validation, and testing. Then, the heart images are transferred to the CNN structure. The CNN directly classifies an image as either normal or abnormal. Their system was given a maximum accuracy of 91.75% and a sensitivity of 92.85%. Moreover, Garate-Escamila et al. (2020) developed a heart disease prediction system, using principle component analysis (PCA) and the random forest algorithm. Initially, the data are collected from the unique client identifier (UCI) Machine-Learning Repository. Then, the dimension of the dataset is reduced, using PCA. After that, the reduced dataset was given to the CNN classifier to classify the data as either normal or abnormal. The proposed approach attained a maximum accuracy of

98.7% for Cleveland, 99.0% for Hungarian, and 99.4% for Cleveland-Hungarian (CH) datasets.

Thanga Selvi and Muthulakshmi (2020) developed a heart disease classification system, using optimal artificial neural network (OANN). The OANN consist of two major processes, namely distance-based misclassified instance removal (DBMIR) and teaching and learning-based optimisation (TLBO) algorithms for artificial neural network (ANN), called TLBO-ANN. This system was designed based on a big data framework like Apache Spark. Moreover, this system works on two phases, namely offline prediction and online prediction. For offline prediction, they utilised a benchmark dataset, whereas, for online prediction, they utilised a real-time dataset. The performance of the presented OANN model has been tested using a benchmark heart disease dataset from the UCI Repository. Oliver et al. (2021) developed an accurate system for prediction of heart disease based on a biosystem, using a regressive learning-based neural network classifier (RLNNC). The RLNNC system was a fully automated algorithm. The results of this system were accurate for patients with heart disease and the drug benefits of detecting and analysing heart disease. Analysis has shown that the RLNNC-based techniques promote greater efficiency and higher accuracy than traditional methods.

Similarly, Jiao et al. (2020) developed a one-dimensional CNN-based pulse recognition system for detecting patients with cardiovascular disease. Initially, the original data are divided and normalised. The divided dataset is then assigned for training and testing process. Then, the pulse signal is inputted to CNN, which automatically extracts the features (Vyas et al. 2022), which are characterised by a fully attached layer. The final classification accuracy ratio can reach 97.14%, which is better than traditional machine-learning classification methods, such as SVM and KNN, providing new ideas and methods for the classification and objectification of pulse signals.

Alkhodari and Fraiwan (2021) developed a valve heart disease prediction system, using convolutional and recurrent neural networks (RNN) in phonocardiogram recordings. Initially, the signal is pre-processed, using the maximal overlap discrete wavelet transform (MODWT) smoothing algorithm. Then, the signal is transferred to the combination of CNN and RNN, based on bi-directional long short-term memory (BiLSTM). The model is trained and tested following the k-fold cross-validation scheme of 10-folds, using the CNN-BiLSTM network as well as the CNN and BiLSTM networks individually. The highest performance was achieved using the CNN-BiLSTM network with an overall Cohen's kappa, accuracy, sensitivity, and specificity measures of 97.87%, 99.32%, 98.30%, and 99.58%, respectively. Dutta et al. (2020) developed a CNN-based coronary heart disease prediction system. Here, the forecast variables are determined using a less complete abstract and select operator (LASO)-based filtering system. Sub-sample methods are implemented to calculate high-class inequalities. The classifier achieves higher class-wise accuracies than traditional models. The introduced framework was used as a transfer learning model for new data. This method attained a maximum accuracy of 79.5%.

12.3 PROPOSED CARDIAC IMAGE-BASED AUTOMATIC HEART DISEASE DIAGNOSIS MODEL

Cardiac imaging plays an important role in diagnosing heart disease. The unavailability or shortage of radiologists and physicians in various countries, for a number of reasons, is a significant factor in barriers to early diagnosis of this high-mortality disease. Among the various efforts to develop end-support systems, computational intelligence is a growing trend in the field of clinical imaging for prognosis and diagnosis. This helps radiologists and clinicians to get relief from the heavy burden and reduce the delays in achieving timely diagnoses of patients. Therefore, in this study, automatic heart disease prognosis was proposed using a deep neural network. The proposed approach consists of four stages, namely pre-processing, feature extraction, feature selection, and classification. The cardiac image-based automatic heart disease diagnosis model is described in Figure 12.1.

12.3.1 PRE-PROCESSING

Consider the cardiac image $I_{i,j}$, which includes some noise. To remove the noise present in the input image, a median filter is applied. The median filter is typically used to lessen noise in an image. It is a non-linear filter that computes median of the pixel set that falls within the filter mask. Each pixel is addressed, and it is replaced by means of statistical median of its $m \times n$ neighborhood. Since the median value is computed from the neighboring pixel, it is more robust to outliers and does not create a new realistic pixel value, which would preserve edge

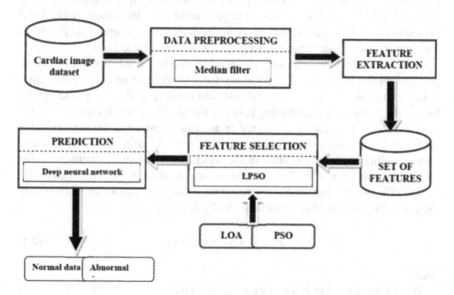

FIGURE 12.1 Proposed cardiac image-based automatic heart disease diagnosis model.

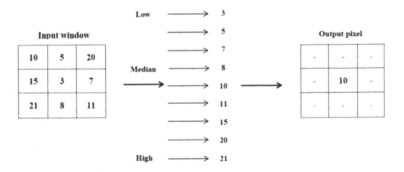

FIGURE 12.2   Graphical representation median filter.

TABLE 12.1

Steps to be followed in median filter

- Place a window over pixels.
- Sort the pixels value ascending or descending.
- Compute the median.
- The median value will be the new value of the center pixel of the window.
- Repeat the above process for all corrupting image area.

---

blurring and loss of image detail. It preserves the sharp high- frequency details. It is well suited to eliminate salt-and-pepper noise from the image. A graphical presentation of the median filter operation is depicted in Figure 12.2. The steps for applying the median filter algorithm are as follows (Table 12.1).

This filter works by analysing the neighborhood of pixels around an origin pixel, as shown in Figure 12.2, for every valid pixel in an image. For this case, a 3 × 3 window of pixels is used to calculate the output. For every pixel in the image, the window of neighboring pixels is found. As shown in Figure 12.2, the pixel values in the window are sorted in ascending order and the median value is chosen; in this case the median value is 50. Next, the pixel in the output image corresponding to the origin pixel in the input image is replaced with the value specified by the filter order. The value in the origin, which is 70, is replaced by 50.

The effect of the median filter in removing noise increases as the window size increase. The median filter is mathematically depicted as follows:

$$\hat{Z}(i, j) = \underset{(s,t)\in S_{ij}}{\mathrm{median}}\{g(s,t)\} \tag{12.1}$$

where

$Z(i, j)$ = median filter at a given coordinate, and

S_{ij} = coordinate of sub-image window of size $m \times n$

12.3.2 Feature extraction

After pre-processing, the texture features are extracted from each image. In this chapter, the gray-level co-occurrence matrix (GLCM) is used to extract the texture features. The GLCM gives a joint distribution of gray-level pairs of neighboring pixels within an image (Rajakumar & George 2013). For the computation of GLCM, first, a spatial relationship is established between two pixels, one being the reference pixel, and other a neighbor pixel.

Let $M(u, v)$ be the element of GLCM of a given image A of size $a \times b$, containing the number of gray levels G^L ranging from 0 to G^L-1. Then, M cab is defined as the matrix element and given by:

$$M(u,v) = \sum_{i=1}^{u} \sum_{j=1}^{v} \begin{cases} 1 & if \quad A(a,b) = u \text{ and } I^{in}(a+\Delta a, b+\Delta b) = v \\ 0 & \text{otherwise} \end{cases}$$

(12.2)

where, (a, b) and $(a+\Delta a, b+\Delta b)$ are the locations of the reference pixel and its neighboring pixel, respectively. Each element of GLCM, $M(u,v|\Delta a, \Delta b)$, represent the relative frequency of two pixels in a given neighborhood separated by a distance $(\Delta a, \Delta b)$ and having gray-level values x and y, respectively (Esteva et al. 2019). It can be represented as $q(u, v | D^D, \theta)$, where the parameter D^D is the distance of separation between two neighborhood resolution cells, with two pixels having intensities u and v in the image. The other parameter θ represents the direction of the neighboring pixel with respect to the reference pixel. The parameter D^D is also called the set distance as it specifies the distance of all neighboring resolution pairs contained in a set. For the texture calculation, the GLCM must be symmetrical and each entry of the GLCM should be a probability value. In this paper, twenty two GLCM features are extracted from each image, namely angular second moment, contrast, inverse difference moment, entropy, correlation, variance, sum average, sum variance, sum entropy, difference entropy, inertia, cluster shade, cluster prominence, dissimilarity, homogeneity, energy, autocorrelation, maximum probability, inverse difference normalised, inverse difference moment normalised, information measure of correlation I, and information measure of correlation II.

12.3.3 Feature selection using the LPSO algorithm

After the feature extraction process, the important features are selected using the LPSO algorithm. The feature selection process is to limit the number of input features to achieve optimum accuracy and also reduce computation complexity. For feature selection, in this chapter, the LPSO algorithm is used. The LPSO is a combination of the lion optimization and PSO algorithms.

Step 1: Initialisation. Initialization is an important process for all optimization algorithms. For feature selection, initially the solutions are randomly selected. In

TABLE 12.2
Solution format

Images	Features					
	F^1	F^2	F^3	F^4	,,,,	F^{22}
l_1	0	0	1	0		1
l_1	1	0	0	1		0
:						
:						
l_1	0	1	0	1		0

this scheme, every single solution is called a "Lion". The initial solution format is shown in Table 12.2.

Among the N number of solutions, some of the solutions are randomly generated, as nomad lions. The remaining population is randomly divided into P prides. Every solution in this algorithm is a specific gender, which remained constant during the optimisation process. Over the searching process, every lion marks its best-visited position. According to these marked positions, every pride's territory is formed. So, for each pride, marked positions ("best-visited positions") by its members form that pride's territory.

Step 2: Fitness calculation. After solution initialisation, the fitness of each lion is calculated. The classification accuracy is regarded as the fitness function. The fitness function is given in Eqn. 12.3.

$$\text{Fitness} = \text{Max}\left(\text{Accuracy}\right) \tag{12.3}$$

$$\text{Accuracy} = \frac{T^P + T^N}{T^P + T^N + F^P \_ F^N} \times 100 \tag{12.4}$$

Step 3: Hunting process. For the hunting process, the hunters are divided randomly into three sub-branches. The group with highest fitness is considered to be the middle and the other groups are considered as the right and left wings. Throughout hunting, if a hunter improves its own fitness, **PREY** (P) will escape from hunter and new position of **PREY** (P′) is obtained as follows:

$$P' = P + rand\left(0,1\right) \times \%I \times \left(P - H\right) \tag{12.5}$$

Where;

    P→ current position of prey,

    H→ position of hunter who attack to prey and PI is the percentage of improvement in the fitness of hunter.

The new position of the hunter which are having a place in both left and right wings,

$$H' = \begin{cases} rand(H,P), & H < P \\ rand(P,H), & H > P \end{cases} \qquad (12.6)$$

where (H,P) indicates the random value

The new position of the female lion is calculated as follows:

$$P_F' = P_F + 2d \times rand(0,1)\{SP_1\} + U(-1,1) \times \tan(\theta) \times D_d \times \{SP_2\} \qquad (12.7)$$

$$\{SP_1\} \cdot \{SP_2\} = 0, \quad \|\{SP_2\}\| = 1 \qquad (12.8)$$

$P_F \rightarrow$ Position of female lion,

$D_d \rightarrow$ Distance between the female lion and the point chosen by tournament selection among the pride territory,

$\{SP_1\} \rightarrow$ Previous location of female lion and its direction is towards the selected point,

$\{SP_2\} \rightarrow$ Perpendicular to $\{SP_1\}$.

Step 4: Roaming operation. Roaming is a solid local search and helps the lion optimisation algorithm to search for a solution to enhance it. The lion pushes towards the chosen region of region by 'n' units, where 'n' is a random number with uniform distribution.

$$n \sim U_d(0, 2 \times D) \qquad (12.9)$$

'D' indicates the distance between male lion position and the selected area of territory.

Also, nomad lions move haphazardly in search of space. The new position of nomad lions is produced as follows:

$$L_{ij} = \begin{cases} L_{ij} & \text{if } rand_j > prob_i \\ RAND_j & \text{otherwise} \end{cases} \qquad (12.10)$$

Where L_{ij} is the current position of the nomad lions and $rand_j$ is the uniform random number between [0, 1].

$rand(j)$ is the random generated vector and $prob_i$ is the probability value.

The probability value ia calculated for every nomad lion independently as described in 12.11:

$$prob_i = 0.1 + \min\left(0.5, \frac{(N_{O_i} - Bst_{N_O})}{Bst_{N_O}}\right) \quad i = 1, 2, \dots M \qquad (12.11)$$

where

N_{O_i} and Bst_{N_O} represents the minimum delay of the current position of the ith lion of the nomads

M represents the number of lion nomads

Step 5: Mating operation. Mating is the vital operation that guarantees the lions' survival. The mating operator is a direct blend of guardians for delivering two new offspring. The new cubs are created subsequently to choosing the female and male lions involved in mating,

$$\text{Offspring}_j 1 = \chi \times F_j + \sum \frac{1-\chi}{\sum\limits_{i=1}^{N_R} SU_i} \times M_j \times SU_i \qquad (12.12)$$

$$\text{Offspring}_j 2 = (1-\chi) \times F_j + \sum \frac{\chi}{\sum\limits_{i=1}^{N_R} SU_i} \times M_j \times SU_i \qquad (12.13)$$

Here, 'j' is the dimension. If male of 'i' is selected for mating, then $SU_i=1$, otherwise $SU_i=0$.

N_R represents the resident males in a pride, χ is a random number with a uniform distribution with mean value is 0.5, and standard deviation is 0.1.

By mating, the lion algorithm shares the data between genders, while the new cubs acquire characters from the two parents.

Step 6: Updating using PSO. To enhance the performance of the lion optimisation algorithm, the position of each lion is further updated, using the PSO algorithm. The position of each lion is updated in the search space using 12.14.

$$Lp_i^{New} = Lp_i + V_i^{New} \qquad (12.14)$$

$$V_i^{new} = V_i + \phi_1.r_1.(pbest_i - Lp_i) + \phi_2.r_2.(gbest_i - Lp_i) \qquad (12.15)$$

where

ϕ_1, ϕ_2 = learning rate,

r_1, r_2 = random numbers in the range of [0, 1],

V_i = current velocity, and

Lp_i = current position.

The overall flow diagram of the proposed MLO algorithm is shown in Figure. 12.2.

Step 7: Termination criterion. In the long run, the best solution is selected. The maximum fitness value is considered to be the best solution. The corresponding feature of the selected solution is given to the input of the DNN classifier to classify an image as either normal or abnormal.

12.3.4 Deep-Neural-Network-Based Heart Disease Prediction

After the feature selection process, the selected features are given to the DNN classifier to classify data as either normal or abnormal. The DNN classifier is a typical structure that follows an ANN, which is a complex network model. But it can represent hierarchies in a simple form to create the model. Having 'n' hidden layers, it processes the elements of data from the previous layer, that is the input layer. After each epoch, with the help of the learning rate "alpha", the error of the input will be reduced gradually by weight adjustment of each node. This continued by back-propagation of the network when there is an error followed by fine-tuning until better results are achieved. Input can have any number of input nodes and there is no limit because the increase in input nodes will increase the learning process. As there are output nodes in the output layer, the number of outputs can be known individually. The step-by-step process of the deep neural network classifier is as follows:

Step 1: Read the number of 'n' input nodes (F_1, F_2, F_3 ... F_n) for the input layer. The number of input nodes is the same as the number of selected features.

Step 2: Assign the number of layers in the hidden layer that need to be trained with data. The input layer and the hidden layer connected with the help of the weighted value which is represented as W_{ij}^H. Similarly, the weight between hidden layer and output layer is represented as W_{ij}^O.

Step 3: Initialise the bias and learning rate values for each node and the weighting will be selected arbitrarily in forward-propagation.

Step 4: Define the number of epochs to make values of the back-propagation from the output to the input direction.

Step 5: In the first hidden layer, the weighted values of input are provided to the summing function with the bias of the neuron as in Equation 12.16.

$$C_{H\_1}(i = 1, 2.., K) = \left(\sum_{m=1}^{M} W_{ij}^h R_m \right) + b_x \tag{12.16}$$

Step 6: The activation function is applied to the output of the first hidden layer as:

$$F\left(C_{H\_1}(i)\right) = \frac{1}{\left(1 + e^{-C_{H\_1(i)}}\right)} \tag{12.17}$$

where $F(\bullet)$ is the sigmoid activation function.

Step 7: Similarly, the operation of nth hidden layer output is calculated as follows:

$$C_{H\_n}(i) = \left(\sum_{z=1}^{K} W_{ij}^o F\left(C_{H\_(n-1)}(z)\right) \right) + b_p \tag{12.18}$$

where b_p is the bias of pth, the hidden node, W_{ij} is the interconnection weight between the $(n-1)^{th}$ hidden layer and the $(n)^{th}$ hidden layer with K hidden nodes.

The activation function, which is the output of the nth hidden layer, is given as:

$$F\left(C_{H\_n}(i)\right) = \frac{1}{\left(1 + e^{-C_{H\_n}(i)}\right)} \qquad (12.19)$$

Step 8: At the output layer, the output of nth, the hidden layer, is again multiplied with the interconnection weights (i.e., weight between the nth hidden layer and the output layer) and then summed up with the bias (b_q) as:

$$C(k) = F\left(\sum_{j=1}^{K} W_{jk}^{O} \ f\left(C_{H\_y}(j)\right) + b_q\right) \qquad (12.20)$$

where W_{jk} represents the interconnection weight at the nth hidden layer and the output layer having j^{th} and k^{th} nodes, respectively. The activation function at the output layer acts as the output of the whole model.

Step 9: After the output calculation, the network error is calculated. The error calculation is given in equation (12.21).

$$\text{Error}\,(m) = \frac{1}{M}\sum_{m=1}^{M}\left(\text{Actual}(C_m) - \text{Target}(C_m)\right)^2 \qquad (12.21)$$

where Target (C_m) is the estimated network output and Actual (C_m) is the actual output. The error must be minimised for obtaining the optimal network structure. Hence, the weighting values must be adjusted until the error decreases at each iteration. By calculating this error function, input features of patients are classified as either normal or abnormal. In this approach, the value of 1 is set as a target for classifying normal data, and 0 is set as a target for classifying abnormal data.

12.4   RESULTS AND DISCUSSION

The performance of proposed cardiac image-based automatic heart disease diagnosis, using DNN, is analysed in this section. The proposed approach is implemented in MATLAB version 7.12. The proposed approach is done in a Windows PC having an Intel Core i5 processor with speed 1.6 GHz and 4 GB RAM. The experimental sample cardiac image used is shown in Figure 12.3.

12.4.1   EVALUATION METRICS

The performance of the proposed heart disease classification approach is analysed in terms of different metrics, which are listed in Table 12.3.

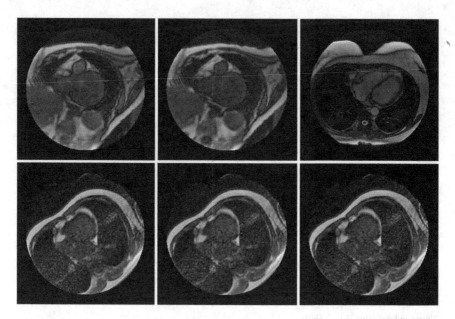

FIGURE 12.3 Experimental used sample images.

12.4.2 EXPERIMENTAL RESULTS

The experimental results obtained by the proposed approach is analysed in this subsection. Figures 12.4–12.7 show the screenshot of experimental results. Figure 12.8 shows the confusion matrices of different methods.

12.4.3 COMPARATIVE ANALYSIS

The main objective of the proposed approach is cardiac image-based automatic heart disease diagnosis, using DNN. This proposed approach consists mainly of two stages, namely feature selection and classification.

12.4.3.1 Comparative analysis based on the classification algorithm

To assess the effectiveness of the proposed approach, we compare our approach with different methods. For comparison, in this chapter, four methods are used, namely DNN, ANN, KNN, and SVM.

In Figure 12.9, the performance of the proposed approach is analysed in terms of accuracy, sensitivity, and specificity. When analysing Figure 12.9, the proposed approach attained a maximum accuracy of 96.55%, compared with 95.74% for DNN-based heart disease prediction, 81.57% for ANN-based heart disease prediction, 80.16% for KNN-based heart disease prediction and 80.56% for SVM-based heart disease prediction. From the results, it's clear that the proposed LPSO+DNN-based heart disease prediction attained better results than the other algorithms. This is due to the LPSO-based feature selection. Moreover, in Figure

TABLE 12.3
Performance metrics

Metrics	Formulae
Accuracy (A)	$A = \dfrac{T^P + T^N}{T^P + T^N + F^P \_ F^N} \times 100$
Sensitivity _(S)	$S = \dfrac{T^P}{T^P + F^N} \times 100$
Specificity (S_p)	$S_P = \dfrac{T^N}{T^N + F^N} \times 100$
Precision _(P)	$P = \dfrac{T_P}{T_P + F_P} \times 100$
Recall _(R)	$R = \dfrac{T_P}{T_P + F_P} \times 100$
F1-Score _(T)	$F = 2 \times \dfrac{\text{Precision} \times \text{Recall}}{\text{Precision} + \text{Recall}}$
Negative Predictive Value _(NPV)	$PPV = \dfrac{T^P}{T^P + F^P}$
False positive rate _(FPR)	$FPR = \dfrac{F^P}{F^P + T^P}$
False negative rate _(FNR)	$FNR = \dfrac{F^N}{F^N + T^P}$
False rejection rate _(FRR)	$FRR = \dfrac{F^N}{F^N + T^P}$
False discovery rate _(FDR)	$FNR = \dfrac{F^P}{F^P + T^P}$

12.9, the specificity of the proposed approach is analysed. According to Figure 12.9, the proposed approach attained a maximum specificity of 97.7%, compared with 97.16% for DNN-based heart disease prediction, 87.71% for ANN-based prediction, 86.77% for KNN-based prediction, and 87.04% for SVM-based prediction. Similarly, our proposed approach attained a maximum sensitivity of 93.11% which is high, compared with the existing approach. In Figure 12.10, the performance of the proposed approach is analysed in terms of precision, recall, and F-measure. When analysing Figure 12.10, our proposed LPSO+DNN-based heart disease prediction attained the maximum precision of 92.11%, compared with 89.49% for DNN-based prediction, 62.15% for ANN-based prediction, 60.32% for KNN-based prediction and 62.13% for SVM-based prediction. Similarly, our proposed approach attained a maximum recall of 94.11% and an F-measure

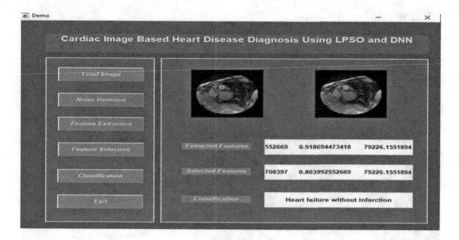

FIGURE 12.4   Heart failure without infarction (abnormal).

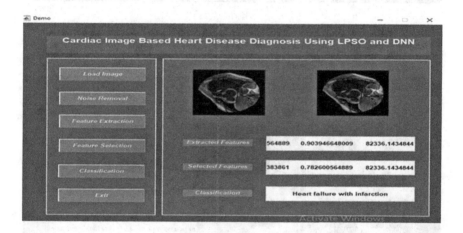

FIGURE 12.5   Heart failure with infarction (abnormal).

of 93.11%. In Figure 12.11, the performance of the proposed approach is analysed in terms of net present value (NPV). When analysing Figure 12.11, the proposed approach attained a maximum NPV of 0.97 which is high compared with approaches such as DNN, ANN, KNN, and SVM. According to Figure 12.11, the DNN-based and LPSO+DNN-based approaches give the most similar results, although, compared with DNN-based prediction, the proposed LPSO+DNN approach attained the better results.

The performance of the proposed approach is analyzed in terms of false positive rate (FPR) in Figure 12.12, according to which, the proposed approach attained the minimum FPR of 0.0229, compared with 0.028 for DNN-based prediction, When the proposed approach is analysed in terms of false negative rate (FNR), Figure 12.13 shows that the proposed approach attained the minimum

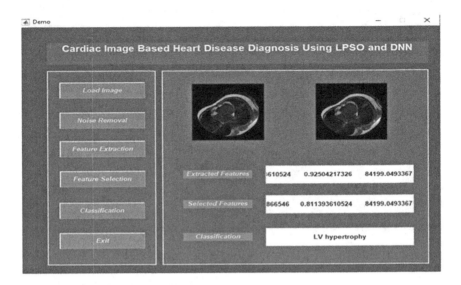

FIGURE 12.6   Left ventricular hypertrophy.

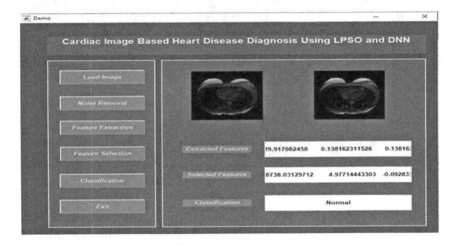

FIGURE 12.7   Normal classification.

FNR of 0.0688. Similarly, in Figure 12.14, the proposed approach attained the lowest false rejection rate of all the algorithms evaluated. This superiority is due to a feature selection process, which decreases the computation complexity and reduces the error rate. In Figure 12.15, the performance of the proposed approach is analysed in terms of the false rejection rate (FRR) measure, where the proposed approach also achieved the lowest FRR, compared with the existing approaches.

Total=246	Normal	Abnormal
Normal	TP = 57	FP=4
Abnormal	FN=4	TN=181

(a)

Total=246	Normal	Abnormal
Normal	TP = 56	FP=5
Abnormal	FN=5	TN=180

(b)

Total=246	Normal	Abnormal
Normal	TP = 39	FP=23
Abnormal	FN=22	TN=162

(c)

Total=246	Normal	Abnormal
Normal	TP = 37	FP=25
Abnormal	FN=24	TN=160

(d)

Total=246	Normal	Abnormal
Normal	TP = 37	FP=24
Abnormal	FN=24	TN=161

FIGURE 12.8 Confusion matrix for different classifiers (a) LPSO+DNN, (b) DNN, (c) ANN, (d) KNN and (e) SVM.

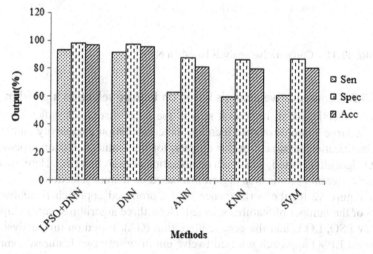

FIGURE 12.9 Performance analysis based on accuracy, sensitivity, and specificity.

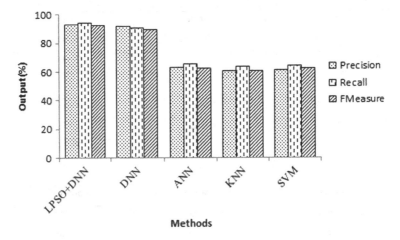

FIGURE 12.10 Performance analysis based on precision, recall, and F-measure.

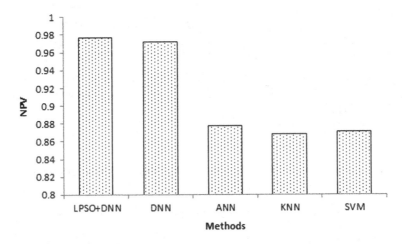

FIGURE 12.11 Comparative analysis based on NPY.

12.4.3.2 Comparative analysis based on feature selection algorithm

Feature selection is an important step in the heart disease classification stage, because large volumes of data increase the computation complexity and reduce the classification accuracy. In this chapter, for the feature selection process, the LPSO algorithm is used, which is a combination of LOA and PSO. Here, we analyse the different optimisation algorithms based on feature selection.

In Figure 12.16, the performance of the proposed approach is analysed in terms of the number of features selected. Here, three algorithms were compared, namely PSO, LOA, and the genetic algorithm (GA). Based on this analysis, our proposed LPSO approach selected twelve out of twenty two features, compared

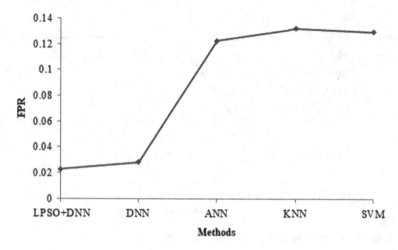

FIGURE 12.12 Performance analysis based on FPR.

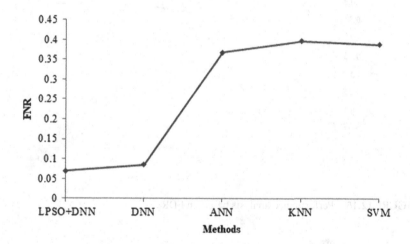

FIGURE 12.13 Performance analysis based on FNR.

with sixteen features selected by the PSO algorithm, fourteen features by LOA, and seventeen features by GA. In Figure 12.17, the performance of the proposed LPSO+DNN approach is analysed in terms of accuracy, sensitivity, and specificity. When analyzing Figure 12.17, our proposed LPSO+DNN approach attained the greatest accuracy of predicting heart disease of 96.55%, compared with 90.87% for LOA+DNN, 87.58% for PSO+DNN, and 85.43% for GA+DNN, due to the superiority of the hybrid LPSO-based feature selection; the other methods used only single-algorithm-based feature selection. Similarly, our proposed LPSO+DNN approach attained the greatest sensitivity and specificity compared with the other algorithms. In Figure 12.18, the performance of the proposed

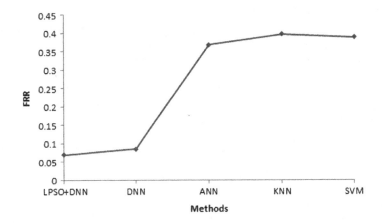

FIGURE 12.14 Performance analysis based on FRR.

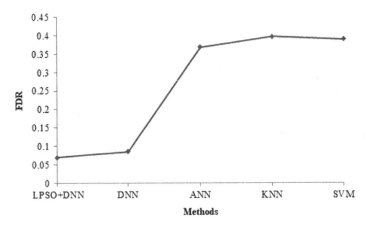

FIGURE 12.15 Performance analysis based on FDR.

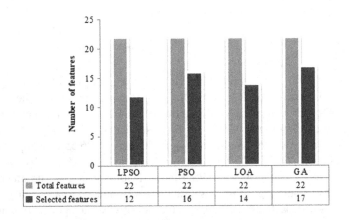

FIGURE 12.16 Performance analysis based on feature selection.

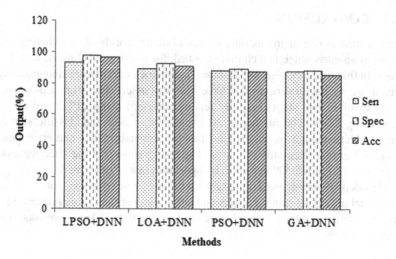

FIGURE 12.17 Comparative analysis based on different feature selection algorithms.

approach is analysed in terms of precision, recall, and F-measure by various optimisation algorithms. In this analysis of the classification DNN algorithm and feature selection process, different optimization algorithms were compared with LPSP+DNN, namely LOA, PSO, and GA. When analyzing Figure 12.18, the proposed LPSO+DNN approach achieved the greatest precision of 93.11%, the greatest recall of 94.11%, and the highest F-measure of 92%. From Figure 12.18, it's clear that proposed approach achieved the best results of the four approaches evaluated.

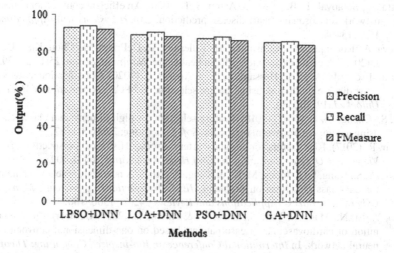

FIGURE 12.18 Graphical plot for precision, recall, and F-measure based on different feature selection approach.

12.5 CONCLUSION

Heart disease is one of the leading causes of death worldwide. Predicting heart disease at an early stage is a challenging task for physicians, clinicians, and scientists. In this study, cardiac image-based automatic heart disease diagnostic systems, using deep neural networks, have been discussed. The proposed approach largely involves two stages, namely feature selection using LPSO and classification using DNN. The mathematical expression of both the classification and feature selection stages is clearly illustrated. The performance and error rate of the classification system are evaluated. The results show that the effectiveness of the proposed LPSO+DNN approach is superior to that of other methods. The proposed in-depth learning model predicts all types of heart diseases with accuracy. This model provides accurate results and helps with patients being prescribed the correct meditation. More research needs to be done to broaden the results to different approaches.

REFERENCES

Ali, L., Rahman, A., Khan, A., Zhou, M., Javeed, A., & Khan, J. A. (2019). An automated diagnostic system for heart disease prediction based on X^2 statistical model and optimally configured deep neural network. *IEEE Access*, 7, 34938–34945.

Alkhodari, M., & Fraiwan, L. (2021). Convolutional and recurrent neural networks for the detection of valvular heart diseases in phonocardiogram recordings. *Computer Methods and Programs in Biomedicine*, 200, 105940.

Baggen, V. J. M., Venema, E., Živná, R., van den Bosch, A. E., Eindhoven, J. A., Witsenburg, M., ... Roos-Hesselink, J. W. (2019). Development and validation of a risk prediction model in patients with adult congenital heart disease. *International Journal of Cardiology*, 276, 87–92. https://doi.org/10.1016/j.ijcard.2018.08.059. Epub 2018 Aug 22. PMID: 30172474.

Dutta, A., Batabyal, T., Basu, M., & Acton, S. T. (2020). An efficient convolutional neural network for coronary heart disease prediction. *Expert Systems with Applications*, 159, 113408.

Esteva, A., Robicquet, A., Ramsundar, B., Kuleshov, V., DePristo, M., Chou, K., ... Dean, J. (2019). A guide to deep learning in healthcare. *Nature Medicine*, 25(1), 24–29.

Gárate-Escamila, A. K., El Hassani, A. H., & Andrès, E. (2020). Classification models for heart disease prediction using feature selection and PCA. *Informatics in Medicine Unlocked*, 19, 100330.

Gu, S., Cheng, R., & Jin, Y. (2018). Feature selection for high-dimensional classification using a competitive swarm optimizer. *Soft Computing*, 22(3), 811–822.

Hajar, R. (2017). Risk factors for coronary artery disease: Historical perspectives. *Heart Views: The Official Journal of the Gulf Heart Association*, 18(3), 109.

Jeong, Y. S., Kang, I. H., Jeong, M. K., & Kong, D. (2012). A new feature selection method for one-class classification problems. *IEEE Transactions on Systems, Man, and Cybernetics, Part C (Applications and Reviews)*, 42(6), 1500–1509.

Jiao, Y., Li, N., Mao, X., Yao, G., Zhao, Y., & Huang, L. (2020, October). Pulse recognition of cardiovascular disease patients based on one-dimensional convolutional neural network. In *International Conference on Bio-inspired Computing: Theories and Applications* (pp. 298–308). Singapore: Springer.

Liu, X., & Tang, J. (2013). Mass classification in mammograms using selected geometry and texture features, and a new SVM-based feature selection method. *IEEE Systems Journal*, 8(3), 910–920.

Oliver, A. S., Ganesan, K., Yuvaraj, S. A., Jayasankar, T., Sikkandar, M. Y., & Prakash, N. B. (2021). Accurate prediction of heart disease based on bio system using regressive learning based neural network classifier. *Journal of Ambient Intelligence and Humanized Computing*, 1–9.

Pham, H. V., Son, L. H., & Tuan, L. M. (2020). A proposal of expert system using deep learning neural networks and fuzzy rules for diagnosing heart disease. In *Frontiers in Intelligent Computing: Theory and Applications: Proceedings of the 7th International Conference on FICTA (2018), Volume 1* (pp. 189–198). Singapore: Springer.

Pradhan, M. (2023). Cardiac image-based heart disease diagnosis using bio-inspired optimized technique for feature selection to enhance classification accuracy. In L. Panigrahi, S. Biswal, A. Bhoi, A. Kalam, & P. Barsocchi (Eds.), *Machine Learning and AI Techniques in Interactive Medical Image Analysis* (pp. 151–166). IGI Global. https://doi.org/10.4018/978-1-6684-4671-3.ch009

Pradhan, M., & Bhuiyan, A. (2023). Automatic heart disease diagnosis based on MRI image using deep neural network: Adaptive bacterial foraging optimization algorithm-based feature selection. In T. Connolly, P. Papadopoulos, & M. Soflano (Eds.), *Diverse Perspectives and State-of-the-art Approaches to the Utilization of Data-driven Clinical Decision Support Systems* (pp. 212–233). IGI Global. https://doi.org /10.4018/978-1-6684-5092-5.ch010

Rajakumar, B. R., & George, A. (2013, July). On hybridizing fuzzy min max neural network and firefly algorithm for automated heart disease diagnosis. In *2013 Fourth International Conference on Computing, Communications and Networking Technologies (ICCCNT)* (pp. 1–5). IEEE.

Rodríguez, J., Prieto, S., & Ramírez López, L. J. (2019). A novel heart rate attractor for the prediction of cardiovascular disease. *Informatics in Medicine Unlocked*, 15, 100174. https://doi.org/10.1016/j.imu.2019.100174

Rojas-Albarracin, G., Chaves, M. Á., Fernandez-Caballero, A., & Lopez, M. T. (2019). Heart attack detection in colour images using convolutional neural networks. *Applied Sciences*, 9(23), 5065.

Shen, Q., Diao, R., & Su, P. (2012). Feature selection ensemble. *Turing-100*, 10, 289–306.

Singh, D. A. A. G., Balamurugan, S. A. A., & Leavline, E. J. (2015). A novel feature selection method for image classification. *Optoelectronics and Advanced Materials-Rapid Communications*, 9(November–December 2015), 1362–1368.

Suganya, R., Rajaram, S., Abdullah, A. S., & Rajendran, V. (2016). A novel feature selection method for predicting heart diseases with data mining techniques. *Asian Journal of Information Technology*, 15(8), 1314–1321.

Thanga Selvi, R., & Muthulakshmi, I. (2021). An optimal artificial neural network based big data application for heart disease diagnosis and classification model. *Journal of Ambient Intelligence and Humanized Computing*, 12(6), 6129–6139.

Vyas, S., Gupta, S., Bhargava, D., & Boddu, R. (2022). Fuzzy logic system implementation on the performance parameters of health data management frameworks. *Journal of Healthcare Engineering*, 2022.

WHO. (2017). World health organization, media centre, cardiovascular diseases fact sheet webpage. https://www.who.int/mediacentre/factsheets/fs317/en/

13 Super-resolution in a world of scarce resources for medical imaging applications

A. Deshpande, V. V. Estrela, P. Patavardhan, G. Kallimani

CONTENTS

13.1 INTRODUCTION

Medical imaging (MI) engenders more intelligent, diversified, and useful representations of the human body's internal organs for clinical investigation and effective medical intervention. MI makes internal structures visible and reveals problems buried by the layers of bones and skin, helping in diagnosis and treatment. The influential non-invasive MI characteristics from Computed Tomography (CT) and Magnetic Resonance (MR) Imaging (MRI) achieve accurate, compelling health scrutiny and interpretation (Ogawa & Lee 1990). Body parts, like tissues, bones, heart, brain, muscles, and tumors, can be observed. However, low spatial resolution is an unrelenting problem (Onesimu & Karthikeyan 2020; Ayubi et al. 2015; Andrew 2020, affecting the diagnosis process and post-processing. Image acquirement time and equipment are the limited MI spatial resolution constraints. High-quality images are often challenging due to long sampling times, patient discomfort, stronger magnetic field, and higher expenses. Thus, to address these associated problems without affecting the hardware and scanning process, super-resolution

DOI: 10.1201/9781003244592-13

(SR) assures promising outputs. SR methods aim to increase the images' spatial resolution and improve MI quality without an additional scanning process via low-resolution (LR) image(s) to construct a high-resolution (HR) image. Acquisition process losses can be recovered from the SR process' high-frequency (HF) content. The main SR algorithm goal is to reconstruct HR images from the observations of under-sampled LR images. SR through Deep Learning (DL) can help fight many maladies, e.g., the coronavirus disease (COVID-19). This SR via DL review can help identify superior artificial intelligence (AI)-based tools (Mondal 2021). Literature searches for keywords like AI, COVID-19, machine learning (ML), CT, MRI, forecasting, DL, and X-rays are all related to detailed imaging. To improve the scrutiny of patients, mining could merge SR with semiotics/semantics to better describe findings and to speed up studies since HR demands network resources and storage. Working with various MI datasets improves and delivers different diagnosis stages, viz., subdivision, pre-processing, and feature extraction. Densely connected convolutional neural networks (CNNs) provide admirable abilities to improve the accuracy and resolution of images (Vyas & Bhargava 2021).

The 2D imaging model is shown by:

$$g_k(m, n) = d(h_k(w_k(f(x, y)) + \eta_k(m, n) \qquad \text{(Eqn. 13.1)}$$

where k corresponds to the number of LR images. The function $g()$ for $k=1$ is given by

$$g(m,n) = \frac{1}{q^2} \sum_{x=qm}^{(q+1)m-1} \sum_{y=qn}^{(q+1)n-1} f(x,y). \qquad \text{(Eqn. 13.2)}$$

g is an acquired LR image, d is a down-sampling parameter, the warping function is w, h is a blurring function, and η is additive noise. f represents the fundamental HR image; q is a sub-sampling parameter or decimation factor equal in both horizontal and vertical directions. x and y are the HR image coordinates and m and n of the LR images, the size of which is $L_1{\times}L_2$, and the HR image has the size $H_1{\times}H_2$, where $H_1= qL_1$ and $H_2= qL_2$. ?The MI model in Ogawa (1990) states that an LR-observed image has been attained by averaging over a q^2-pixel area. Other MI process parameters can be considered, i.e., blurring, warping (geometric transformation), and noise. Let g, f, and η represent k-dimensional vectors. All the warping factors belong to matrix A. A more realistic vector-form model becomes $g = A f +$ high-quality SR images mitigate noisy, blurred images, artifacts, and degraded effects i) with fewer costs, ii) without fancy hardware, repurposing existing LR imaging systems, and iii) with high flexibility. SR has various applications (Deshpande et al. 2020; Deshpande et al. 2021) in realms viz. biometrics, MI analysis, unmanned aerial vehicles (UAVs), and many more. Table 13.1 classifies SR's threefold major strategies.

The previous three-class classification works for still images and videos. Single-image SR (SISR) processes rely heavily on learning algorithms to infer the missing data, resulting in super-resolved pictures utilising the connection between LR

TABLE 13.1

Classification of SR methods

	Methods	Algorithms	Gains	Disadvantages
1	Interpolation-based (Frank 1982; Markov 2008)	a. Nearest-neighbor interpolation b. Bi-cubic interpolation c. Bilinear interpolation	Simple and easy to achieve fast computation	Perform well in low-frequency areas but poorly in edge (HF) areas prone to blurring and jaggy artifacts along edges.
2	Reconstruction-based (Bertero 1998; Liu 2017)	a. Maximum *a posteriori* b. Markov random field c. Kernel steering d. Total Variation (TV)	Image overlay, change detection	Small discontinuity and pixel losses near the edges.
3	Example-based (Qu et al. 2013; Li 2016)	e. Markov random field g. Sparse coding h. Gaussian process regression	High magnification factor	Require a huge image database. Increased execution time due to searching test image patches from databases

and HR images from a training database. Multiple-image SR (MISR) algorithms typically assume a targeted HR image, and the LR observations include equivalent geometric or photometric shifts from the intended HR image. In general, these algorithms use the differences between the LR observations to rebuild the desired HR picture, i.e., they are reconstruction-based SR algorithms. Reconstruction-based SR algorithms consider the SR issue to be inverted. Consequently, as with other inverse situations, a forward-imaging model is required.

The latest performance achieved with deep-learning (DL) algorithms has facilitated super-resolving LR images. The primary DL aim is to learn an often-superior representation of data hierarchy compared to other machine-learning (ML) algorithms. A few existing SR frameworks constructed via convolutional neural networks (CNNs) appear in Section 13.2. DL-based SR procedures emerge in Section 13.3, whereas Sections 13.4 and 13.5 cover the discussion and conclusion of the chapter, respectively.

13.2 SUPER-RESOLUTION CONVOLUTIONAL NEURAL NETWORK (SRCNN) ARCHITECTURES

A convolutional neural network (CNN) is a type of artificial neural network used in image recognition and processing that is specifically designed to process pixel data.

13.2.1 SRCNN

The first DL SISR method is the SRCNN. Thus, LR and HR images are directly learned in end-to-end mapping.

The layout of the network structure is presented in Figure 13.1. The network carries three layers, where each layer contains a layer of convolution by adding

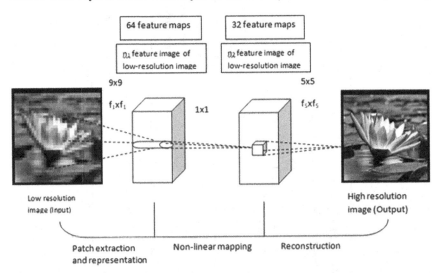

FIGURE 13.1   Network structure layout of SRCNN (medium.com 2022).

an activation function and a bi-cubic LR interpolation of the same size as the HR image. The network's input image is a, and the output is a super-resolved image.

13.2.2 FAST SRCNN (FSRCNN)

The upgraded SRCNN version is the fast SRCNN (FSRCNN). The HR reconstruction speed increases in FSRCNN, the structure of which consists of five elements: feature extraction, shrinking, mapping, expanding, and de-convolution.

Figure 13.2 shows the FSRCNN structure. Not enlarging the input image size improves the speed and reduces computation.

13.2.3 VERY DEEP SR CONVOLUTIONAL NETWORKS (VDSR)

VDSR reveals extra improvements in SR performance. Higher-depth networks influence convergence significantly. Learning residuals are better since LR and HR images convey more information, improving performance and speed as shown in Figure 13.3.

13.2.4 DEEPLY RECURSIVE CONVOLUTIONAL NETWORKS (DRCN)

DRCN gives SR reconstruction with deep recursive layers. Depth might improve performance; paradoxically, convolution layers prevent an increase in parameters.

The reconstruction results from weighing the average fallouts from the recursive convolution layers. The DRCN network structure from Figure 13.4 represents the SR for MRI and was conducted by Fiat (2001) to achieve the following:

(1) For a 2D image from a 3D slice of 3D/4D MRI, the in-plane enhancement of the resolution (Holden 2000; Malczewski 2008) provides a solution for resolution information that is missed (cf. Table 13.2); and

(2) Among several 3D/4D MRI slices, the through-plane resolution enhancement (Jiang 2007; Rousseau 2005) eliminates alias and reduces the slice depth. In comparison, the in-plane resolution for multiple slice 2d acquisitions is higher than the through-plane resolutions for 3D acquisitions.

13.3 DL-BASED SR METHODS

MI processing uses DL-based SR to produce high spatial and high-quality resolution images without extra scans. CNN-reliant SR applies to MI, for example, retinal images (Reeth 2012; Zhang 2019) and MRIs (Pham 2017; Chaudhari 2020), due to rapid DL development. The studies in Pham (2017, 2019) utilised SRCNN for brain MRI analysis (Deshpande and Patavardhan 2016a, 2016b, 2016c). An SR network for brain MRIs, inspired by a densely connected network (Mahapatra 2018), was reported by Chen (2018). Fast SR for retina images and efficient SR for knee MRIs appear in Mahapatra (2018), using the network with the same structure, with three SRCNN hidden layers and a convolutional layer of sub-pixels

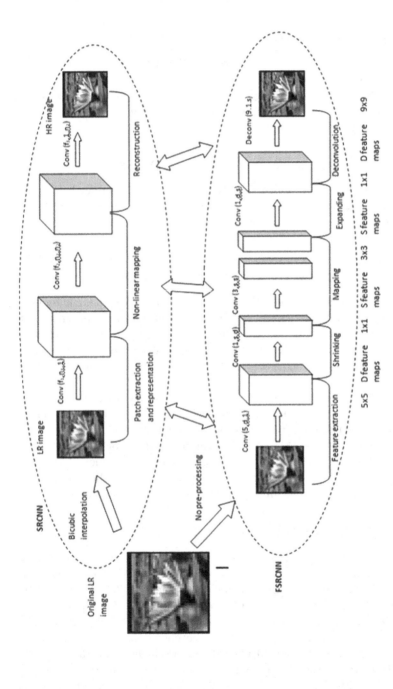

FIGURE 13.2 Network structure of FSRCNN (towardsdatascience.com 2022).

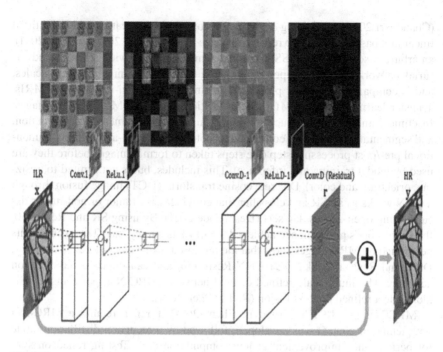

FIGURE 13.3 Network structure of VDSR (towardsdatascience.com 2022).

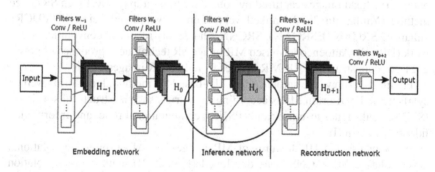

FIGURE 13.4 Network structure of DRCN (medium.com 2022).

TABLE 13.2
In-plane SR of MRI

Class	Approach	Limitation
Deterministic regularisation	Low-rank TV, direct acquisition, bi-linear interpolation	Noise vulnerability
Projection Onto Convex Sets (POCS)	Wavelet-based POCS	High computation cost
Back projection	Iterative back projection	Noise vulnerability

(Chaudhari 2020) for pairing 20-layer 3D convolution operators with a rectified linear unit based on the deep resolve for knee MRIs (Huang 2017). In Zhu (2021), an arbitrary-scale SR (MIASSR) combines meta-learning with generative adversarial networks (GANs), super-resolves MI with various magnification scales, and is compared with SISR processes on single- and multi-modal brain MRIs. Transfer learning enabled MIASSR to tackle SR cardiac MR and CT images. In clinical analysis tasks, such as image quality enhancement, reconstruction, and segmentation, MIASSR confirmed its potential as an up-and-coming foundational pre-/post-processing step (the steps taken to format images before they are used by model training and inference). This includes, but is not limited to, resizing, orienting, and color). Discrete cosine transform (DCT) image fusion through a CNN works as an SR and classifier that could classify tumor or non-tumor tissues, using open-access datasets (Deshpande 2021). By using SR and ResNet50, the framework's performance achieved a 98.14% accuracy rate. The experiments performed on MRI images show that the proposed SR framework relies on CNN, DCT, and ResNet50 (aka DCT-CNN-ResNet50) and can improve classification accuracy. The multi-scale refined context network (MRC-Net) performs the SR alongside a refined context fusion (RCF) (Chen 2021).

MRC-Net and RCF emerged in Chen (2021). First, a recursive MRC-Net with temporal context was developed, followed by a recursion distillation mode for performance improvement at low computation cost. Testing relied on synthetic and real histopathology and capsule endoscopy LR images. To enhance optic nerve head images captured by coherence tomography (OCT), an SR-based method (Yamashita 2020) ranked very deep convolutional network (VDCR), enhanced SRGAN (ESRGAN), SRCNN, and deeply recursive convolutional network (DRCN). Autoencoder-based MR image SR technique is proposed (Andrew 2021) to reconstruct the HR MR images from LR MR images.

Figure 13.5 shows the autoencoder (AE)-based SR method. It performs well on synthetic and real-brain MRIs according to metrics, such as structural similarity (SSIM), peak signal-to-noise ratio (PSNR), computational time, and information fidelity criterion (IFC).

Between LR and HR features of MR images, an AE-inspired convolutional network-based SR (ACNS) was developed (Park 2021), with a de-convolution

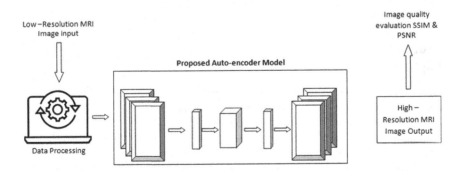

FIGURE 13.5   Autoencoder (AE)-based MRI SR technique (Andrew 2021).

layer, which extrapolates the missing spatial information by CNN-based nonlinear mapping. With four volunteers, the proposed method was tested with thoracic MRI and virtual phantoms. The PSNR, SSIM, IFC, [DEFINE], and computational time were compared with SRCNN; FSRCNN and deeply recursive convolutional network (DRCN) performed well compared with these methods. The study implies that the ACNS has a potential application to the real-time enhancement of the resolution of 4D MRI for MRI-guided radiation therapy. Two in-parallel progressive learning streams (Xue 2020), one stream focusing on reconstructing refined MRIs, and the other stream learning missed HF residuals by the sub-band residual learning (RL) unit (ISRL). These two parallel streams are complementary, enabling one to learn complex mappings between LR and HR MRI, introducing progressive sub-band learning and brain-like ways to emphasize the MRI variant textures. The proposed PSR-SRN model shows performance superior to traditional and DL MRI SR methods. It is a cascaded DL framework, a down-sampling network (DSN), a de-noising autoencoder (DAE), and an SR generative model (SRG) (Chun 2019). Clinical LR noisy MRI scan in DAE training and DSN training used a small amount of paired LR/HR volunteers' data, and SRG cascaded with data generated by the DSN that maps LR inputs to HR outputs. An RL-built SR process for MRI emerges (Shi 2018) as a shallow network block-based local RL (LRL) to learn local residuals effectively, i.e., in capturing HF details. Algorithm evaluation relies on two real MRI datasets and a simulated MRI dataset. Experimental fallouts proved that the proposed SR algorithm achieved superior performance in this study compared with the other entire CNN-established SR algorithms.

13.4 DISCUSSION AND FUTURE WORK

As DL models knowledge from information, profound data comprehension and representation are vital to building data-driven intelligent medical cyber-physical systems in particular applications. Realistically speaking, evidence comes in various forms:

(i) Images entail vectors, matrices, and tensors, representing pixels, voxels, depth, and deformations, which are essential traits or fundamental parameters in MI. The first category can represent MI in 1D, 2D, 3D, 4D, and even higher-dimensional tensors if one considers hyperspectral images.

(ii) Sequential data are records where the order is relevant, i.e., a collection of sequences like text, streaming, audio fragments, video clips, and time-series data. The successive nature of input data must be accounted for while building a model.

(iii) Tabular datasets hold columnar information as in a database table. Each field (column) must include a name. Each column only has a defined data type. It is a logically organised data arrangement, encompassing rows and columns, built on information properties or features. DL models can learn effectively on tabular data and permit one to craft data-driven intelligent systems.

DL typically depends on big data(BD) to foster a data-driven model aimed at a certain condition. Scarce data hinder DL algorithms, but this caveat can be circumvented via pre-processing steps, such as data augmentation and meta-heuristics. A Graphical Processing Unit (GPU) works mostly to optimise the computational operations powerfully. Consequently, DL depends more on high-performance equipment containing GPUs than on standard ML methods. Feature engineering unearths features (i.e., properties, characteristics, and attributes) from crude data, utilising domain awareness. A central peculiarity between DL and other ML practices is the effort to extract high-level elements straight from data. As a result, DL downsizes time and struggles to build a feature extractor. Execution time and model training are long due to many DL parameters.

Most DL model pieces of training occur through openly accessible annotated (aka tagged, labeled, or categorised) datasets. Still, raw data from significant sources are needed to handle a different problem domain or a current data-driven situation. Categorising a colossal raw data volume is paramount and difficult. This hindrance happens especially when deploying discriminative DL models or supervised tasks. Automatic and dynamic data labeling replaces manual categorisation or employing human annotators. They are paramount for large datasets, can work more effectively for supervised learning, and reduce human effort. Hence, a more in-depth examination of ways of data gathering and annotation or introducing an unsupervised learning solution can be promising research directions in DL modeling. Binaural beats (BB) perception and appropriate algorithm choice are hard to explain for DL, i.e., the outcomes or how DL gets the conclusive decisions for a certain model are unclear. Although DL models accomplish major operations through learning from outsized datasets, this BB view of DL modeling normally denotes weak statistical understanding, which could be a keynote issue. Conversely, ML algorithms, above all rule-based ML practices, deliver clear logic rules (e.g., IF-THEN) for elaborating verdicts that are easy to explain, update or delete, consistent with the target applications. If one chooses the wrong learning algorithm, unforeseen outcomes may take place, prompting the model to lose efficacy, work rate, and accuracy; in view of the model performance, intricacy, accuracy, and applicability will all suffer. Therefore, selecting the appropriate model for the intended application is essential, if demanding. An in-depth breakdown is necessary for better comprehension and decision-making.

Supervised or discriminative DL networks, predominantly adopting multi-layer perceptrons (MLPs), CNNs, RNNs, and their variants, are widely used in innumerable health domains. However, planning new developments or their variants by allowing for applicability, model optimization, or accuracy, in line with the target real-world purposes and the data type, can be a novelty, which can also become an important future attribute in supervised or discriminative learning. DL networks aimed at generative or unsupervised learning can perform major tasks in healthcare. They permit portrayal of the high-order correlation characteristics (or properties) in data or generation of new data representations, utilizing exploratory investigations. Unlike supervised learning, it does not demand labeled data, owing to its knack for getting insights straight from the information and data-driven decision-making. Therefore, it can be a pre-processing stage for supervised, discriminative modeling in addition to semi-supervised learning that safeguards learning accuracy and model know-how.

Major DL tasks can comprise hybrid collaborative modeling and uncertainty management. A successful hybridisation can outperform other frameworks as regards performance and uncertainty management in high-risk uses. This hybrid-ization by-product happens because mixed-model development associates genera-tive with discriminative learning gains. Hybridisation can help train ANNs with different parameters or with distinct sub-sampling training datasets. Hybridisation of such procedures, like DL with DL or meta-heuristics or ML, can play a key part in healthcare. So, combining effective discriminative and generative models, instead of a naïve scheme, can be a crucial research enhancement. This strategy helps solve several everyday concerns covering semi-supervised learning actions in addition to model uncertainty. Dynamism in deciding on hyper-parameter val-ues, thresholds, and network configurations with computational efficacy generally affects the relationship between performance, model intricacy, and computational necessities and is a key issue in DL modeling and uses. A mixture of algorithmic improvements with enhanced accuracy and preserved computational effectiveness, i.e., reaching the maximum throughput while expending the least resources without brutal information loss, can grant a breakthrough in DL modeling effectiveness in imminent real-world uses. The notion of incremental approaches or recent learning paradigms might be the best under several circumstances, contingent on the nature of the imaging applications. Accordingly, a data-driven scheme to dynamically pick them up can work better while building a DL model, with respect to performance and hands-on applicability. Such data-driven automation can produce a forthcom-ing generation of DL models with added intelligence so that these deployments can significantly boost future models as essential research contributions.

Trivial DL modeling, aimed at the Internet of Things (IoT), involves many intelligent, communication-based healthcare-related things. Mobile technolo-gies are popular for detecting and collecting human and environmental material (e.g., geo-information, climate data, biodata, anthropological behaviors, etc.) for various intelligent medical services and usages. These pervasive smart devices or gadgets spawn large amounts of data daily, necessitating speedy data process-ing on different smart portable devices. DL technologies can discover underlying properties and handle large volumes of sensor and actuator information. These information pieces can be related to various IoT applications, comprising health surveillance and disease diagnoses, and working simultaneously with smart towns, traffic flow estimates, transportation monitoring, smart transport, manufacturing inspection, fault assessment, and many more. Although DL methodologies can be powerful tools for handling big data, lightweight modeling remains indispens-able for resource-constrained technologies, thanks to their high computational burden and substantial memory overhead. Consequently, several processes, such as optimisation, generalisation, compression, pruning, simplification, and feature extraction, etc., might help several cases. For that reason, creating lightweight DL practices founded on a baseline network structural design to adjust the DL model for the next generation of portable, IoT, or resource-limited devices and uses can represent a significant future feature in healthcare.

Integrating domain knowledge into DL modeling, as opposed to a general or domain-independent connection, demands familiarity with a specialised subject or field. For example, natural language processing (NLP) may evaluate the English language properties that differ from other languages, like Bengali, Japanese, and

Arabic, among others. As a result, a DL model incorporating domain-based restrictions can deliver better outcomes for such a particular purpose. Transfer learning can be an effective manner to start a different challenge by employing domain knowledge. Contextual information, akin to societal, spatial, temporal, or ecological contexts, can also perform a vital role in incorporating context-aware processing with an understanding of domains for smart decision-making and crafting adaptive and smart context-aware structures. Understanding domain familiarity and effectively slotting them into the DL model can be a different research direction. Designing all-purpose DL structures for different target domains is a promising research direction to generate frameworks handling data variety, countless dimensions and scales, stimulus forms, etc. This framework must have an attention model (AM), that identifies the most relevant input parts, and ways to obtain latent features. These traits can represent the image distinctively and informatively. AMs are a popular research subject owing to their intuitive, versatile, and interpretable nature. They are employed in various areas like computer vision, word-based or image-based classification, NLP, recommender systems, emotion research, customer profiling, etc. Learning algorithms viz. reinforcement learning can help devise AMs to find the most advantageous parts while carrying out a policy search. Likewise, CNNs and proper AMs can merge to generalise classification. In the last case, a CNN can learn and capture features at innumerable levels along with ranges.

13.5 CONCLUSION

This chapter discussed SR and its importance in health applications. Detailed information is paramount to complex tasks such as forecasting, screening, and diagnosing Covid-19, while DL also provides invaluable help to researchers and health experts, but there are too many things still to be tried. From recent literature studies, it was obvious that SR has attracted a lot of attention, with DL-based SR tactics predominating. In addition, various state-of-the-art DL-based SR approaches have been proposed and successfully developed. Ultimately, this paper highlights the challenges, including noisy data, regulations, and the reliability of large datasets, facing future research directions in AI-based disease management approaches.

REFERENCES

Andrew, J. (2020). Spine magnetic resonance image segmentation using deep learning techniques. In *Proceedings 6th International Conference on Advanced Computing and Communication Systems* (pp. 945–950). Coimbatore, India.

Andrew, J., Mhatesh, T. S. R., Sebastin, R. D., Sagayam, K. M., Eunice, J., Pomplun, M., & Dang, H. (2021). Super-resolution reconstruction of brain magnetic resonance images via lightweight autoencoder. *Informatics in Medicine Unlocked*, 26, 100713.

Ayubi, S., Bajwa, U. I., & Anwar, M. W. (2015). Super-resolution based enhancement of cardiac mr images. *Current Respiratory Medicine Reviews*, 11, 105–113.

Bertero, M., Boccacci, P. & De Mol, C. (2021). *Introduction to inverse problems in imaging*. CRC press.

Chaudhari, A. S., et al. (2020). Utility of deep learning super-resolution in the context of osteoarthritis MRI biomarkers. *Journal of Magnetic Resonance Imaging*, 51(3), 768–779.

Chen, Y. (2018, April). Brain MRI super resolution using 3D deep densely connected neural networks. In *Proceedings 15th IEEE ISBI* (pp. 739–742).

Chen, Z., Guo, X., Woo, P. Y., & Yuan, Y. (2021). Super-resolution enhanced medical image diagnosis with sample affinity interaction. *IEEE Transactions on Medical Imaging*, 40(5), 1377–1389.

Chun, J., Zhang, H., Gach, H. M., Olberg, S., Mazur, T., Green, O., ... Park, J. C. (2019). MRI super-resolution reconstruction for MRI-guided adaptive radiotherapy using cascaded deep learning: In the presence of limited training data and unknown translation model. *Medical Physics*, 46(9), 4148–4164.

Deshpande, A., & Patavardhan, P. (2016a, July). Gaussian process regression based iris polar image super resolution. In *IEEE International Conference on Applied and Theoretical Computing and Communication Technology*.

Deshpande, A., & Patavardhan, P. (2016b). Segmentation and quality analysis of long range captured iris image. *Journal on Image and Video Processing*, 6(4), 1280–1283.

Deshpande, A., & Patavardhan, P. (2016c). Single frame super resolution of non-cooperative iris images. *Journal on Image and Video Processing*, 7(2), 1362–1365.

Deshpande, A., & Patavardhan, P. (2020). Superresolution and recognition of unconstrained ear image. *International Journal of Biometrics*, 12(4), 396–410.

Deshpande, A., Patavardhan, P., Estrela, V. V., & Razmjooy, N. (2020). Deep learning as an alternative to super-resolution imaging in UAV systems.. *Imaging and Sensing for Unmanned aircraft systems*, 2, 9.

Fiat, D. (2001, September 25). Method of enhancing an MRI signal, US Patent 6 294 914 B1.

Franke, R. (1982). Scattered data interpolation: Tests of some methods. *Mathematics of Computation*, 38(157), 181–200.

Holden, J. E., Unal, O., Peters, D. C., & Oakes, T. R. (2000). Control of angular undersampling artifact in projection-based MR angiography by iterative reconstruction. In *Proceedings 8th Annual Meeting ISMRM*. Denver, CO, USA (p. 1).

https://medium.com/coinmonks/review-srcnn-super-resolution-3cb3a4f67a7c, Accessed on 5 January 2022.

https://towardsdatascience.com/review-fsrcnn-super-resolution-80ca2ee14da4, Accessed on 6 January 2022.

https://towardsdatascience.com/review-vdsr-super-resolution-f8050d49362f, Accessed on 11 January 2022.

https://medium.datadriveninvestor.com/review-drcn-deeply-recursive-convolutional-network-super-resolution-f0a380f79b20, Accessed on 15 January 2022.

Huang, G., Liu, Z., Van Der Maaten, L., & Weinberger, K. Q. (2017, July). Densely connected convolutional networks. In *Proceedings IEEE Conference CVPR* (pp. 4700–4708).

Jiang, S., et al. (2007). MRI of moving subjects using multislice snapshot images with volume reconstructtion (SVR): Application to fetal, neonatal, and adult brain studies. *IEEE Transactions on Medical Imaging*, 26(7), 967–980.

Li, X., Chen, J., Cui, Z., Wu, M., & Zhu, X. (2016). Single image super-resolution based on sparse representation with adaptive dictionary selection. *International Journal of Pattern Recognition and Artificial Intelligence*, 30(7), 1654006.

Li, X., & Nguyen, T. Q. (2008). Markov random field model-based edge directed image interpolation. *IEEE Transactions PAMI*, 17(7), 1121–1128.

Lijun, S., Yun, X. Z., & Hua, H. (2010). Image super-resolution based on MCA and wavelet domain HMT. In *Proceedings IEEE International Forum on Information Technology and Applications (IFITA)*, vol. 2.

Liu, L., Huang, W., & Wang, C. (2017). Texture image prior for SAR image super resolution based on total variation regularization using split Bregmaniteration. *International Journal of Remote Sensing*, 38(20), 5673–5687.

Mahapatra, D., Bozorgtabar, B., Hewavitharanage, S., & Garnavi, R. (2018, May 21). Retinal vasculature segmentation using local saliency maps and generative adversarial networks for image super resolution. arXiv:1710.04783v3 [cs.CV].

Malczewski, K. (2008, May). MRI image enhancement by PROPELLER data fusion. in *Proceedings IEEE International Workshop on Medical Measurements and Applications* (pp. 29–32).

Mondal, M. R., Bharati, S., & Podder, P. (2021). Diagnosis of COVID-19 using machine learning and deep learning: A review. *Current Medical Imaging*, 17(12), 1403–1418.

Ogawa, S., Lee, T. M., Kay, A. R., & Tank, D. W. (1990, December). Brain magnetic resonance imaging with contrast dependent on blood oxygenation. *Proceedings of the National Academy of Sciences of the United States of America*, 87(24), 9868–9872.

Onesimu, J. A., & Karthikeyan, J. (2020). An efficient privacy-preserving deep learning scheme for medical image analysis. *Journal of Information Technology Management*, 12 (Special Issue: The Importance of Human-Computer Interaction: Challenges, Methods and Applications.), 50–67. doi: 10.22059/jitm.2020.79191.

Park, S., Gach, H. M., & Kim, S. (2021). Autoencoder-inspired convolutional network-based super-resolution method in MRI. *IEEE Journal of Translational Engineering in Health and Medicine*, 9, 1–13.

Pham, C. H., Ducournau, A., Fablet, R., & Rousseau, F. (2017, April). Brain MRI super-resolution using deep 3D convolutional networks. In *2017 IEEE 14th International Symposium on Biomedical Imaging (ISBI 2017)* (pp. 197–200). IEEE.

Pham, C. H., et al. (2019, October). Multi-scale brain MRI super-resolution using deep 3D convolutional networks. *Computerized Medical Imaging and Graphics*, 77, Art. no. 101647.

Qu, Y. Y., Liao, M. J., Zhou, Y. W., Fang, T. Z., Lin, L., & Zhang, H. Y. (2013). Image super resolution based on data-driven Gaussian process regression. In *Intelligence Science and Big Data Engineering: 4th International Conference, IScIDE 2013, Beijing, China, July 31–August 2, 2013, Revised Selected Papers 4* (pp. 513–520). Berlin Heidelberg: Springer.

Van Reeth, E., Tham, I. W., Tan, C. H., & Poh, C. L. (2012). Super-resolution in magnetic resonance imaging: A review. *Concepts in Magnetic Resonance Part A*, 40(6), 306–325.

Rousseau, F., et al. (2005, October). A novel approach to high resolution fetal brain MR imaging. In *Proceedings International Conference on Medical Image Computing and Computer Assisted Intervention, MICCAI* (vol. 3749, pp. 548–555).

Shi, J., Liu, Q., Wang, C., Zhang, Q., Ying, S., & Xu, H. (2018). Super-resolution reconstruction of MR image with a novel residual learning network algorithm. *Physics in Medicine & Biology*, 63(8), 085011.

Vyas, S., & Bhargava, D. (2021). *Smart Health Systems: Emerging Trends*.

Xue, X., Wang, Y., Li, J., Jiao, Z., Ren, Z., & Gao, X. (2020). Progressive sub-band residual-learning network for MR image super resolution. *IEEE journal of biomedical and health informatics*, 24(2), 377–386.

Yamashita, K., & Markov, K. (2020). Medical image enhancement using super resolution methods. In V. V. Krzhizhanovskaya, et al. (Eds.), *Proceedings 2020 International Conference on Computational Science* (ICCS) (pp. 496–508).

Zhang, S., Liang, G., Pan, S., & Zheng, L. (2018). A fast medical image super resolution method based on deep learning network. *IEEE Access*, 7, 12319–12327.

Zhu, J., Tan, C., & Guang, J. Y. (2021). Arbitrary scale super-resolution for medical images. *International Journal of Neural Systems*, 31(10), 2150037.

14 Legal and ethical implications of edge-AI-enabled IoT healthcare monitoring systems

Ridoan Karim, Sonali Vyas

CONTENTS

14.1 INTRODUCTION: BACKGROUND AND DRIVING FORCES

The introduction of artificial intelligence (AI) and its recent developments have fundamentally changed how society functions. It brings up a wide range of possibilities for enhancing the quality of life in all spheres, from education to healthcare to banking and financial industries, by ensuring efficient automation and control over technological factors. AI has several advantages for the healthcare industry, including better monitoring with intelligent sensors, instant access to vital signs, remote health monitoring, and effective disease diagnosis (Davenport & Kalakota 2019).

Pandemic conditions like COVID-19 provide us with a dimension to prepare for a new healthcare era (Naudé 2020), in which the healthcare service providers need to utilise technologies for early illness diagnosis, which eventually will lead to effective treatments capable of saving lives (Islam 2021). It can be done even

DOI: 10.1201/9781003244592-14

with the existing set-up (Kim & Huh 2020); however, the introduction of edge-AI requires minor changes (Nguyen Gia et al. 2020). For such, healthcare providers can utilise the existing health monitoring tools, such as temperature monitors, to identify irregularities in patient physical behavior (Rathi et al. 2021). The essence is that such data will be transmitted to a linked hospital, allowing it to start treatment immediately (Rathi et al. 2021). This would be very helpful in stopping the disease's impact and further spread on a large scale. The question arises of how such edge-AI works.

The AI-enabled Internet of Things (IoT) is a highly regarded technology tool that provides a way to integrate different electronic gadgets (Sodhro & Zahid 2021). The gadgets have the ability to communicate and collect data while also causing other devices to take appropriate actions (Sodhro & Zahid 2021). It has numerous uses in various industries, including agriculture (Gupta et al. 2020), manufacturing (Wan et al. 2021), and inventory management (Oosthuizen et al. 2021). Numerous sensors may be used in the healthcare industry to gather information about a patient's health (including images of the patient), and, when necessary, an emergency reaction can be initiated (Zhu et al. 2019). It is reasonably simple to check someone's health remotely and offer aid with these gadgets (Rathi et al. 2021). The IoT and AI-built smart technologies have been shown to be incredibly beneficial in the healthcare industry (Rathi et al. 2021). Edge-enabled IoT, in which a sizable portion of sensing and IoT applications link to deliver various services to the healthcare industry, has the potential to treat chronic illnesses by diagnosing and detecting conditions at earlier stages to enable convenient cures (Verma & Fatima 2020). Additionally, the associated medical expenses decrease (Verma & Fatima 2020). Hence, edge-AI and IoT convergence can categorise and cluster an enormous volume of IoT data, predict outcomes, and provide preliminary insights. This might deal with the anticipated pandemics and provide fast and effective solutions.

Nevertheless, there remain legal and regulatory challenges when it comes to edge-AI implementation in healthcare, mainly in terms of consumer protection, data protection, intellectual property, cybersecurity, and liabilities. Hence, this chapter evaluates the existing legal and regulatory challenges of an edge-AI-enabled IoT healthcare monitoring system and provides insights that can make both theoretical and practical contributions to ensure the timeliness of the technology in healthcare. Therefore, this study possesses the potential to greatly impact upon the policy-making process in strengthening the health infrastructure through comprehensive legal and regulatory considerations.

14.2   ETHICAL DEBATE ON EDGE-AI-ENABLED IOT HEALTHCARE MONITORING SYSTEMS

The use of AI for decision-making in the medical field will have a significant impact in the future on how diagnoses and treatments are carried out. In fact, some individuals now view AI as a co-diagnostic partner with doctors (Yin et al. 2021). Nevertheless, AI may even create a new medical standard (Savadjiev et al. 2019). However, humans always doubted and still will have doubts about AI's behavior and the rationale behind the decision-making process (Rigby 2019). That is why AI may not substitute for the whole existing system; rather, it can provide collaborative support that extends beyond the manual check of the physicians to provide an overall effective support system.

AI solutions have a major positive impact on the medical and healthcare industries. They enable the collection, processing, and use of patient records, medical data, diagnosis discoveries, and medical research in a way that enhances the public health system and boosts prevention and treatment of diseases (Islam 2021). AI technology may also be used for patient monitoring, considering the national demographics (Rathi et al. 2021). With e-health, which includes the use of information and communication technology for health, new areas of health services are emerging, particularly mobile health apps (m-health) (Istepanian 2022). The implementation of a trustworthy AI regulatory framework should include participation in research funded by the government (Stix 2021). Additionally, coordination of general AI ethical guidelines with appropriate legislative measures is vital to respond to the changing technological environment (Stahl et al. 2021).

Then again, the drastic need to educate citizens on the new risks, benefits, and ethical concerns of AI on the medical and health sector should not be discounted either (Stahl et al. 2021). Different governments are planning to create a shared library of health data that will be used to understand better and treat chronic diseases (Sodhro & Zahid 2021). Linking genomic libraries and creating rare illness registries will become a dimension that medical science is aiming for (Rath et al. 2012). In these situations, AI could be used as a tool to help clinical research, improve diagnoses, and support decision-making. Additionally, the information at the core of AI systems used in medicine is regarded as having a sensitive nature, pertaining to the most private and intimate parts of the patient's life. Additionally, there are worries about the judgments made by the AI-based software's interpretability.

The mediated function of AI in the diagnostic environment calls for attention. For instance, when presented with an alternate interpretation from an AI system, doctors – especially less experienced ones – may be reluctant to challenge the machine's authority. It is certainly challenging. The ability to interface with an AI system, train it, and achieve ongoing maintenance and result verification are all steps that must be taken before the system can be trusted as a diagnostic partner. Additionally, AI systems engage with patients largely as disembodied measurable statistics. Patients themselves must be vocal about their unique histories and contextual circumstances to ensure that their experiences do not get lost in the mountains of data, even while this increases the doctor's obligation to actively search for aspects not recommended by the AI decision assistance.

It's crucial that AI laws serve to specify the boundaries of such partnerships to firmly ground doctors and patients in their relationship with this technology, even when institutional and legal discourse promotes human-AI collaboration rather than AI replacing the human decision-making process. The fundamental concept of human-AI collaboration requires digital literacy, namely the capacity to critically analyse the signals which AI systems convey and contextualize them (Berberich et al. 2020). Patients must be informed about the level of AI engagement in their care, any potential hazards, and the division of corporate and medical duties (He et al. 2019). However, informed consent forms are already complex papers that need to be explained to patients or guardians by medical experts (Amann et al. 2020). The best ways to explain the role of AI in a patient's treatment plan must be taught to staff members, and plans must be made to reduce the possibility of imposing new epistemic hierarchies between patients and medical professionals. Additionally, while discussing digital literacy in relation to human-AI interaction, it is important to consider the digital divide by considering the ideals of justice, equality, and inclusion. Depending on the kind of robotic or software AI program employed, and the kind of activity or service supplied with the aid of such an application, the liability schemes may vary. There are circumstances under which manufacturers, doctors, or even patients may be held accountable in the case of m-health solutions (Sadegh et al. 2018). However, these are issues that are often governed by national laws, and some applications could include a contractual obligation clause.

Then again, there are strict national laws in many countries relating to the usage and collection of data through medical devices (Pesapane et al. 2018). A uniform regulation EU 2017/ 745634 is in effect in the EU currently. The broad definition of medical devices under the law creates a strict policy for adherence by the companies behind the application of AI (manufacturer or importer), which states that they must comply with the detailed quality management system, failure of which may create liability litigation. They might also be charged for clinical data breaches due to defective medical devices. It is also important to note that, in addition to strict regulations, the Commission often issues "MEDDEVs", which are non-binding recommendations for medical device law (Contardi 2019). These strictly regulated environments may hinder AI developments, particularly in the healthcare industry.

Whatever it is, we cannot deny the prospects of edge-AI for healthcare. The edge computing architecture could process numerous data collected from different gateways (edge nodes) or devices (end-nodes). Such architecture and its application will reduce processing time, and data traffic, and provide critical analysis and medical monitoring system to support fast responses from healthcare providers. The development and design of edge nodes are the focus of several applications related to patient monitoring (Greco et al. 2020). In a healthcare setting, the end nodes can be further distinguished (Priyadarshini et al. 2021). Interactive devices may also refer to any fixed hardware or a mobile component that promotes interaction between the user's environment and the user (Venkatesan et al. 2021). All these devices are analyzed with AI algorithms (edge-AI) and provide a satisfactory analysis of data for medical responses.

Researchers assess edge intelligence, which focuses on the categorisation of health data with the detection and tracking of vital signs, using deep-learning technology, where billions of edge devices are connected (Rathi et al. 2021). Privacy breaches lead not only to legal consequences, but also to a security threat.

The use of a hierarchical edge-based computing system has been shown to have several benefits, including scalability, low latency, and the fortification of model data linked to training, which enables the researchers to evaluate diseases with a dependable local edge server (Sodhro & Zahid 2021). Edge intelligence is not a single form of technology. Rather, it is a comprehensive platform comprising other innovative tools – for example, deep learning (DL), decoupled blockchain, and multi-access edge computing (MEC). However, there are still unanswered questions that future research will be required to resolve, and the topics mainly are model/algorithm flexibility, data consistency, reward systems, and privacy and security (Amin & Hossain 2021).

14.3 LEGAL AND REGULATORY CHALLENGES

With every dramatic transition of new technologies, edge-AI poses a range of legal concerns to the healthcare industry. Legal concerns vary from data privacy to liability and consumer protection to intellectual property, based on the nature and scope of the AI applications. Some of the legal concerns of edge-AI relating to healthcare are highlighted in this section.

14.3.1 DATA PROTECTION

All algorithmic technologies – and machine learning in particular – are data-driven and necessitate a well-functioning data ecosystem underpinned by a solid legislative framework that fosters trust and data accessibility while preserving privacy rights. By enacting personal data protection laws in so many jurisdictions, policymakers have played a crucial role in establishing the desired perspective on data privacy as a fundamental human right. General Data Protection Regulation (GDPR) is such an example, and it serves not only Europe but also the entire world. With a focus on individual liberties, European ideals, and trust, it has set a new global norm (Rustad & Koenig 2019).

Most privacy laws worldwide consider six major principles. First and foremost, personal data must be handled honestly, legally, and transparently. Second, it must be gathered for clear, stated, and legal reasons. Third, the "data minimisation" principle requires that personal data be sufficient, relevant, and restricted to what is required for the processing purpose. Fourth, personal information must be relevant and correct. Fifth, it must only be stored for the time that is necessary. Finally, the processing of personal data should be conducted with the utmost integrity and secrecy, allowing for the necessary level of security and protection against improper or unlawful processing. However, it could be particularly challenging to satisfy the standards of specific data protection laws in an edge-AI-driven healthcare system.

To begin with, using skewed health data raises questions about data security and accuracy. It must be emphasised that developing AI will be a multidisciplinary effort. A restriction on the purpose of the data may provide another difficulty (Xiang & Cai 2021). AI systems frequently make use of data that has been gathered incidentally for their primary goal. In this situation, the data collector must get extra consent from the data subjects to comply with data protection regulations. Then again, the data minimisation rule poses another challenge. Finally, transparency and the right to information are the two issues that provide the greatest challenge to data protection compliance (Asan et al. 2020).

Many scholars believe the solution is simple as they state that, in the involvement of automated data process, the data controller must give the data subject meaningful information about the logic involved, as well as the significance and the anticipated consequences of the processing of the personal data (Murdoch 2021). However, the right to explanation, in principle, is not that simple to comprehend. The question here is how to convey the message to the data subject as to what amount of "relevant" information regarding the underlying logic should be disclosed to the data subject. What will happen if the hackers understand the system and the patterns of AI? Are there more threats to data security if the information of AI processing is disclosed with the data subject? These questions should be evaluated from the viewpoint of the person requesting the information as it is somewhat subjective in nature. Hence, when striving to adhere to international data protection standards, healthcare practitioners who use personal information for AI may experience difficulties (Murdoch 2021).

Several nations even have stringent data protection regulations that prohibit the use of AI and automated decision-making when making decisions concerning personal data (Wachter et al. 2017). Healthcare providers trying to adhere to the fairness principle may face difficulties due to the intricacy of the AI approaches being deployed. Also, skewed results may be caused by inadequate data, data oddities, and algorithmic mistakes. An algorithm that uses information from one region of the world, for instance, might not work well elsewhere. As a result, the GDPR advises organisations using automated data processing, such as AI, to take certain precautions, such as using the right mathematical or statistical techniques for profiling, putting in place organisational and technical measures to address causes of inaccurate personal information, and reducing the likelihood of errors (Casey et al. 2019). The Federal Trade Commission (FTC) Guidance mandates that healthcare industries using AI must ensure that their decisions are fair, requiring them to give patients/consumers access to and control over information used in decision-making and implement access controls and other safeguards to protect their algorithms from unauthorised use (Wagner 2020).

14.3.2 LIABILITY REGIME

The liability and the legal obligations of people involved in developing AI technologies remain as one the fundamental questions when analysing the legal framework for edge-AI. There is a general belief among legal practitioners that investors or, more generally, producers acting on behalf of investors, should be held firmly accountable for any flaws in AI technology (Čerka et al. 2015). That should also be taken to mean that they are responsible even if the flaws are discovered after the product has been used, providing they are in charge of technical software updates (Čerka et al. 2015). Hence, in most cases, strict liability will be imposed on the producer of the edge-AI products, regardless of whether those defects are based on hardware or software.

Edge-AI innovations and products will also be subject to the general rule of product liability. The general principles related to product liability dictate a fair distribution of risks and benefits resulting from commercial production, which calculates the costs of individual harm and an attributable responsibility for the prevention of harm (Schönberger 2019). This means that, if it is established that a specific AI product has caused harm, the burden of proving that the producer/investors have done everything appropriate to prevent harm lies with them. In any case, the investor is still liable if the flaw stems from software, hardware, or service offered with the product (Bathaee 2020). Hence, the responsibility of timely updates, of both software and hardware, lies with the producer/investor even after the release of the edge-AI system to maintain the required level of safety and efficacy. In the case of edge-AI, it is always challenging to forecast a product's performance due to the interconnectedness of appliances and cybersecurity concerns. As the edge-AI system connects different devices, the system will have to accommodate different devices manufactured by different companies/manufacturers. Hence, applying product or strict liability provides a broad framework but does not specify specific legal/practical concerns.

It is also hard to perceive the level of safety a user is entitled to anticipate due to the unpredictable nature of edge-AI systems. The same holds true for determining anything that may be categorised as a failure to achieve the desired degree of safety in the system. These traits may lead to circumstances in which it is simpler for the producer to substantiate important data. The imbalance between the investor, the producer acting in their capacity, and the user (healthcare providers) supports shifting the burden of proof to the user to prove that the system failed to perform with the standard criteria. Additionally, the user's/healthcare provider's responsibility to decide on the edge-AI system outcome relies on the probable accurate function of the system. Hence, if the system fails, the medical decision taken by the user will also fail, so that it will be easier for the aggrieved party (patient) to bring a legal suit against the healthcare provider rather than bringing a lawsuit against the producer/manufacturer/investor. (Reed 2018). Producers must therefore ensure that the design, description, and marketing of edge-AI devices enable operators to carry out their responsibilities. The rules requiring operators to perform their duties comprehensively have been implemented in several jurisdictions under tort law, mainly in common law countries (Cabral 2020; Sullivan & Schweikart 2019). Software developers should be held accountable for the harm caused by flaws in their services, much like manufacturers of digital technology goods and services (Schönberger 2019). Hence, there are three main aspects of liability in this edge-AI environment that ought to be considered for implementation.

First, there should be a mandatory liability to ensure that victims may obtain compensation and that prospective tortfeasors are protected from the danger of liability in situations where there is a possibility that third parties may be exposed to an elevated risk of injury. Second, as healthcare is a sensitive industry, a more refined duty of care should be imposed on the manufacturer, user, operator, and developer, which will eventually help the victims with the claim of damages. Third, the burden of proof should initially lie with the manufacturer, operator, and developer that they have taken standard measures to ensure the safety of the system and the patient, and, if they fail as such to prove, the victim/aggrieved party should receive compensable damage.

The appropriate and just response of law and regulatory requirements to the liability questions should be worked out regardless of the complications imposed by the edge-AI in healthcare. Nevertheless, the policymakers should not hesitate to make any essential modifications and alterations to the current liability regimes to introduce a more comprehensive legal and regulatory structure of edge-AI. It may be necessary to develop several solutions rather than a single, all-encompassing one, taking into account a wide range of dangers linked with edge- AI and its numerous intricacies. However, notwithstanding the diversity of available options, identical risks should be covered by equivalent liability structures. These rules should eventually make it apparent whether losses are recoverable and to what amount. Both product and strict liability should continue to exist, as with other available remedies. That ought to make it possible for a victim to file claims for damages against many defendants. Rules on numerous tortfeasors should thus apply. Additionally, contractual liability or other compensation regimes may apply alongside or in place of tortious responsibility.

14.3.3 CONSUMER PROTECTION

In AI-driven healthcare, the patients as customers/consumers need special consideration. In many scholarly discussions on patient empowerment and involvement, the terms "patient" and "consumer" are sometimes used interchangeably (Goldstein & Bowers 2015). However, the question arises whether the two phrases represent the same thing, or is a "consumer" an informed, deliberate decision-maker and a "patient" a passive player in the healthcare system? However, the recent commercialisation of healthcare dictates that the two words correspond to one another. Hence, when we talk about AI-driven impact on patients, we should also understand how patients as a consumer would fit into the technological transition. Generally, there are several concerns about the consumer's position in the algorithmic environment, which include the increased vulnerability in biased decision-making, invasion of privacy, deception, commercialisation, and exploitation.

Consumer protection through EU legislation primarily aims to protect consumers by taking control over the decision-making process with adequate information (Busch et al. 2016). The law also enshrines the principles of transparency, freedom of choice, equality, etc. (Busch et al. 2016). Most of the consumer protection laws address specific consumer protection issues in banking, real estate, tourism, or other financial institutions. There are, however, additional regulations that are more general in nature and that, regardless of how particular they are, must be implemented in all AI-enabled systems, even the healthcare industry. For example, in the EU, directive 2019/216/EU on better enforcement of consumer protection, directive 2011/83/EU on consumer rights, and directive 2005/29/EC on unfair commercial practices (UCPD) may be similarly applicable for edge-AI-driven healthcare system.

Our goal is not to analyse these legal acts in-depth but rather to pinpoint the pertinent concerns from the consumer's or user's perspective of edge-AI-based healthcare services or products and place them within the context of the current legal framework, which is meant to offer some guidance on the moral and legal use of algorithmic systems. The following broad principles of consumer law should be advantageous to patients, with protection of the weaker party, controlled autonomy, non-discrimination (equal treatment), and privacy. Autonomy and privacy data protection seem to be the most crucial ones when we talk about edge-AI in healthcare.

The term "autonomous consumer" refers to a person who makes decisions independently and considers all available information and possibilities (Jabłonowska & Pałka 2020). Consumers should receive clear information on the usage, features, and qualities of acquired items when it comes to edge-AI-enabled healthcare services, just like they would in any other type of transaction. That means that even an edge-AI healthcare system should provide a patient with the option to choose whether he or she wants to be admitted to a hospital or, if yes, which one he/she wants to choose. It is not always that the physician will be notified by the AI system that his patient is in a vulnerable condition, and the physician can take autocratic medical decisions on behalf of the patient. It is also important that the patient provides consent to be the subject of algorithmic analysis, which is based on the data provided by the patient. If the researchers require to save the data and reuse it for research purposes, it is equally important that they have taken the consent from the patient.

14.3.4 INTELLECTUAL PROPERTY

There are several ways in which intellectual property law, AI, and healthcare are closely related. AI-related products' patentability may significantly affect how businesses in the healthcare industry safeguard their intellectual property, particularly their patents. Recent healthcare-related choices have made the problem even more complicated. The various intricacies involved in patenting AI and ideas produced by AI are highlighted by a recent Western District of Texas ruling in the US regarding machine-learning technology (Ben-Ari et al. 2017). A Texas court ruled in Health Discovery Corp. v. Intel Corp. that two patents covering the use of extremely sophisticated machine-learning systems, to aid humans in intelligently and automatically analysing and finding patterns in genes and other biological systems, were directed to non-patentable subject matter under 35 U.S.C. 101. In Alice Corp. Pty. v. CLS Bank Int'l, 573 U.S. 208 (2014), the Supreme Court outlined multiple processes for deciding whether a patent application asserts an unpatentable idea (Hsiao 2019). The Court must look at whether a claim of the patent is classified under the natural laws or it is just an abstract concept; if it is an abstract idea, then the Court must analyse the claim's character and its usefulness sufficiently to qualify as a patent-eligible application (Hsiao 2019). The second phase is often met when a patent claim is made for the healthcare industry (Hsiao 2019). Due to the difficulty in determining whether a patent actually covers invalid subject matter or not, Alice Corp.'s application by the courts remains unpredictable and inconsistent, especially in the case of the healthcare industry (Hsiao 2019).

Health Discovery Corp. contributes to further guidance on Alice's application to AI, despite the fact that patenting in healthcare industry is still challenging (Hsiao 2019). When it comes to AI, a claim must be made that "improves an existing technical or computer feature" in order for it to be patentable (Hsiao 2019). For instance, just enhancing a process with computer capabilities to make it faster or more effective does not make an otherwise abstract notion patentable. Furthermore, a claimed invention does not automatically become patentable only because it produces better data quality or accurate information as compared with traditional techniques. In reality, a judge is more likely to agree that a machine-learning invention qualifies for patent protection when the claims are expressed as an advancement of a novel idea, such as a new piece of hardware or software (Hsiao 2019). However, where the claims are made in terms of improvements to a mathematical algorithm rather than improvements to a technology that uses a mathematical algorithm, as was the case in Health Discovery Corp., the invention is more likely to be deemed to be just an improvement of an abstract concept.

According to conventional wisdom, patents promote inventive and creative labor by granting inventors monopoly (or exclusive) rights over their ideas for predetermined amounts of time. The patent system plays a significant role in fostering technical advancement. There is also a different viewpoint, which states that the societal costs connected to patent rights have largely been overlooked while the incentives they give have been greatly overstated (Roin 2014). Nevertheless, whatever it is, we cannot deny that the major technology players will not jump to edge-AI in healthcare and develop the overall technology if they do not see the commercial benefits. By limiting access to individual ideas, patents effectively provide the effort that is needed to achieve their full potential value. In the fast-paced, knowledge-driven, and highly interconnected world, novel ideas and inventions tend to have very short shelf lives. Hence, it will need the combined efforts of a sizable network of participants to access one another's knowledge and ideas to realise commercial value from these discoveries in a reasonable amount of time. The era of innovation requires an easy patent process to safeguard the information-driven healthcare industry. However, the establishment of a seamless patent process remains a monumental aspiration and challenge for the healthcare industry.

14.4 POLICY RECOMMENDATIONS

Generally, the existing legal provisions worldwide ignore historical disparities that have impeded the development of AI technologies and led to uneven access to digital resources (Mohamed et al. 2020). Legal implementation of edge-AI also has further technical challenges. For example, it is important to understand how the law would work when healthcare providers over-rely on or over-interpret AI; how patients perceive the utilisation of edge-AI; how data are collected, analysed, and updated to achieve the best possible performance, etc. Some of the policy recommendations in the following subsections might answer some of the above questions.

14.4.1 AI AND LAW LITERACY

Ethical and legal principles of AI mandate that healthcare providers inform the patients directly about automated data processing. For instance, Articles 13 and 14 of the GDPR mandate that healthcare providers notify people when automated decision-making, such as profiling, is being used and where such decision-making may have substantial implications for the data subject's rights or other interests. Regulators have not yet provided instructions on how much data users of AI must disclose about their algorithms. Most of the time, firms can give people enough information regarding AI and other automated processing. Organisations are seen to gain more credibility and face less objection to their use of personal information if they are more open about how AI functions and the functions it serves. This situation will be like the healthcare services as well. When developing edge-AI, healthcare providers may encounter difficulties defining the purpose of processing because it is impossible to foresee what algorithms will learn and how the resulting data will be used. For instance, algorithms could find unexpected relationships that allow for new uses of the data. Healthcare providers must constantly evaluate whether they are using personal data in AI for the same or similar reasons to those that were communicated to the data subject when the data were being collected. They must amend their privacy notifications to reflect the new processing purpose and take one or more steps if the new processing is incompatible with the original purpose, which are gaining renewed consent and discovering a different legal justification for the processing. Healthcare providers must determine in advance the range of data that will be important and essential for creating an effective algorithm. Overall, an appropriate and just response of law and regulatory implementation to data protection, liability, consumer protection, and intellectual property are required in relation to edge-AI in healthcare.

14.4.2 STANDARDISATION

Standards for AI-based products have been published or established by international standards organisations (ISO and IEC, CEN/CENELEC) (Sharkov et al. 2021). Work on standardisation covers topics including software testing for AI, ethics and human issues, and neural network robustness (Sharkov et al. 2021). These standardisations aim to establish more rigorous criteria that may apply to a wide range of AI application fields, not just healthcare. Furthermore, a lot of well-known general standards, including those for quality management (ISO9000 series), medical software lifecycle standards (IEC 62304), software testing, health software safety and security (IEC 82304), human usability of medical devices (IEC 62366), and medical device risk management (ISO 14791), contain some content that is highly pertinent to the development of AI-based products and conformity evaluations.

14.4.3 RESEARCH

Even while the ethical disparities brought on by AI are receiving attention, such as the potential for AI to either eliminate or raise inequalities or racial prejudices in healthcare with new paradigms, the legal implications have not yet been examined or addressed. However, it is vital to remember that the legal challenges of health AI or edge-AI in healthcare are not entirely different from the legal challenges of AI implementation in other industries.

14.5 CONCLUSION

Edge-AI in healthcare still needs human interaction, which might cause problems, even if it depends on computers, math, and technology to function. Additionally, AI models might be faulty, just like any other digital health technology, posing dangers to patient safety. These flaws may result from a variety of sources, including errors with the data needed to create the algorithm, the decisions made by programmers while creating and training the model, and the final implementation of the AI-enabled program – all of which include human participation. We still need to understand the effects of edge-AI on healthcare, as the technology is still relatively new. The extent to which healthcare providers must inform patients about the intricacies of AI, particularly the types of data inputs and the potential for biases or other flaws in the data being utilised, is a crucial ethical question to be considered in this context. Developers must ensure two critical factors in order to fully exploit the potential of edge AI: (1) The authenticity and trustworthiness of the data sets; and (2) Transparency. The datasets must first be valid and dependable. The performance of AI will improve with greater testing and training. Transparency is crucial, too. Although, in a perfect world, all data and algorithms would be made available to the public, there are real concerns about safeguarding healthcare data as they are sensitive in nature, while also avoiding an increase in cybersecurity risk. Additionally, AI software developers must be sufficiently open and honest about the types of data utilised and any software flaws.

REFERENCES

Amann, J., Blasimme, A., Vayena, E., Frey, D., & Madai, V. I. (2020). Explainability for artificial intelligence in healthcare: A multidisciplinary perspective. *BMC Medical Informatics and Decision Making*, 20(1). https://doi.org/10.1186/s12911 -020-01332-6

Amin, S. U., & Hossain, M. S. (2021). Edge intelligence and internet of things in health-care: A survey. *IEEE Access*, 9. https://doi.org/10.1109/ACCESS.2020.3045115

Asan, O., Bayrak, A. E., & Choudhury, A. (2020). Artificial intelligence and human trust in healthcare: Focus on clinicians. *Journal of Medical Internet Research*, 22(6). https://doi.org/10.2196/15154

Bathaee, Y. (2020). Artificial intelligence opinion liability. *Berkeley Technology Law Journal*, 35 , 113–170.

Ben-Ari, D., Frish, Y., Lazovski, A., Eldan, U., & Greenbaum, D. (2017). "Danger, will Robinson"? Artificial intelligence in the practice of law: An analysis and proof of concept experiment. *Journal of Law Technology*, 23(2), 3–35.

Berberich, N., Nishida, T., & Suzuki, S. (2020). Harmonizing artificial intelligence for social good. *Philosophy and Technology*, 33(4). https://doi.org/10.1007/s13347-020 -00421-8

Busch, C., Franceschi, A. De, Luzak, J., Mak, V., Carvalho, J. M., Nemeth, K., Wallis, I. D., Busch, I. C., & Schulte-nölke, H. (2016). The rise of the platform economy: A new challenge for EU consumer law? *Journal of European Consumer and Market Law*, 5(1), 3–10.

Cabral, T. S. (2020). Liability and artificial intelligence in the EU: Assessing the adequacy of the current Product Liability Directive. *Maastricht Journal of European and Comparative Law*. https://doi.org/10.1177/1023263X20948689

Casey, B., Farhangi, A., & Vogl, R. (2019). Rethinking explainable machines: The GDPR'S "right to explanation" debate and the rise of algorithmic audits in enter-prise. *Berkeley Technology Law Journal*, 34(1), 143–188.

Čerka, P., Grigiene, J., & Sirbikyte, G. (2015). Liability for damages caused by artificial intelligence. *Computer Law and Security Review*. https://doi.org/10.1016/j.clsr.2015 .03.008

Contardi, M. (2019). Changes in the medical device's regulatory framework and its impact on the medical device's industry: From the medical device directives to the medical device regulations. *Erasmus Law Review*, 12(2). https://doi.org/10.5553/elr.000139

Davenport, T., & Kalakota, R. (2019). The potential for artificial intelligence in health-care. *Future Healthcare Journal*, 6(2). https://doi.org/10.7861/futurehosp.6-2-94

Goldstein, M. M., & Bowers, D. G. (2015). The patient as consumer: Empowerment or commodification? Currents in contemporary bioethics. *Journal of Law, Medicine and Ethics*, 43(1). https://doi.org/10.1111/jlme.12203

Greco, L., Percannella, G., Ritrovato, P., Tortorella, F., & Vento, M. (2020). Trends in IoT based solutions for health care: Moving AI to the edge. *Pattern Recognition Letters*, 135. https://doi.org/10.1016/j.patrec.2020.05.016

Gupta, N., Khosravy, M., Patel, N., Dey, N., Gupta, S., Darbari, H., & Crespo, R. G. (2020). Economic data analytic AI technique on IoT edge devices for health moni-toring of agriculture machines. *Applied Intelligence*, 50(11). https://doi.org/10.1007 /s10489-020-01744-x

He, J., Baxter, S. L., Xu, J., Xu, J., Zhou, X., & Zhang, K. (2019). The practical implemen-tation of artificial intelligence technologies in medicine. *Nature Medicine*, 25(1). https://doi.org/10.1038/s41591-018-0307-0

Hsiao, J. I.-H. (2019). Patent eligibility of predictive algorithm in second generation per-sonalized medicine. *SMU Science and Technology Law Review*, 22, 23.

Islam, S. (2021). Artificial intelligence in healthcare. *International Journal of Engineering Materials and Manufacture*, 6(4). https://doi.org/10.26776/ijemm.06.04.2021.08

Istepanian, R. S. H. (2022). Mobile health (m-Health) in retrospect: The known unknowns. *International Journal of Environmental Research and Public Health*, 19(7). https:// doi.org/10.3390/ijerph19073747

Jabłonowska, A., & Pałka, P. (2020). EU consumer law and artificial intelligence. *The Transformation of Economic Law.* https://doi.org/10.5040/9781509932610.ch-006

Kim, S. K., & Huh, J. H. (2020). Artificial neural network blockchain techniques for healthcare system: Focusing on the personal health records. *Electronics (Switzerland),* 9(5). https://doi.org/10.3390/electronics9050763

Mohamed, S., Png, M. T., & Isaac, W. (2020). Decolonial AI: Decolonial theory as sociotechnical foresight in artificial intelligence. *Philosophy and Technology,* 33(4). https://doi.org/10.1007/s13347-020-00405-8

Murdoch, B. (2021). Privacy and artificial intelligence: Challenges for protecting health information in a new era. *BMC Medical Ethics,* 22(1). https://doi.org/10.1186/s12910-021-00687-3

Naudé, W. (2020). Artificial intelligence vs COVID-19: Limitations, constraints and pitfalls. *AI and Society,* 35(3). https://doi.org/10.1007/s00146-020-00978-0

Nguyen Gia, T., Nawaz, A., Peña Querata, J., Tenhunen, H., & Westerlund, T. (2020). Artificial intelligence at the edge in the blockchain of things. Lecture Notes of the Institute for Computer Sciences, Social-Informatics and Telecommunications Engineering, LNICST, 320 LNICST. https://doi.org/10.1007/978-3-030-49289-2_21

Oosthuizen, K., Botha, E., Robertson, J., & Montecchi, M. (2021). Artificial intelligence in retail: The AI-enabled value chain. *Australasian Marketing Journal,* 29(3). https://doi.org/10.1016/j.ausmj.2020.07.007

Pesapane, F., Volonté, C., Codari, M., & Sardanelli, F. (2018). Artificial intelligence as a medical device in radiology: Ethical and regulatory issues in Europe and the United States. *Insights into Imaging,* 9(5). https://doi.org/10.1007/s13244-018-0645-y

Priyadarshini, R., Barik, R. K., Dubey, H. C., & Mishra, B. K. (2021). A survey of fog computing-based healthcare big data analytics and its security. *International Journal of Ambient Computing and Intelligence,* 12(2). https://doi.org/10.4018/IJACI.2021040104

Rath, A., Olry, A., Dhombres, F., Brandt, M. M., Urbero, B., & Ayme, S. (2012). Representation of rare diseases in health information systems: The orphanet approach to serve a wide range of end users. *Human Mutation,* 33(5). https://doi.org/10.1002/humu.22078

Rathi, V. K., Rajput, N. K., Mishra, S., Grover, B. A., Tiwari, P., Jaiswal, A. K., & Hossain, M. S. (2021). An edge AI-enabled IoT healthcare monitoring system for smart cities. *Computers and Electrical Engineering,* 96. https://doi.org/10.1016/j.compeleceng.2021.107524

Reed, C. (2018). How should we regulate artificial intelligence? *Philosophical Transactions of the Royal Society A: Mathematical, Physical and Engineering Sciences,* 376(2128). https://doi.org/10.1098/rsta.2017.0360

Rigby, M. J. (2019). Ethical dimensions of using artificial intelligence in health care. *AMA Journal of Ethics,* 21(2). https://doi.org/10.1001/amajethics.2019.121

Roin, B. N. (2014). Intellectual property versus prizes: Reframing the debate. *University of Chicago Law Review,* 81(3), 999–1078.

Rustad, M. L., & Koenig, T. H. (2019). Towards a global data privacy standard. *Florida Law Review,* 71, 18–16.

Sadegh, S. S., Khakshour Saadat, P., Sepehri, M. M., & Assadi, V. (2018). A framework for m-health service development and success evaluation. *International Journal of Medical Informatics,* 112. https://doi.org/10.1016/j.ijmedinf.2018.01.003

Savadjiev, P., Chong, J., Dohan, A., Vakalopoulou, M., Reinhold, C., Paragios, N., & Gallix, B. (2019). Demystification of AI-driven medical image interpretation: past, present and future. *European Radiology,* 29(3). https://doi.org/10.1007/s00330-018-5674-x

Schönberger, D. (2019). Artificial intelligence in healthcare: A critical analysis of the legal and ethical implications. *International Journal of Law and Information Technology*, 27(2). https://doi.org/10.1093/ijlit/eaz004

Sharkov, G., Todorova, C., & Varbanov, P. (2021). Strategies, policies, and standards in the EU towards a roadmap for robust and trustworthy AI certification. *Information & Security: An International Journal*, 50. https://doi.org/10.11610/isij.5030

Sodhro, A. H., & Zahid, N. (2021). Ai-enabled framework for fog computing driven E-healthcare applications. *Sensors*, 21(23). https://doi.org/10.3390/s21238039

Stahl, B. C., Andreou, A., Brey, P., Hatzakis, T., Kirichenko, A., Macnish, K., Laulhé Shaelou, S., Patel, A., Ryan, M., & Wright, D. (2021). Artificial intelligence for human flourishing – Beyond principles for machine learning. *Journal of Business Research*, 124. https://doi.org/10.1016/j.jbusres.2020.11.030

Stix, C. (2021). Actionable principles for artificial intelligence policy: Three pathways. *Science and Engineering Ethics*, 27(1). https://doi.org/10.1007/s11948-020-00277-3

Sullivan, H. R., & Schweikart, S. J. (2019). Are current tort liability doctrines adequate for addressing injury caused by AI? *AMA Journal of Ethics*. https://doi.org/10.1001/amajethics.2019.160

Venkatesan, M., Mohan, H., Ryan, J. R., Schürch, C. M., Nolan, G. P., Frakes, D. H., & Coskun, A. F. (2021). Virtual and augmented reality for biomedical applications. *Cell Reports Medicine*, 2(7). https://doi.org/10.1016/j.xcrm.2021.100348

Verma, P., & Fatima, S. (2020). Smart healthcare applications and real-time analytics through edge computing. In *Internet of Things Use Cases for the Healthcare Industry*. https://doi.org/10.1007/978-3-030-37526-3_11

Wachter, S., Mittelstadt, B., & Floridi, L. (2017). Why a right to explanation of automated decision-making does not exist in the general data protection regulation. *International Data Privacy Law*, 7(2). https://doi.org/10.1093/idpl/ipx005

Wagner, J. K. (2020). The federal trade commission and consumer protections for mobile health apps. *Journal of Law, Medicine and Ethics*, 48(1_suppl). https://doi.org/10.1177/1073110520917035

Wan, J., Li, X., Dai, H. N., Kusiak, A., Martinez-Garcia, M., & Li, D. (2021). Artificial-intelligence-driven customized manufacturing factory: Key technologies, applications, and challenges. *Proceedings of the IEEE*, 109(4). https://doi.org/10.1109/JPROC.2020.3034808

Xiang, D., & Cai, W. (2021). Privacy protection and secondary use of health data: Strategies and methods. *BioMed Research International*, 2021. https://doi.org/10.1155/2021/6967166

Yin, J., Ngiam, K. Y., & Teo, H. H. (2021). Role of artificial intelligence applications in real-life clinical practice: Systematic review. *Journal of Medical Internet Research*, 23(4). https://doi.org/10.2196/25759

Zhu, X., Zhang, G., & Sun, B. (2019). A comprehensive literature review of the demand forecasting methods of emergency resources from the perspective of artificial intelligence. *Natural Hazards*, 97(1). https://doi.org/10.1007/s11069-019-03626-z

15 The prospective role of artificial intelligence in the development dynamic of healthcare sectors

Biswajit Basu, Bhupendra Prajapati,
Ayon Datta, Jigna B. Prajapati

CONTENTS

DOI: 10.1201/9781003244592-15

15.1 INTRODUCTION

Insuring people's health is a major obligation of the healthcare systems, which are essential to both healthy societies and people. Such systems have existed ever since people began attempting to maintain their health and treat illnesses. Donev et al. (2013) assert that there are two fundamental goals for healthcare: finding the correct diagnosis and specifying an appropriate course of action. In Sweden, a wrong, delayed, or indeterminate diagnosis is the root of 10 to 20% of all major injuries treated by healthcare professionals. The emergency room is where diagnostic mistakes are most common, and it's a known stressful place to work (Kubota et al. 2016). High patient flow and longer stays are associated with higher mortality, decreased patient safety, more misdiagnoses, higher risk of comorbidities, and lower patient satisfaction (Chen & Decary 2020). Reporting incidents that may have caused or may have seriously injured a patient is referred to as "lex Maria". Cases from the emergency room and primary care make up between 40 and 50% of total lex Maria registrations (Kubota et al. 2016). AI simply refers to the intelligence of machines and the branch of computer science that aims to generate it (Boden 1998). AI has the potential to better organise patient flow or therapeutic strategies and give doctors virtually all the data they require to make intelligent medical and healthcare decisions (Fogel & Kvedar 2018). Healthcare is just beginning to undergo a dramatic change as a result of AI, starting with the design of treatment strategies and moving through the augmentation of repetitive tasks through medication management or drug creation (Ranganath et al. 2014). Doctors no longer need to memorise nearly as much information as they did fifty years ago. Doctors, nurses, and researchers may now devote more mental energy to patient care and higher-level cognitive work, thanks to digital technology (Murali & Sivakumaran 2018). AI is prepared to advance this to the next stage. "Thinking" time was used to set oneself up for thought, decision-making, and research (Shulman & Bostrom 2012). Information was discovered or acquired, not digested, far more quickly. To get the data into comparable form, more than a few hours of computation were needed. The decision was made quickly when they were in a comparable condition (Ramesh 2004). Digital technologies have made it possible to manage complex networks effectively by enhancing factors like connectivity, communication, and information flow (Belliger & Krieger 2018). Despite these developments in technology, misdiagnosis and missed diagnoses continue to plague the field, particularly in the emergency room. AI technology has been demonstrated to provide significant advantages in several fields, including healthcare. However, it has difficulties in at least three areas: technical, moral, and legal issues (Morley 2019). Healthcare AI guarantees patients' honourable remuneration. Researchers must assess comprehensive patient data along with more general aspects to track and identify sick and generally healthy people to decide on the best approach for customising medicine (Ahmed & Zeeshan 2020). AI has the potential to manage a range of patient care functions as well as administrative processes involving suppliers, payers, and pharmaceutical companies (Thomas et al. 2020).

15.1.1 HEALTHCARE TYPES, SERVICES, SECTORS

Medical imaging and (electronic) health records are just two examples of the traditional, data-intensive clinical health sectors on which the advances in AI can have a significant positive impact. According to WHO (2017), fewer than three nurses and midwives are addressed in less than one-half of WHO Member Countries, and fewer than one nurse and midwife are reported in less than one-quarter of WHO Member Countries. In addition, nurses are more prone to exhaustion, burnout, and job discontent as daily working hours exceed ten (Massaro 2017). According to another study, nurses reported more decision error reports due to weariness, daytime sleepiness, difficulty to recover between shifts, and poor sleep quality than nurses who were well rested (Lee et al. 2018; Massaro 2017). According to research, the development of AI-supported health information technology would aid nurses in multitasking work environments, such as vital sign checking and data gathering, prescription management, infectious disease supervision, and other tasks. Nurse workloads can be reduced by assigning non-value-added nursing activities and duties to others involved in the healthcare delivery process. Nurses' responsibilities will shift, and they'll spend more time with patients. With the use of technology, nurses will deliver healthcare in a more effective and efficient manner (Yen & Kelkye 2018)

15.1.2 THE INSUFFICIENCY OF THE HEALTHCARE SYSTEM

Global public health has always been deeply concerned with patient safety. A patient has a good likelihood of experiencing non-lethal damage while receiving treatment. It is one of the key causes of the burden of sickness on the entire planet. Feedback provided from patients regarding any inaccuracies also makes it easier for practitioners to improve serices (Bell et al. 2017). Innovations in the electronic healthcare record decreased the amount of clicking required and streamlined the handling of medical data. As a result of spending more time with patients, medical staff burnout has decreased, and patient safety has increased. Adverse occurrences not only compromise the health of the patients but also squander a significant amount of medical expenditure. With the advancement of machine learning (ML) technology and the large amount of medical data related to physiology, behavior, lab testing, and medical images, both patients and medical professionals can profit more (Howard 2019). According to a study by OECD nations, some administrative procedures were useless. There is no obvious correlation between health system performance and the roughly 14% of health costs that make up administrative costs in OECD nations, compared to the 3% global average. This indicates that 11% or so of costs have no value. An e-health telemedicine platform system can send the patient's evaluated data from home to a clinic while emphasising homecare assistance and decreasing hospital-based expenditure (Massaro & Maritati 2018). The cloud-based electronic medical record system significantly improves the integrity of antenatal data and makes it possible for outpatient clinics, hospitals, and public health agencies to communicate high-quality and comprehensive medical information, supporting informed health decisions (Haskew et al. 2015). Additionally, it promotes early treatment for HIV patients and closes HIV care gaps in western Kenya (Haskew et al. 2015). Based on AI, expert systems can help clinicians, in areas with a shortage of medical resources, diagnose patients, develop treatment plans, and even take the role of a human doctor if one is not available (Reis et al. 2004).

15.1.3 ARTIFICIAL INTELLIGENCE

It is stated that the phrase "artificial intelligence" is widely used to describe creating systems that have human-like abilities, such as the capacity for reasoning, i.e., discovery, generalisation, or learning from prior experience (Honavar 2019; Copeland 2020).

15.1.4 EXPERT SYSTEM, NLP

Statistical NLP is based on ML, specifically deep-learning (DL) neural networks, and has helped to improve the recognition of accuracy recently (Lee & Logsdon 2018). The generation, comprehension, and classification of clinical documentation and published research are the primary applications of NLP in the field of healthcare. NLP systems are able to conduct conversational AI, create reports (for example, on radiological examinations), analyse unstructured clinical notes on patients, and record patient interactions (Hussain & Malik 2014).

15.1.5 ML-DL

ML is a technique where a programme trains and learns from data without using conventional programming by using mathematical models based on statistics and probability. The learning algorithm or software can then be fed unlabeled data to create predictions once the labeled data have been utilised as a foundation

(Bohr & Memarzadeh 2020). The input layer, hidden layer, and output layer are the three layers that make up an artificial neural network (ANN). The input layer collects the data and sends them to the hidden layer, where mathematical models are used to extract patterns. The output layer is where the outcome is produced and shown after the data have been processed in the hidden layer (Shahid et al. 2019). The benefit of ANN is the ability to link and integrate both experimental and literature-based data. It can also function with missing information, generalise to analogous undiscovered data, and learn with an inductive technique from training data (Agatonovic-Kustrin & Beresford 2000). The algorithm can then effectively identify a nodule in an image once the system has had enough training. Particularly for data like images, audio, and video, DL is adequate (Bohr & Memarzadeh 2020). A study that combined data from electroic health records (EHRs) and mammograms presented a deep-learning-based algorithm for predicting breast cancer. Because of its accuracy, the Assuta Medical Center recommended their technique as a backup tool for radiologists. To increase the model's accuracy, the authors of the study suggest that more data be included (Habib 2021).

15.1.6 Robotics

More recently, robots have improved their ability to work cooperatively with people and are simpler to teach by having them perform a desired activity. Additionally, they are developing greater intelligence as additional AI capabilities are integrated into their "brains" (really, their operating systems). It would appear reasonable that, over time, physical robots would include the same advances in intelligence that we have seen in other branches of AI (Etienne & Harry 2020). Surgical robots give surgeons "superpowers", enhancing their vision, capacity to make precise, minimally invasive incisions, close wounds, and other surgical procedures. Robots can protect the economy and infrastructure, in addition to the medical profession, by working for staff of significant businesses like factories, waste management, or power generation. A robot named "Mitra" has been created by an Indian business called Invento Robotics, Bengaluru, to help patients connect with their loved ones (Singh et al. 2021). Medical robots can assist with supported living, social contact, assisted surgery, and more. AI-assisted surgical robots are among the most frequently utilised medical robots because they can physically direct a surgeon's tool in real time during an operation by analysing data from pre-operative medical records (Crawford 2019). Robots have also been employed to deliver medical supplies and equipment, assist in the care of the elderly, and aid in the rehabilitation of stroke patients (Chen & Decary 2020). It is logical to assume that, someday, machines will be able to keep track of a patient's vital signs and respond appropriately when necessary (Weng 2001). Robotic process automation (RPA) primarily uses server-based software rather than actual robots (Schaal 1999). They are employed in the healthcare industry for routine duties like billing, prior authorisation, and patient record updates (Etienne 2020). They can be used to extract data from, say, faxed photographs and feed it into transactional systems when paired with other technologies, like image recognition (Robert 2019).

Through incisions, surgeons can execute a variety of surgical procedures, using robot-assisted surgical equipment. This kind of surgery can assist in reducing pain, blood loss, scars, infections, and post-operative recovery time when compared with typical surgical procedures (Hussain 2014). Robotic technology development has transformed controlled access surgery by addressing some of the drawbacks of the laparoscopic method (Thomas et al. 2020). Robotic systems offer the capabilities to increase flexibility and ergonomic performance; they do not, however, replace the surgeon or perform tasks independently. They are (a) the master console, which has a user port that enables the operator to view a 3D representation of the operating area, manipulators for monitoring instruments, and a monitor panel for adjusting camera position and focus; and (b) the slave unit, which is mounted on the patient's side and houses the connected instruments and camera and is controlled by robotic arms (Singh et al. 2021).

15.2   TRANSFORMATION OF HEALTHCARE

Life expectancy has increased, as have expectations for healthcare itself, thanks to significant advances in scientific understanding, public health, disease prevention, healthcare delivery, and technology. We must deliver care that is better, faster, and more cost-effective, and we must offer more and better services to more people as healthcare prices continue to climb exponentially and outpace GDP growth. According to the WHO, there will be a 9.9 million shortage of doctors, nurses, and midwives worldwide by 2030 (Sinha & Al Huraimel 2020). Automation and AI have the power to completely change the way healthcare is provided, meeting the need for better, more cost-effective treatment as well as helping to make up some of the staffing shortages. AI can contribute and hasten new biomedical discoveries, diagnosis, and therapy access in such a setting (Vyas & Bhargava 2021). The potential for AI to transform healthcare holds true for all aspects of the framework, including self-care and prevention, triage and diagnosis, clinical decision-making support, care delivery in hospitals or at home, chronic care management, population health, operational improvement, and advancing healthcare innovation, such as in R&D (Sinha & Al Huraimel 2020).

- The initial stage involves designing and developing AI solutions for the appropriate challenges, utilising a human-centered AI and experimentation methodology while involving the necessary stakeholders, particularly the healthcare consumers themselves (Andrews et al. 2011)
- A multidisciplinary team is created with computer and social scientists, operational and research mentorship, clinical stakeholders (physicians, caregivers, patients), and subject experts (for example, biomedical scientists). The technical, strategic, and operational expertise needed to

establish issues, objectives, success indicators, and interim milestones is brought about by a multi-stakeholder team (Junaid & Usman 2021).

- A human-centred AI strategy integrates AI with an ethnographic understanding of healthcare systems. Understanding the main issues through user-designed research is the first step. The next stage after defining critical challenges is to determine which problems AI can address effectively and whether there are any relevant datasets available to create and later evaluate AI (Junaid & Usman 2021).

- The development of new stepwise experiments should be the primary focus, with strong feedback effects from stakeholders enabling quick experiential learning and gradual modifications. The experiments would enable the simultaneous testing of several novel concepts to determine which one works and to discover what works and why. The expected end-users and the potential negative and ethical ramifications of the AI system for them (for example, data privacy, security, equity, and safety) will be clarified through experimentation and feedback (Davahli & Waldemar 2021).

- The predictions made by the AI tool must then be iteratively evaluated and validated to see how well the tool is performing. Assessment is based on three criteria: statistical validity, clinical utility, and economic utility. Understanding the performance of AI on parameters like accuracy, dependability, robustness, stability, and calibration is statistical validity (Davahli & Waldemar 2021).

- Based on the patient population unique to that region and environment, many AI systems are initially developed to tackle a problem at one healthcare system. When scaling up AI systems, deployment methods, model updates, the regulatory system, system differences, and the reimbursement environment demand special consideration (Nachev & Herron 2019).

- Collecting and analysing the pertinent datasets for AI performance, clinical and safety-related concerns, and adverse events requires collaboration between healthcare organisations, regulatory agencies, and AI developers (Nachev & Herron 2019).

15.2.1 CURRENT TRENDS IN HEALTHCARE

15.2.1.1 Prediction of disease "data mining" with AI

In the age of pervasive technology, data play a crucial role in fostering creativity. To extract insights and patterns from huge databases, data mining is used. Patient records are collected in vast quantities by the healthcare sector. The healthcare industry can handle a variety of disorders before they are manifest by the proper analysis of these data, utilising ML methods. Medical records are mined for data or decoded to retrieve the information, including voice- and non-voice-based interactions between doctors and patients (Mindfields 2018).

15.2.1.2 AI in "medical imaging" for diagnosis

AI has significantly advanced in the fields of medical imaging and diagnostics during the past few years, allowing medical researchers and practitioners to provide faultless clinical practice (Vyas 2023). Additionally, AI is enhancing medical imaging evaluation to identify conditions like cancer and diabetic retinopathy (DR). Recently, General Electric (GE) Healthcare, in comparison with traditional cardiac magnetic resonance (MR) scans, has integrated advanced technologies into the cardiac assessment process, allowing them to be completed in a fraction of the time (Mindfields 2018).

15.2.1.3 AI in "lifestyle management"

Increased digitalisation makes it possible for people to take control of their own comfort and health. The data produced by digitization power future AI technology. A start-up company called Fedo just discovered a way to address people's risks for lifestyle diseases. They have created an algorithm for risk classification, to determine a person's risk of seven non-communicable diseases (Jason 2017).

15.2.1.4 AI in "nutrition"

Nutritional apps can provide personalised recommendations and suggestions based on a person's interests and habits, with the incorporation of AI. The London-based start-up VITL uses AI to identify patients' dietary demands and inadequacies. It also offers consumers a personalised diet plan and daily vitamin pack in addition to the diagnosis. The start-up uses an AI engine dubbed LANA (Live and Adaptive Nutritional Advisor), which makes use of a variety of lifestyle and dietary data points, to simulate the reasoning and thought processes of human nutrition experts (Jason 2017).

15.2.1.5 AI in emergency room and surgery

The FDA approved the da Vinci Surgery System as the first surgical robot for general use. The newest surgical robots are currently being developed. powered by AI and ML. To answer a surgeon's questions, IBM Watson possesses cutting-edge medical cognitive and NLP skills. Additionally, similar AI tools help with real-time blood monitoring, recognising the body's physiological reaction to pain, and helping navigation during arthroscopy and open surgery (Nordlinger et al. 2020).

15.2.1.6 AI in hospital information system (HIS)

Most hospitals and clinics currently use HIS software to manage appointment scheduling, treatment follow-up, and other administrative tasks by linking with patient EHRs. These systems have significant potential for providing excellent healthcare. Additionally, AI in healthcare helps clinicians with real-time predictive analytics and resolves operational issues across all hospital activities. Additionally, it eliminates paper-based operations, saves staff time, and automates data gathering, analysis, reporting, and communication (Nordlinger et al. 2020).

15.2.1.7   AI in research

Healthcare professionals can now digitally profile patients, thanks to AI. This may aid in the understanding of the immune sequence and lead to the development of a new class of immunological diagnostics for oncology. Additionally, it is being utilised to carry out repeatable research in the fields of genetics, life science, and bioinformatics (Nachev & Herron 2019).

15.2.1.8   AI in mental health

Mental problems are one of the main causes of disability and poor health in our society. Some of the most significant advances in AI have recently occurred in the field of healthcare, a sector which has been somewhat hesitant to adopt new technology, including the early diagnosis of mental health issues. Wysa, an emotionally intelligent AI-based penguin created by Touchkin, can chat, listen, and assist users in developing mental toughness. Within three months, Wysa has helped 50,000 individuals overcome mental health issues while carrying out a million talks with them. Some of these individuals had attempted suicide, while others suffered from PTSD, social anxiety disorder (SAD), depression, or bipolar disorder (Nachev & Herron 2019).

15.2.1.9   AI in pharma

The approach by which pharmaceutical companies develop novel medications is being revolutionised by AI. To understand how a medicine may impact a patient's tissues or cells, AI probes biological systems. An AI platform developed by the pharmaceutical start-up BERG analyses biological data to track how healthy cells become cancerous. The software makes use of nearly 14 trillion data points in a single tissue, as well as data from the 2003 Human Genome Project. Through this study, BERG was able to create a brand-new cancer medication with the potential to stop this progression (Sunarti & Rahman 2021).

15.2.1.10   AI in virtual assistant

AI and virtual assistants are being developed to support and improve human-like interactions and save time and costs. For the 500,000 physicians who use Dragon Medical every day for their clinical paperwork, Nuance, a business that has created a Medical Virtual Assistant, improves clinical operations. It makes it possible for those who use specialist medical terminology to communicate naturally and accurately (Sunarti & Rahman 2021).

15.2.1.11   Wearables with AI

Wearables like smartwatches, clothing, and shoes will become increasingly popular soon because of the forthcoming trend in AI applications of miniaturisation. The data from a product would be worthless to the user without an AI engine. As a result, AI engines are being incorporated into the product's health solutions to gather personal health insights. Therefore, consumers can consult a doctor or choose an AI doctor if clinical grade wearable technology detects an issue (Sunarti & Rahman 2021).

15.2.2 VIRTUAL AND IN-PERSON SERVICES

Numerous factors make it possible for doctors in any specialism to gain from integrating AI into their daily routines. First, even though medical knowledge is doubling every few months and growing tremendously, doctors don't have enough free time to read and keep their knowledge up to speed. AI is a potential "partner" in learning. Second, AI can facilitate organisation and the treatment of chronic illnesses in many people, particularly because they have more pertinent information from several sources, including genetic sequencing and wearable technology (Chang 2020). Digital health and medicine are ushering in an era of technological advancements that include applications, wearable technology and remote monitoring, telemedicine and communication tools, and other diagnostic tools to improve care quality and speed-up response times under any circumstance (Banaee et al. 2013). The sensor-based, quantifiable, unambiguous, and user-friendly Parkinson's disease assessment system has the potential to displace current qualitative and interpretive human assessments (Steven & Topol 2016). The central subjects in AI-enabled data capture and interpretation in digital health and medicine are organising, storing, and understanding the enormous volumes of data collected by the devices to facilitate acute and chronic disease diagnosis and management (Kubota et al. 2016).

15.2.3 ADVANCED PRECISION MEDICINE

Like other fields, precision medicine is expanding quickly. Initially, the National Research Council described the development as based on "a new taxonomy of human disease", via molecular biology, or the start of a healthcare revolution by using information from the human genome sequence. Healthcare professionals can now use precision medicine to find and communicate data that can either confirm or change the course of a medical choice from one that is based on the evidence for the average patient to one that is based on the individual's unique traits (Ziegelstein 2017). Early disease detection and the development of individualised treatments are two examples of how advances in precision medicine have a real-world impact on healthcare (Johnson et al. 2021). Genotype-guided therapy is now one of the effects of precision medicine on healthcare that has perhaps received the most research. Genotype data have been used by clinicians, for example, as a guide to assist in establishing the ideal warfarin dose. When precision medicine is applied to healthcare, it can produce more accurate diagnoses, identify disease risks before symptoms appear, and create specialised treatment regimens that maximize efficiency and safety (Haskew et al. 2015). Although AI and precision medicine have a lot of potential, more work needs to be done to evaluate, validate, and alter current treatment methods. The adoption of unified data formats, such as Fast Healthcare Interoperability Resources, the acquiring of enough high-quality labeled data for algorithm training, and meeting sociocultural, legal, and regulatory standards are hurdles for researchers (Caudle & Klein 2014).

15.2.4 REMOTE MONITORING

Remote patient monitoring satisfies the desire to observe the signals and actions of those with chronic illnesses, who are susceptible to acute symptoms. The patient benefits from better treatment, certainty that sudden health attacks are being tracked, and a decrease in hospital visits. Real-time and ongoing symptom monitoring, early illness identification or prevention, lower healthcare expenses, more knowledge about health concerns, and finally, more opportunities for service and emergency medical care are just a few of the benefits of doing remote monitoring (Vegesna & Melody 2017; Malasinghe et al. 2019).

As Figure 15.1 indicates, remote patient monitoring can benefit a range of medical problems, including diabetes, cardiovascular disease, and neurological illnesses, by lowering mortality, preventing hospitalisation, and delivering better care and services (Klersy & Annalisa 2009). Lack of monitoring after treatment episodes is likely to raise the risk of readmission as well as morbidity for persons with heart failure. Compared with professional visits in person, remote patient monitoring is a more affordable option. ECG, blood pressure, heart rate, and weight measures are frequently combined with telephone monitoring and consultations to form the monitoring process. Some of these rely on telemonitoring, whereas others rely on videoconferencing or monitoring and interventions using mobile phones (Jeddi & Bohr 2020).

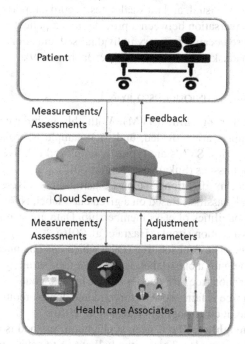

FIGURE 15.1   Remote patient monitoring.

15.2.5 AI ADAPTATION

AI comprises systems that can analyse patterns in unstructured data. Production, marketing, supply chain, human resources, and financial choices are made in SMEs. AI employs algorithms to analyze both organized and unstructured data collections. Studies from the past confirm that AI technologies enhance organisational effectiveness and efficiency. Small- and medium-sized businesses are the backbone of the nation's economy, yet they fall far behind in the use of AI. The effects of AI adaptability have been the subject of extensive investigation in the past. However, because SMEs operate in various environments, generalised findings cannot be applied to them (Ingalagi et al. 2021).

15.3 ML/DL IN HEALTHCARE

Numerous health-related applications of ML solutions include helping clinicians find various patient-specific medications and treatments, as well as helping patients determine when or whether they need to schedule follow-up consultations (Bhardwaj et al. 2017). There is currently a vast amount of information available in the healthcare industry. It includes electornic medical records (EMRs) that are made up of information, both structured and unstructured. Most of the medical information is as unstructured data; among the many different types are fully diverse auditory, visual, and musical notes, records, reports, and summaries of discharge. A conversation between a provider and a patient is very difficult to quantify and analyse because it is very individualised and could go in a lot of different directions (Hauskrecht 2010; Shailaja & Jabbar 2019).

15.3.1 DIFFERENT TECHNIQUES USED BY ML

- **Support vector machine (SVM).** With this technique, a variety of training samples are provided, and each sample is broken down into various categories. SVMs are typically employed to solve classification and regression issues (Sukanya & Kumar 2017).
- **Naïve Bayes classification.** The best illustration of a Bayesian classifier is a statistical classifier. Based on a given class label, Naïve Bayes calculates the probabilities of class membership. Data are scanned just once, making classification simple (Hazra et al. 2016).
- **Decision tree.** The decision tree (DT), which has one interior node and one leaf node with a class label, is the most-used strategy for classification. The decision tree's root nodes are the highest nodes. The creation of the decision tree is fairly straightforward and doesn't require any parameters, making it quite popular (Hazra et al. 2016).
- **K-nearest neighbor.** The K-nearest neighbour method is a popular one for classifying samples. This method allows us to calculate the distance measure, using N training samples (Yadav 2019).

- **Fuzzy logic.** Fuzzy set theory gives rise to fuzzy logic. These numbers fall between 0 and 1. It is a technique that is frequently utilised in engineering applications (Yadav 2019).
- **Classification and regression tree methodology (CART).** The goal variable is expressed as a continuous and categorical variable in classification and regression trees. To forecast values in the tree, these variables are needed (Shailaja 2019).

15.3.2 DEEP-LEARNING ARCHITECTURES IN THE HEALTHCARE SECTOR

- **Neural Network.** Nodes make up the layers in neural networks. A node is a location where processing takes place and is loosely modeled after a neuron in the human brain. Nodes fire when they receive enough stimuli. A node will provide significant inputs in relation to the method it is trying to learn by combining input from the data with weights that can either amplify or dampen the input (Manne & Kantheti 2021).
- **Convolutional Neural Network (CNN).** CNNs are used to classify, segment, and recognise images. CNNs' primary responsibilities include classifying visual content, recognising items that are fed into it, and grouping the detected objects into clusters. CNNs use subsampling after relying on connections and weights among the units. One convolutional layer, a pooling layer, and occasionally fully linked layers for supervised prediction make up the fundamental components of CNN architecture (Manne & Kantheti 2021).
- **Input layer.** The image's data should be in the CNN's input layer. Images are nothing more than three-dimensional matrices that must first be converted into a single column before being submitted. Each layer's output will be fed into the one below it (Murali & Sivakumaran 2018).
- **Convolutional layer.** The activity starts in the convolutional layer. This layer describes the characteristics of a picture, such as color, shape, and object elements, etc. The ReLu layer is a CNN extension layer. This layer increases the nonlinearity of the image. At this layer, improved feature extraction is accomplished. Following the convolutional layer, the pooling layer lowers the spatial volume of the input image (Murali & Sivakumaran 2018).
- **Fully connected layer.** Weights, neurons, and biases are all present in this layer.Using completely connected layers, neurons in one layer are connected to neurons in another layer. At this layer, categories are created for images using training data (Samyuktha & Geetha 2020)
- **Output layer.** The fully connected (FC) layer is just below the Softmax layer, which is utilised for binary classification. CNN is used in the healthcare industry for medical image analysis. Using CNN for medical image classification, it is possible to precisely identify anomalies in MRI and X-ray pictures (Samyuktha & Geetha 2020)

TABLE 15.1

Classification of robots used in healthcare (Fosch-Villaronga & Drukarch 2021)

Sl. No	Robots used in healthcare	Examples
1.	Surgical robots	Surgery robots, surgery automation, telesurgery robots
2.	Socially assistive robots	Therapeutic robots, care robots
3.	Physically assistive robots	Rehabilitation robots, nurse-assisted robots
4.	Healthcare service robots	Routine task robots, nurse-assisted robots, disinfectant robots

15.4 ROBOTICS IN HEALTHCARE

In healthcare contexts, physical robotic devices are integrated with cloud-based services. The legal and regulatory ramifications of the increasing interaction and interdependence between physical and virtual elements in cyberphysical systems for use in healthcare are becoming more apparent (Fosch-Villaronga & Drukarch 2021). The need to increase access to healthcare and the desire to enhance patient outcomes and prevention are the two main social objectives for better health care that robotic technology can address. Robotic technology has demonstrated a significant potential for accelerating the development of novel treatments for a wide range of diseases and disorders, expanding the quality and accessibility of care, and improving patient outcomes (Fosch-Villaronga & Drukarch 2021). The usage of robots in the healthcare industry spans a range of autonomy levels and also includes associated technology, such as sensor systems, data-processing algorithms, and cloud services as listed in Table 15.1 (Fosch-Villaronga & Albo-Canals 2019).

15.5 MONITORING HEALTH THROUGH WEARABLES AND PERSONAL DEVICES

Wearables are electronic technology or devices built into clothing that can be comfortably worn on the body. Wearable technology is a general phrase for such electronics. These wearable tech gadgets are used to track data in real time, as shown in Figure 15.2. They have motion sensors that capture an image of your daily activity and sync it with laptops or mobile devices. Although there are many kinds of wearable technology, activity trackers and smart watches are among the gadgets most often used. Apple Watch, Fitbit, chest straps, shoes, helmets, glasses, lenses, rings, patches, textiles, hearing aids, etc., act as administrators of healthcare or as professionals keeping an eye out for worrying patterns that call for treatment (Chawla 2020).

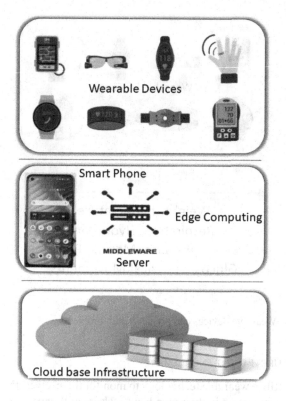

FIGURE 15.2 Wearable device application model.

Some gadgets merely urge users to update friends and colleagues on their health progress via social media platforms, whereas a patient's physical changes can be immediately detected by a wearable medical gadget. Numerous industries have been impacted by wearable technology, but the healthcare industry has benefited the most (Chawla 2020). Figure 15.3 demonstrates how wearable device can predict health problem.

Hospitals and clinics can benefit on a variety of levels and in a variety of roles by implementing wearable technologies. Some of these advantages are outlined in the following subsections.

15.5.1 Promotes preventive healthcare

There is promise of a more pro-active approach to healthcare with wearable technology. This is because wearables can be used to act before health issues become serious rather than reacting to them after they have already started to cause difficulties. Health abnormalities can be found in those who are already predisposed to them before they become concerns (Sabry & Tamer 2022).

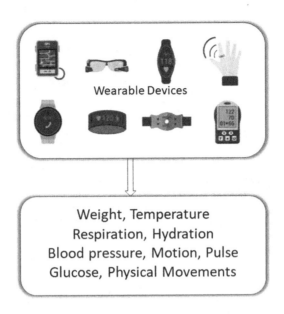

FIGURE 15.3 Wearable devices can predict health problems

15.5.2 Ensures patient engagement

If people can utilise wearable technology to monitor themselves, they will be considerably more interested in their own health. Users will have access to real-time data that is continuously gathered through a wearable device, allowing them to be informed about their own health situation (Sabry & Tamer 2022).

15.5.3 Monitors patients who are at risk

Wearable technology can be used by healthcare professionals to monitor vulnerable people who are more likely to have medical problems. Wearable technology can be used to keep an eye on them at home if they are at danger but not seriously unwell enough to be in hospital (Sabry & Tamer 2022).

15.5.4 Enhance patient satisfaction and care

Wearable technology gives surgeons and doctors the vital information they need to make better decisions while expanding the chance to connect with patients, such as the use of smart glasses to monitor patient vitals and pertinent data while carrying out surgery without looking away from the patient (Sabry & Tamer 2022).

15.5.5 Benefits for employers and healthcare providers

The potential advantages for healthcare professionals of wearable technology are significant. Medical personnel can gain a more comprehensive understanding of the problems affecting their patients by employing wearable devices to monitor patient data over an extended period. They can then utilise the information to diagnose a patient more precisely than they could have done without the equipment (Sabry & Tamer 2022).

15.6 REVOLUTIONISING CLINICAL DECISION-MAKING WITH AI

The principles of the AI smart support system which are being developed and put into place in our hospitals aid clinical decision-making processes include computer identification of a clinical problem, quick data collection from EHRs and algorithm evaluations, real-time predictions, and links with clinical recommendation. AI has been shown to detect patients at risk of multidrug-resistant infections at the outset of febrile neutropenia and provide advice in line with predictions made to overcome the difficulties described before about clinical settings (Garcia-Vidal & Sanjuan 2019).

15.7 CONCLUSION

AI is a burgeoning scientific field with applications in many industries, including the delivery of healthcare services. Studies show that the market for AI in healthcare is fundamentally growing. In this discipline, it can be used for a wide range of things, including data management, medication research, diabetes treatment, and digital consulting. There is some solid evidence that medical AI will be able to assist doctors and patients and offer healthcare much more competently in the twenty-first century.

REFERENCES

Agatonovic-Kustrin, S., & Beresford, R. (2000). Basic concepts of Artificial Neural Network (ANN) modeling and its application in pharmaceutical research. *Journal of Pharmaceutical and Biomedical Analysis*, 22(5), 717–727. https://doi.org/10.1016/S0731-7085(99)00272-1

Ahmed, Z., Mohamed, K., Zeeshan, S., & Dong, X. Q. (2020). Artificial intelligence with multi-functional machine learning platform development for better healthcare and precision medicine. *Database*, 2020, 1–35. https://doi.org/10.1093/database/baaa010

Andrews, M., McConnell, J., & Wescott, A. O. (2011). Development as leadership-led change – A report for the global leadership initiative and the World Bank Institute (WBI). *SSRN Electronic Journal*. https://doi.org/10.2139/ssrn.1551375

Bajwa, J., Munir, U., Nori, A., & Williams, B. (2021). Artificial intelligence in healthcare: Transforming the practice of medicine. *Future Healthcare Journal*, 8(2), e188–e194. https://doi.org/10.7861/fhj.2021-0095

Banaee, H., Uddin Ahmed, M., & Loutfi, A. (2013). Data mining for wearable sensors in health monitoring systems: A review of recent trends and challenges. *Sensors (Switzerland)*, 13(12), 17472–17500. https://doi.org/10.3390/s131217472

Belliger, A., & Krieger, D. J. (2018). *The Digital Transformation of Healthcare* (pp. 311–326). https://doi.org/10.1007/978-3-319-73546-7_19

Bhardwaj, R., Nambiar, A. R., & Dutta, D. (2017). A study of machine learning in health-care. *Proceedings – International Computer Software and Applications Conference* 2, 236–241. https://doi.org/10.1109/COMPSAC.2017.164

Boden, M. A. (1998). Creativity and artificial intelligence. *Artificial Intelligence*, 103(1–2), 347–356. https://doi.org/10.1016/s0004-3702(98)00055-1

Bohr, A., & Memarzadeh, K. (2020). The rise of artificial intelligence in healthcare applications. *Artificial Intelligence in Healthcare*. https://doi.org/10.1016/B978-0-12-818438-7.00002-2

Caudle, K., Klein, T., Hoffman, J., Muller, D., Whirl-Carrillo, M., Gong, L., McDonagh, E., et al. (2014). Incorporation of pharmacogenomics into routine clinical practice: The Clinical Pharmacogenetics Implementation Consortium (CPIC) guideline development process. *Current Drug Metabolism*, 15(2), 209–217. https://doi.org/10.2174/1389200215666140130124910

Chang, A. (2020). The role of artificial intelligence in surgery. *Advances in Surgery*, 54, 89–101. https://doi.org/10.1016/j.yasu.2020.05.010

Chawla, N. (2020). AI, IOT and wearable technology for smart healthcare-a review. *International Journal of Recent Research Aspects*, 7(March), 9–13.

Chen, M., & Decary, M. (2020). Artificial intelligence in healthcare: An essential guide for health leaders. *Healthcare Management Forum*, 33(1), 10–18. https://doi.org/10.1177/0840470419873123

Copeland, B. J. (2020). Artificial intelligence. Encyclopedia Britannica.

Crawford, M. (2019). *Top 6 Robotic Applications in Medicine, the American Society of Mechanical Engineers.*2016 (9).

Davahli, M. R., & Waldemar, K. (2021). Controlling safety of artificial intelligence-based systems in healthcare. *Symmetry*, 13(1), 1–25. https://doi.org/10.3390/sym13010102

Davenport, T., & Kalakota, R.. (2020). The potential for artificial intelligence in health-care. *SSRN Electronic Journal*, 6(2), 94–98. https://doi.org/10.2139/ssrn.3525037

Donev, D., Kovacic, L., & Laaser, U. (2013). The role and organisation of health system. In *Health: Systems – Lifestyle – Policies, A Handbook for Teachers, Researchers and Health Professionals* (Vol. I). https://www.researchgate.net/publication/257830385_The_Role_and_Organization_of_Health_Care_Systems

Etienne, H., Hamdi, S., Le Roux, M., Camuset, J., Khalife-Hocquemiller, T., Giol, M., Debrosse, D., & Assouad, J. (2020). Artificial intelligence in thoracic surgery: Past, present, perspective and limits. *European Respiratory Review*, 29(157), 1–11. https://doi.org/10.1183/16000617.0010-2020

Fogel, A. L., & Kvedar, J. C. (2018). Artificial intelligence powers digital medicine. *Npj Digital Medicine*, 1(1), 3–6. https://doi.org/10.1038/s41746-017-0012-2

Fosch-Villaronga, E., & Albo-Canals, J. (2019). 'I'll take care of you,' said the robot. *Paladyn, Journal of Behavioral Robotics*, 10(1), 77–93. https://doi.org/10.1515/pjbr-2019-0006

Fosch-Villaronga, E., & Drukarch, H. (2021). *On Healthcare Robots: Concepts, Definitions, and Considerations for Healthcare Robot Governance.* https://www.researchgate.net/publication/352208794_On_Healthcare_Robots_Concepts_definitions_and_considerations_for_healthcare_robot_governance

Garcia-Vidal, C., Sanjuan, G., Puerta-Alcalde, P., Moreno-García, E., & Soriano, A. (2019). Artificial intelligence to support clinical decision-making processes. *EBioMedicine*, 46, 27–29. https://doi.org/10.1016/j.ebiom.2019.07.019

Habib, M., Faris, M., Alomari, A., & Faris, H. (2021). Altibbivec: A word embedding model for medical and health applications in the arabic language. *IEEE Access*, 9, 133875–133888. https://doi.org/10.1109/ACCESS.2021.3115617

Hartmaier, R. J., Albacker, L. A., Chmielecki, J., Bailey, M., He, J., Goldberg, M. E., Ramkissoon, S., et al. (2017). High-throughput genomic profiling of adult solid tumors reveals novel insights into cancer pathogenesis. *Cancer Research*, 77(9), 2464–2475. https://doi.org/10.1158/0008-5472.CAN-16-2479

Haskew, J., Rø, G., Saito, K., Turner, K., Odhiambo, G., Wamae, A., Sharif, S., & Sugishita, T. (2015). Implementation of a cloud-based electronic medical record for maternal and child health in rural Kenya. *International Journal of Medical Informatics*, 84(5), 349–354. https://doi.org/10.1016/j.ijmedinf.2015.01.005

Hauskrecht, M., Valko, M., Batal, I., Clermont, G., Visweswaran, S., & Cooper, G. F. (2010). Conditional outlier detection for clinical alerting. *AMIA. Annual Symposium Proceedings/AMIA Symposium. AMIA Symposium*, 2010, 286–290.

Hazra, A., Kumar, S., & Gupta, A. (2016). Study and analysis of breast cancer cell detection using Naïve Bayes, SVM and ensemble algorithms. *International Journal of Computer Applications*, 145(2), 39–45. https://doi.org/10.5120/ijca2016910595

Honavar, V. G. (2019). Artificial intelligence: An Overview. In *Cutting Edge Technologies and Microcomputer Applications for Developing Countries* (pp. 61–65). https://doi.org/10.4324/9780429042522-6

Howard, J. (2019). Artificial intelligence: Implications for the future of work. *American Journal of Industrial Medicine*, 62(11), 917–926. https://doi.org/10.1002/ajim.23037

Hussain, A., Malik, A., Halim, M. U., & Ali, A. M. (2014). The use of robotics in surgery: A review. *International Journal of Clinical Practice*, 68(11), 1376–1382. https://doi.org/10.1111/ijcp.12492

Ingalagi, S. S., Mutkekar, R. R., & Kulkarni, P. M. (2021). Artificial Intelligence (AI) adaptation: Analysis of determinants among Small to Medium-Sized Enterprises (SME's). *IOP Conference Series: Materials Science and Engineering*, 1049(1), 012017. https://doi.org/10.1088/1757-899X/1049/1/012017

JASON. (2017). Artificial intelligence for health and health care. The MITRE Corporation 7508 (December), 65. https://www.healthit.gov/sites/default/files/jsr-17-task-002_aiforhealthandhealthcare12122017.pdf

Jeddi, Z., & Bohr, A. (2020). Remote patient monitoring using artificial intelligence. *Artificial Intelligence in Healthcare. INC.* https://doi.org/10.1016/B978-0-12-818438-7.00009-5

Johnson, K. B., Wei, W. Q., Weeraratne, D., Frisse, M. E., Misulis, K., Rhee, K., Zhao, J., & Snowdon, J. L. (2021). Precision medicine, AI, and the future of personalized health care. *Clinical and Translational Science*, 14(1), 86–93. https://doi.org/10.1111/cts.12884

Klersy, C., De Silvestri, A., Gabutti, G., Regoli, F., & Auricchio, A. (2009). A meta-analysis of remote monitoring of heart failure patients. *Journal of the American College of Cardiology*, 54(18), 1683–1694. https://doi.org/10.1016/j.jacc.2009.08.017

Kubota, K. J., Chen, J. A., & Little, M. A. (2016). Machine learning for large-scale wearable sensor data in Parkinson's disease: Concepts, promises, pitfalls, and futures. *Movement Disorders*, 31(9), 1314–1326. https://doi.org/10.1002/mds.26693

Lee, S. I., Celik, S., Logsdon, B. A., Lundberg, S. M., Martins, T. J., Oehler, V. G., Estey, E. H., ... & Becker, P. S. (2018). A machine learning approach to integrate big data for precision medicine in acute Myeloid Leukemia. *Nature Communications*, 9(1). 42. https://doi.org/10.1038/s41467-017-02465-5

Malasinghe, L. P., Ramzan, N., & Dahal, K. (2019). Remote patient monitoring: A comprehensive study. *Journal of Ambient Intelligence and Humanized Computing*, 10(1), 57–76. https://doi.org/10.1007/s12652-017-0598-x

Manne, R., & Kantheti, S. C. (2021). Application of artificial intelligence in healthcare: Chances and challenges. *Current Journal of Applied Science and Technology*, 40(6), 78–89. https://doi.org/10.9734/cjast/2021/v40i631320

Massaro, A., Maritati, V., Savino, N., Galiano, A., Convertini, D., De Fonte, E., & Di Muro, M. (2018). A study of a health resourses management platform integrating neural networks and dss telemedicine for homecare assistance. *Information*, 9(7), 176.

Massaro, M., Lazzara, G., Milioto, S., Noto, R., & Riela, S. (2017). Covalently modified halloysite clay nanotubes: Synthesis, properties, biological and medical applications. *Journal of Materials Chemistry B*, 5(16), 2867–2882. https://doi.org/10.1039/c7tb00316a

Mindfields. (2018). Artificial intelligence in healthcare table of contents abbreviations, 1–27. https://www.cpaaustralia.com.au/-/media/corporate/allfiles/document/employers/ai-in-healthcare-mindfields.pdf?la=en&rev=c50cc09afb0648859a5c407063baa444

Morley, J., Machado, C., Burr, C., Cowls, J., Taddeo, M., & Floridi, L. (2019). The debate on the ethics of AI in health care: A reconstruction and critical review. *SSRN Electronic Journal*, no. January. https://doi.org/10.2139/ssrn.3486518

Murali, N., & Sivakumaran, N. (2018). Artificial intelligence in healthcare-a review. *International Journal of Modern Computation, Information and Communication Technology*, 1(6), 2581–5954. http://ijmcict.gjpublications.com.

Nachev, P., Herron, D., McNally, N., Rees, G., & Williams, B. (2019). Redefining the research hospital. *NPJ Digital Medicine*, 2(1), 1–5. https://doi.org/10.1038/s41746-019-0201-2

Nordlinger, B., Villani, C., & Rus, D. (2020). Healthcare and artificial intelligence. *Healthcare and Artificial Intelligence*. https://doi.org/10.1007/978-3-030-32161-1

Ramesh, A. N., Kambhampati, C., Monson, J. R. T., & Drew, P. J. (2004). Artificial intelligence in medicine. *Annals of the Royal College of Surgeons of England*, 86(5), 334–338. https://doi.org/10.1308/147870804290

Ranganath, R., Gerrish, S., & Blei, D. M. (2014). Black box variational inference. *Journal of Machine Learning Research*, 33, 814–822.

Reis, M. A. M., Ortega, N. R. S., & Silveira, P. S. P. (2004). Fuzzy expert system in the prediction of neonatal resuscitation. *Brazilian Journal of Medical and Biological Research*, 37(5), 755–764. https://doi.org/10.1590/S0100-879X2004000500018

Robert, N. (2019). How artificial intelligence is changing nursing. *Nursing Management* (Springhouse), 50(9), 30–39. DOI: 10.1097/01.NUMA.0000578988.56622.21.

Sabry, F., Eltaras, T., Labda, W., Alzoubi, K., & Malluhi, Q. (2022). Machine learning for healthcare wearable devices: The big picture. *Journal of Healthcare Engineering*, 2022. https://doi.org/10.1155/2022/4653923

Samyuktha, P. S., & Geetha, R. V. (2020). Awareness and knowledge about artificial intelligence in healthcare among doctors – A survey. *European Journal of Molecular and Clinical Medicine*, 7(1), 697–708. https://ejmcm.com/article_2238.html%0Ahttp://ovidsp.ovid.com/ovidweb.cgi?T=JS&PAGE=reference&D=emca&NEWS=N&AN=2010164658

Schaal, S. (1999). Is imitation learning the route to humanoid robots? *Trends in Cognitive Sciences*, 3(6), 233–242. https://doi.org/10.1016/S1364-6613(99)01327-3

Shahid, N., Rappon, T., & Berta, W. (2019). Applications of artificial neural networks in health care organizational decision-making: A scoping review. *Plos One*, 14(2), e0212356.

Shailaja, J. (2019). Machine learning in healthcare. *British Journal of Health Care Management*, 25(2), 100–101. https://doi.org/10.12968/bjhc.2019.25.2.100

Shulman, C., & Bostrom, N. (2012). How hard is artificial intelligence? Evolutionary arguments and selection effects. *Journal of Consciousness Studies*, 19(7–8), 103–130.

Singh, S., Dalla, V. K., & Shrivastava, A. (2021). Combating COVID-19: Study of robotic solutions for COVID-19. *AIP Conference Proceedings*, 2341(May). https://doi.org /10.1063/5.0050148

Sinha, S., & Al Huraimel, K. (2020). Transforming healthcare with AI. *Reimagining Businesses with AI*, no. March, 33–54. https://doi.org/10.1002/9781119709183.ch3

Steven, T. (2016). Moving from digitalization to digitalization in cardiovascular care: Why is it important and what can it mean for patients and providers? *Journal of the American College of Cardiology*, 66(13), 1489–1496. https://doi.org/10.1016/j.jacc .2015.08.006

Sukanya, J., & Kumar, S. V. (2017). Applications of big data analytics and machine learning techniques in health care sectors. *International Journal of Engineering and Computer Science*, 6(7), 21963–21967. https://doi.org/10.18535/ijecs/v6i7.11

Sunarti, S., Rahman, F. F., Naufal, M., Risky, M., Febriyanto, K., & Masnina, R. (2021). Artificial intelligence in healthcare: Opportunities and risk for future. *Gaceta Sanitaria*, 35, S67–S70. https://doi.org/10.1016/j.gaceta.2020.12.019

Vegesna, A., Tran, M., Angelaccio, M., & Arcona, S. (2017). Remote patient monitoring via non-invasive digital technologies: A systematic review. *Telemedicine and E-Health*, 23(1), 3–17. https://doi.org/10.1089/tmj.2016.0051

Vyas, S. (2023). Extended reality and edge AI for healthcare 4.0: Systematic study. In *Extended Reality for Healthcare Systems* (pp. 229–240). Academic Press.

Vyas, S., & Bhargava, D. (2021). *Smart Health Systems: Emerging Trends*. https://doi.org /10.1007/978-981-16-4201-2.

Weng, J., McClelland, J., Pentland, A., Sporns, O., Stockman, I., Sur, M., & Thelen, E. (2001). Autonomous mental development by robots and animals. *Science*, 291(5504), 599–600. https://doi.org/10.1126/science.291.5504.599

Yadav, R. (2019). Survey on heart disease prediction by using machine learning technique. *IJCRT*, 7(1), 44–51. www.ijcrt.org.

Yen, P. Y., Kellye, M., Lopetegui, M., Saha, A., Loversidge, J., Chipps, E. M., Gallagher-Ford, L., & Buck, J. (2018). Nurses' time allocation and multitasking of nursing activities: A time motion study. *AMIA: Annual Symposium Proceedings. AMIA Symposium*, 2018, 1137–1146.

Ziegelstein, R. C. (2017). Personomics and precision medicine. *Transactions of the American Clinical and Climatological Association*, 128, 160–168.

16 Edge-AI-empowered blockchain

A game-changer for the medical tourism industry

Amitabh Bhargava, Deepshikha Bhargava, Ajay Rana

CONTENTS

16.1 INTRODUCTION

The term "Tourism" is usually associated with leisure and traveling to local or foreign locations; however, when combined with the term "Medical", its focus changes from leisure travel to means of medical care. Formerly, medical tourism was associated with the medical treatment of patients from richer/developed countries to cheaper/less developed countries. The term "Medical Tourism" is all about patient mobility, where the medical tourists/travelers seek pocket-friendly healthcare/medical care services outside their country of residence. During their stay, they also leverage the traditional tourism activities, such as sightseeing, city tours, leisure, etc. For the past two decades, the majority of developed countries raised their cost of healthcare such as medical treatment, drug prices, medical procedures, and medical

DOI: 10.1201/9781003244592-16

insurance billing. For example, a typical heart bypass surgery is 30–70% cheaper in less-developed countries than in developed countries like the US (OECD Report 2011). At the same time, these countries ensure the quality of services, medical tourist satisfaction, target market segmenting, quality assessment, laid-down procedures, and risk management. Medical tourism provides cost-effective alternatives for medical tourists, such as low-cost treatments, inexpensive travel, advertising and marketing, medical-tour packages, online platforms, and cultural exchanges and leisure trips. The reason is that medical tourism has now become a billion-dollar industry, gaining popularity among medical tourists, hospitality and tourism industries, policymakers, government agencies, researchers, and advertising and media. The coronavirus pandemic interrupted the tourism and travel industry and also medical tourism. With the advent of blockchain, medical tourism is also looking for alternatives to raise their business (Benowitz n.d.).

16.2   WHAT IS MEDICAL TOURISM?

There are various definitions of medical tourism, depending upon the country and their healthcare regulations. The following are a few definitions, imposing restrictions upon medical treatments, such as dental, cosmetic surgery, health spa and wellness, and accidental cases (Bhattacharjee 2019):

- A report from OECD (2011) defined a medical tourist as one who seeks out overseas options for dental, cosmetic, and fertility treatments.
- McKinsey (2008) defined a medical tourist as an individual who seeks medicinal treatment in overseas countries. The definition excludes emergency, health, and wellness tourism.
- Pollard in International Medical Tourism Journal in 2011 defined medical traveler as an individual who travels abroad for medical treatment (Bhattacharjee 2019).

The World Health Organization also emphasised the policy and guidelines for medical tourism and transplant tourism (WHO Resolution WHA59.26 2006) (Etemad 2010). In contrast, the medical tourist prefers medical tourism for treatment of dental care; cardiac, orthopedic and cosmetic surgery; organ, stem cell, and tissue transplantation; cancer treatment; and reproductive technologies, such as surrogate pregnancy, in-vitro fertilization (IVF), to name but a few. During the pandemic, medical tourism also offered medical tour packages includes vaccination (Marketdataforecast.com 2021; Kelley 2013). Popular medical tourism destinations include countries in Europe and Asia. The travelers need to follow country-specific norms, official approvals/license, patient data process, security policies, and quality of drugs/clinical products (CDC.gov n.d.). Medical tourism provides destination countries with improved prospects in terms of economic growth, better job opportunities, improved healthcare services and solutions, emerging technologies, advanced quality of life contributing to global healthcare, information, social and cultural exchanges, increasing foreign revenues, patient-tailored 24/7 medical treatment, support for m-Visa, language translators, local SIM cards, loading and boarding, appointment management and post-treatment follow-ups (Bhattacharjee 2019).

16.3 CATEGORIES OF MEDICAL TOURISM

Medical tourism focuses on treatment, healthcare solutions, and services and covers preventive to therapeutic, and rehabilitation healthcare services. Medical tourism can be broadly categorised as international or domestic classes as mentioned in the following sub-sections (Bhattacharjee 2019):

16.3.1 INTERNATIONAL MEDICAL TOURISM

It includes inbound and outbound international travel for the purpose of medical treatment. International medical tourism is about receiving better healthcare services in a foreign country as compared with his/her own country. The patient prefers this option due to its cost-effectiveness and high quality.

- *Inbound medical tourism.* When a patient belongs to outside origin/foreign country and is entering a particular country, say "X", for medical treatment, then the patient will be inbound in nature for country "X".
- *Outbound Medical Tourism.* When a patient from native country, say "X", travels to an outside origin/foreign country for medical treatment, then the patient will be outbound for country "X".

In other words, the patient, leaving his native country, say "A", to foreign country, say "B", is outbound for country "A" and inbound for country "B". This type of medical tourism includes risk-prone treatments, which are usually costly and need specialisation or better facilities (Bhattacharjee 2019).

International medical tourism includes dental care or dentistry; orthopedics and musculoskeletal treatment; cosmetic/plastic surgery; cardiology such as bypass surgery, electrophysiology, inborn heart diseases, or coronary-artery disease; weight loss or bariatric surgery; reproductive treatments such as IVF; surgery for eyes, nose, ears, throat; organ or tissue transplantation and rehabilitation (Meštrović 2018; Vyas & Gupta 2022).

16.3.2 DOMESTIC/INTRA-COUNTRY-BOUND MEDICAL TOURISM

This type of medical tourism has no international travel. It belongs to interstate, intercity, or inter-region travel of patients within their native country. When a patient belonging to their home city/state/region travels to another city/state/region in his/her country, it is called domestic medical tourism. Usually, domestic medical tourism is preferred by citizens to get better-quality, more reliable, faster or more affordable healthcare services, such as medical, surgical, or dental care etc., than in their home city/state/region. For example, during the COVID-19 pandemic, India witnessed a scarcity of hospitals beds and oxygen in almost all big/metro cities. At this moment, many patients traveled to nearby cities/states for better treatment or availability of beds or oxygen supply. In a few cases, they had to travel to small cities/regions to find the availability of such life-saving options (Meštrović 2018).

16.4 MEDICAL TOURISM: PRE- AND POST-PANDEMIC

Pre-pandemic, the study by the Global Wellness Institute (GWI) shows that the medical tourism industry introduced 800+ health & wellness tours, the majority of them in the Asia- Pacific region (e.g., China, Japan, India, Thailand, Indonesia, Malaysia, and the Philippines) and raised its business value to US$639 billionin 2017. Before the pandemic, global data forecast the health and wellness tourism business to reach (7.5% yearly) to reach $919 billion in 2022. . The COVID-19 pandemic disrupted medical tourism badly, and the sector has been struggling hard to recover. In a survey conducted on 441 respondents by a pharmaceutical technology website, more than 52% of respondents felt that this industry would take the next three years to restore its business to its pre-pandemic level. To combat this disruption and recover the economy in this sector, several reforms in medical tourism have already been initiated in medical tourism in markets such as Sri Lanka and Thailand (Xu et al. 2021).

Post-pandemic, to deal with this decline in the economy of the sector, the medical tourism industry shifted its focus to health and wellness, Ayurveda and yoga, local job creation, and conservation, redirecting from medical treatment to ecotourism along with the offer of vaccination. With the advent of technology, the sector also added several new offerings for the medical tourist, such as an online/digital platform, ensuring patient-data security, contact-less service delivery, social distancing, healthcare and hygiene, locally produced food, artisan products and handicrafts, and entertainment (Tourism Notes 2020).

Post-pandemic, people are more health conscious and looking for high-quality healthcare solutions. A report from the World Health Organization (WHO) mentions that around 40% of people prefer medical tourism because of the cost-effective healthcare solutions combined with advanced technology. On the contrary, a report from the British Association of Plastic Reconstructive and Aesthetic Surgery mentions that around 37% of medical tourists faced issues such as contamination and post-treatment remedial problem. On the other hand, the countries are facing problems of an inadequate workforce, enormous pressure on medical professionals, cancellation of domestic/international flights, and insufficient adoption of technology. In turn, this has an adverse effect on medical tourism. The need is to take these factors into consideration to strengthen the medical tourism market globally. Now, many countries have started investing in medical tourism in the form of inviting members of the medical faculty from Harvard, Cleveland, and Mayo, to name but a few, to their countries. At this moment, countries like Singapore, Thailand, and India have an opportunity in terms of medical tourism, due to their comparatively low cost of medical care (Bhattacharjee 2019).

India is also moving ahead and creating strategies to promote medical, rural, and meetings, incentives, conferences and exhibitions (MICE) tourism. A recent report from The Economic Times highlighted the draft national strategy and roadmap of the Indian Ministry of Tourism to promote wellness and medical tourism, by advertising during conferences, meetings, and exhibitions to attract medical tourists. As part of the "Aatmanirbhar Bharat" mission, the government is planning to leverage our cultural diversity, values, and heritage; ancient therapies of 'AYUSH' (Ayurveda, Yoga and Naturopathy, Unani, Siddha and Homoeopathy); and wellness tourism. The purpose is to ensure affordable, accessible, efficient, and high-quality healthcare and wellness services to attract medical tourists (The Economic Times 2021). On another occasion, during the ASSOCHAM virtual conference, the Minister of State at the Ministry of Tourism and Culture also stressed the target of reviving medical and wellness tourism in India (https://economictimes.indiatimes.com/industry/services/travel/post-pandemic-tourism-ministry-floats-strategy-to-promote-medical-rural-mice-tourism/articleshow/83640800.cms?from=mdr), while a rapid e-medical-visa facility in India provides the support to foreign national people seeking medical treatment India (Bhattacharjee 2019).

16.5 MAPPING THE MARKET FOR MEDICAL TRAVELERS

A report from the Maximize Market Research Company describes the global medical tourism market in regions such as North America, Europe, Asia-Pacific, the Middle East, Africa, and South America. The report forecasts that the medical tourism market would grow by Compound Annual Growth Rate of ~10% in the next five years, specifically peaking in North America and the Asia-Pacific region. The research by Alkire identified the preference for medical tourism as Mexico, Croatia, Poland, Hungary, Turkey, the UAE, Spain, South Korea, Costa Rica, Barbados, Egypt, Australia, Thailand, Brazil, South Africa, and India.

16.6 MARKET PLAYERS IN MEDICAL TOURISM

The market forecasts for medical tourism are encouraging, although only a few countries around the globe are cashing in on this opportunity. For example, China, one of the business giants, is far behind Malaysia in terms of medical tourism. The flourishing medical tourism has now become the driving force for growth across the globe (Tewari 2020).

Developing countries are strengthening their medical facilities and infrastructure, healthcare centres, alliance between private and private hospitals, and other different healthcare solutions and packages to attract medical tourists (IMF 2021).

The major market players in Indian medical tourism include Aditya Birla Memorial Hospital, Apollo Hospitals, Asian Heart Institute, Fortis Healthcare, KPJ Healthcare Berhad, Prince Court Medical Centre, Samitivej etc., to name but a few. These healthcare providers carry out cosmetic surgery, dental care, cardiac surgery, orthopedic and fertility treatments (Vara 2021).

16.7 BLOCKCHAIN CONCEPT

Blockchain is termed as a secure, transparent, and robust system for information sharing. Blockchain includes digital ledger technology, bitcoins, and secure transactions distributed across the network (Wood 2021).

Nofer et al. also describe blockchain technology, which provides secure and immutable data storage and exploits the distributed ledger technology (DLT) to record transactions (Nofer et al. 2017).

Blockchain plays a significant role in the healthcare domain, most specifically medical tourism. The medical tourist's data are stored in the Electronic Health Record (EHR) or Electronic Medical Record (EMR) (Gupta 2017; Ahram et al. 2017; Dagher et al. 2018; Ekblaw et al. 2016; Fan et al. 2018; Jiang et al. 2018; Roehrs et al. 2017). The patient data have to be secure and shared with hospitals. To ensure data privacy, the digital ledger technology in blockchain ensures secure remote patient monitoring and data transfer of EHR or EMR of the patients (Zhang et al. 2018).

In blockchain, features such as decentralisation, confidentiality, and security ensure secure access to EHRs with hospitals across the globe, doctors, ministries, and insurance companies (Ben Fekih & Lahami 2020).

In medical tourism, patient data is vulnerable at various places. Hence, it is necessary to store their personal data securely and confidentially. The blockchain ensures its secure storage, accuracy, and transparency (Daley 2021). In medical tourism, blockchain caters patient-centric interoperability, accessibility, and privacy. With blockchain technology, the patients can access and share tag information of medical data/EMR with outbound hospitals over private blockchain. At the same time, they can make their general information such as medical reactions/drug sensitivity, etc., over public blockchain (Sharma et al. 2021).

16.8 BLOCKCHAIN IN MEDICAL TOURISM: SCOPE, ROLE, AND IMPACT

With advent of technology, hospitality, healthcare, and tourism witnessed significant growth in the field of multi-disciplinary sectors – medical tourism. The technology provides opportunities for the patients to search global options for medical treatment, hospitals, doctors, and healthcare solutions through the internet. At the same time, trust and the quality of healthcare are equally important as hospital facilities, doctors, country-specific procedures, health hazards, risk transparency, and privacy of medical data. The blockchain technology is one of the facilitators for this move in healthcare industry. Blockchain features answers to all these concerns by providing decentralisation, immutability, distribution, encryption and validation of data, transparency, trust, interoperability, privacy and inconsistency without any intervention of brokers. The blockchain technology expedites medical tourists to make informed decisions while selecting their outbound country. At the same point, the transparency feature of blockchain ensures hassle-free movement of patients abroad (Yoon 2019; Rejeb et al. 2020).

Blockchain also provides solutions to various potential challenges to medical tourism, such as wastage of money, logistics issues, insecure record exchanges among stakeholders, and threat to data breach in the inbound (destination) country. At the same point, for medical mobility, a lack of access to the patient's EMR not only slows down the healthcare procedures, it can also ruin the reputation of the facilitators. With the decentralised record system of blockchain, it ensures secure and smooth share of medical data/patient's personal records without any geographical barriers. Patients' smart contracts withstand the ownership of their data and prevention of data breach. Patients can provide authentication and accessibility to any healthcare provider across the globe. Another important element of medical tourism is insurance and claims. Blockchain technology also takes care of broker-free automation of insurance claims and payment process, payment tracking, and the audit of bills (Rejeb et al. 2019).

16.9 BLOCKCHAIN TECHNOLOGIES FOR THE MEDICAL TOURISM ECOSYSTEM

This section discusses the use of blockchain techniques to convey the needed information to the respective healthcare professional based on the grounds of cross-border data sharing. This section primarily focuses on four characteristics of blockchain, namely no-middlemen, data transparency and trust, digitisation and inter-operability, and confidentiality, that directly influence medical tourism. Medical tourism raised the need for mediators or brokers to connect tourist-patients with healthcare service providers (Stephano 2019). The patients have to compromise their personal information and health data with intermediaries to get facilities such as a visa, hospitality, accommodation, travel arrangement, and pre- and post-medical treatment (https://www.magazine.medicaltourism.com/article/blockchain-technology-medical-tourism; Vyas et al. 2022). The blockchain technology facilitates various value-added services such as optimised searching of suitable medical service providers, credible medical and non-medical information, connecting patients directly with medical care providers (Aghaei et al. 2021), negotiating medical packages, document verification of medical professionals, and the patient's information and health data, inclusive assessment of a person's health, payment settlement through cryptocurrency, minimising transaction cost (Connell 2006); and providing secure access and control over their own health data. The blockchain technologies protect a patient's personal data by eliminating mediators, ensuring transparency and trust among patients and service providers, enhancing digitisation and safeguarding the security of patient data.

16.10 EDGE-AI-EMPOWERED BLOCKCHAIN

Medical tourism is dependent upon medical data, which has to be privacy critical, sensitive, and delay free. Data privacy and security are ensured by blockchain technologies, as mentioned in previous sections. At the same time, delays can be minimised with inclusion of artificial intelligence-based edge computing.

Edge-AI ensures massive decision-making with low latency. At the same time, the security at edge devices is ensured through blockchain architecture (Gupta et al. 2021). The edge-AI-based blockchain architecture can keep track of patient data and its analysis, using distributed databases (Nawaz et al. 2019). Also, the edge-AI-empowered blockchain technologies strengthen the Internet of Medical Things for monitoring medical data (Dai et al. 2021).

16.11 CONCLUSION

The main reasons for patients to choose medical tourism are limited medical facilities and accessibility to healthcare services in their home country; low-cost medical treatments in destination countries; ease of mobility; growth of medical services worldwide; and access to technology such as edge-AI and blockchain (Vyas 2023). However, medical tourism also do have a few issues, such as lack of follow-up procedures; cultural and language barriers; fear of organ trafficking, improper healthcare infrastructure such as lack of water, hygiene, power supply and limited food options; lack of trust of medical tourism due to non-uniform medical procedures, rules and regulations, and gaps in the law (Kelley 2013). Hence, with the advent of edge-AI-empowered blockchain, medical tourism has great potential to grow as a strong market player.

REFERENCES

Aghaei, H., Naderibeni, N., & Karimi, A. (2021). Designing a tourism business model on block chain platform. *Tourism Management Perspectives*, 39, 100845.

Ahram, T., Sargolzaei, A., Sargolzaei, S., Daniels, J., & Amaba, B. (2017) Blockchain technology innovations. In *IEEE Technology & Engineering Management Conference (TEMSCON)* (pp. 137–141). IEEE.

Ben Fekih, R., & Lahami, M. (2020). Application of blockchain technology in healthcare: A comprehensive study. In M. Jmaiel, M. Mokhtari, B. Abdulrazak, H. Aloulou, & S. Kallel (Eds.), *The Impact of Digital Technologies on Public Health in Developed and Developing Countries*. ICOST 2020. Lecture Notes in Computer Science (Vol. 12157). Cham: Springer. https://doi.org/10.1007/978-3-030-51517-1_23

Benowitz, I. J. (n.d.). Medical tourism – Chapter 9 – 2020 yellow book | travelers' health | CDC. *CDC.Gov*. Retrieved July 28, 2021, from https://wwwnc.cdc.gov/travel/yellowbook/2020/travel-for-work-other-reasons/medical-tourism

Bhattacharjee, T. (2019, August 11). Top 10 types of medical tourism. *Madre Healthcare*. Retrieved July 28, 2021, from https://www.madrehealthcare.com/top-10-types-of-medical-tourism/

Connell, J. (2006). Medical tourism: Sea, sun, sand and… surgery. *Tourism Management*, 27(6), 1093–1100.

Dagher, G. G., Mohler, J., Milojkovic, M., & Marella, P. B. (2018). Ancile: Privacy-preserving framework for access control and interoperability of electronic health records using blockchain technology. *Sustainable Cities and Society*, 39, 283–297.

Dai, H.-N., Wu, Y., Wang, H., Imran, M., & Haider, N. (2021, June). Blockchain-empowered edge intelligence for internet of medical things against COVID-19. *IEEE Internet of Things Magazine*, 4(2), 34–39. https://doi.org/10.1109/IOTM.0011.2100030

Daley, S. (2021, May 8). How using blockchain in healthcare is reviving the industry's capabilities. *Built In*. https://builtin.com/blockchain/blockchain-healthcare-applications-companies, Accessed on 24 July 2021.

Ekblaw, A., Azaria, A., Halamka, J. D., & Lippman, A. (2016). A case study for blockchain in healthcare: "MedRec" prototype for electronic health records and medical research data. In *Proceedings of IEEE Open & Big Data Conference* Chicago, 2016 (Vol. 13, p. 13).

Etemad, A. (2010, September 10). Competitive prices in medical tourism – Part 1. *Medtalk*. https://emedtravel.wordpress.com/2010/09/09/competitive-prices-in-medical-tourism-part-1/. Accessed on 24 July 2021.

Fan, K., Wang, S., Ren, Y., Li, H., & Yang, Y. (2018). Medblock: Efficient and secure medical data sharing via blockchain. *Journal of Medical Systems*, 42(8), 136.

Global medical tourism market size, share, trends, growth & COVID-19 analysis report – Segmented by treatment type and region – Industry forecast (2021 to 2026) (ID: 1769). (2021, April). *Marketdataforecast.com*. Retrieved July 12, 2021, from https://www.marketdataforecast.com/market-reports/medical-tourism-market

Gupta, S. S. (2017). Blockchain. IBM Online. http://www.IBM.COM. Accessed on 24 July 2021.

Gupta, R., Reebadiya, D., Tanwar, S., Kumar, N., & Guizani, M. (2021). When blockchain meets edge intelligence: Trusted and security solutions for consumers. *IEEE Network*, 35(5), 272–278.

Jiang, S., Cao, J., Wu, H., Yang, Y., Ma, M., & He, J. (2018). BlocHIE: A blockchain-based platform for healthcare information exchange. In *IEEE International Conference on Smart Computing (SMARTCOMP)* (pp. 49–56). IEEE.

Kelley, E. (2013, October 2). Medical tourism. WHO Patient Safety Programme. https://www.who.int/global_health_histories/seminars/kelley_presentation_medical_tourism.pdf. Accessed on 12 June 2021.

Medical tourism: Travel to another country for medical care | Travelers' health | CDC. (n.d.). *CDC.Gov*. Retrieved July 20, 2021, from https://wwwnc.cdc.gov/travel/page/medical-tourism

Meštrović, T. (2018, August 23). What is medical tourism? *News-Medical.Net*. https://www.news-medical.net/health/What-is-Medical-Tourism.aspx. Accessed on 20 July 2021.

Nawaz, A., Gia, T. N., Queralta, J. P., & Westerlund, T. (2019). Edge AI and blockchain for privacy-critical and data-sensitive applications. In *2019 Twelfth International Conference on Mobile Computing and Ubiquitous Network (ICMU)* (pp. 1–2). https://doi.org/10.23919/ICMU48249.2019.9006635

Nofer, M., Gomber, P., Hinz, O., & Schiereck, D. (2017). Blockchain. *Business & Information Systems Engineering*, 59(3), 183–187.

Post-pandemic tourism: Ministry floats strategy to promote medical, rural, MICE tourism. (2021, June 18). *The Economic Times*. Retrieved on July 24, 2021, from https://economictimes.indiatimes.com/industry/services/travel/post-pandemic-tourism-ministry-floats-strategy-to-promote-medical-rural-mice-tourism/articleshow/83640800.cms?from=mdr

Rejeb, A., Keogh, J. G., & Treiblmaier, H. (2019, December). The impact of blockchain on medical tourism. In *Workshop on E-Business* (pp. 29–40). Cham: Springer.

Rejeb, A., Keogh, J. G., & Treiblmaier, H. (2020, August 7). The impact of blockchain on medical tourism. *Middle East Medical Portal*. Retrieved on July 24, 2021, from https://www.middleeastmedicalportal.com/the-impact-of-blockchain-on-medical-tourism/

Roehrs, A., da Costa, C. A., & da Rosa Righi, R. (2017). Omni PHR: A distributed architecture model to integrate personal health records. *Journal of Biomedical Informatics*, 71, 70–81.

Sharma, L., Olson, J., Guha, A., & McDougal, L. (2021). HOW blockchain will transform the healthcare ecosystem. *Business Horizons*, 64(5), 673–682.

Stephano, R.-M. (2019, October). Blockchain technology: A total game-changer in medical tourism. *Medicaltourism.Com*. Retrieved on June 24, 2021. https://www.magazine.medicaltourism.com/article/blockchain-technology-medical-tourism

Tewari, S. (2020, December 17). India to benefit from medical tourism post covid: MoS, Tourism. *Mint*. https://www.livemint.com/news/india/india-to-benefit-from-medical-tourism-post-covid-mos-tourism-11608209710018.html. Accessed on 13 June 2021.

Tourism in a post-pandemic world. (2021, February 24). *IMF*. https://www.imf.org/en/News/Articles/2021/02/24/na022521-how-to-save-travel-and-tourism-in-a-post-pandemic-world. Accessed on 24 June 2021.

Tourism Notes. (2020, August 9). Medical tourism- Definition, history, types, importance, issues, and challenges. *Tourism Notes*. https://tourismnotes.com/medical-tourism/. Accessed on 21 July 2021.

Vara, V. (2021, March 9). Medical tourism industry will take up to three years to bounce back to pre-pandemic levels: Poll. *Pharmaceutical Technology*. https://www.pharmaceutical-technology.com/news/medical-tourism-industry-will-take-up-to-three-years-to-bounce-back-to-pre-pandemic-levels-poll/. Accessed on 24 July 2021.

Vyas, S. (2023). Extended reality and edge AI for healthcare 4.0: Systematic study. In *Extended Reality for Healthcare Systems* (pp. 229–240). Academic Press.

Vyas, S., & Gupta, S. (2022). Case study on state-of-the-art wellness and health tracker devices. In *Handbook of Research on Lifestyle Sustainability and Management Solutions Using AI, Big Data Analytics, and Visualization* (pp. 325–337). IGI Global.

Wood, L. (2021, July 7). Global medical tourism market (2021 to 2026) – Industry trends, share, size, growth, opportunity and forecasts – ResearchAndMarkets.com. *Business Wire*. https://www.businesswire.com/news/home/20210707005561/en/Global-Medical-Tourism-Market-2021-to-2026---Industry-Trends-Share-Size-Growth-Opportunity-and-Forecasts---ResearchAndMarkets.com. Accessed on 20 July 2021.

Xu, Q., Purushothaman, V., Cuomo, R. E., & Mackey, T. K. (2021). A bilingual systematic review of South Korean medical tourism: A need to rethink policy and priorities for public health?. *BMC Public Health*, 21(1), 1–17.

Yoon, H. J. (2019). Blockchain technology and healthcare. *Healthcare Informatics Research*, 25(2), 59–60.

Zhang, P., White, J., Schmidt, D. C., Lenz, G., & Rosenbloom, S. T. (2018). FHIRChain: Applying blockchain to securely and scalably share clinical data. *Computational and Structural Biotechnology Journal*, 16, 267–278.

https://globalwellnessinstitute.org/press-room/press-releases/new-study-reveals-wellness-tourism-now-a-639-billion-market/

17 System for secure edge healthcare monitoring based on artificial intelligence

Sunil Gupta

CONTENTS

17.1 INTRODUCTION

Bandwidth constraints, unstable networks, and latency problems can have a negative impact on results when processing healthcare and life science data remotely. When timing is crucial, such delays can be critical. Innovative healthcare companies are implementing edge computing, which allow data to be examined and used right away, to allay these worries. By bringing data processing and storage closer to the point of origin and giving clinical and research teams access to real-time insights, AI-powered instruments, medical devices, and edge technologies are revolutionising healthcare and the life sciences. On-demand insights support teams in making critical choices concerning patients, which is crucial for the delivery of healthcare (Vyas & Gupta 2022). The use of edge-AI computing has become popular in recent years. In 2020, the market was already worth US\$9 billion and, by 2030, it was expected to reach US\$60 billion (Allied Market Research).

Edge-AI outperforms the more prevalent cloud AI as a solution. The numerous advantages it offers serve to highlight its superiority. Consider real-time data analysis as an example. Edge-AI performs local data analysis. Because the data do not need to be sent to the cloud, there is less latency, allowing for real-time decision-making. This skill may be essential for factory robots, self-driving automobiles, and other devices. In comparison with cloud AI, edge-AI can result in significantly lower costs for data communication because it doesn't require a connection. The same holds true for energy usage. This makes it possible to develop better wearable technology, which has a lot of potential for application in hospitals. Additionally, this has a privacy component. There is less privacy risk because most of the data remains on the premises. Because data is transmitted and stored in the cloud with cloud AI, vulnerabilities may arise (Gundi 2022).

The goal of edge computing, which has become a popular computing paradigm, is to reduce the time for data transfer between end users and the cloud. The low latency provided by edge computing benefits a variety of artificial intelligence applications.

17.2 APPLICATION OF EDGE-AI IN THE HEALTHCARE SECTOR

The contemporary healthcare sector is being shaped in part by edge computing. Adopting edge-AI has numerous advantages, as was already mentioned. It may be crucial in the healthcare sector for both patients and healthcare professionals. Some of the strong arguments that make edge-AI the obvious choice for this sector are described in the following sub-sections.

17.2.1 AUTONOMOUS HOSPITAL ROOM MONITORING

The ability to automate processes is one of AI's main selling points in general. A wide range of sensors can be used to gather data that AI systems can then analyse to determine the best course of action. Edge-AI takes this to the next level. It provides autonomous monitoring of hospital rooms and patients by utilising computer vision and data from other sensors.

17.2.2 NEW RADIOLOGY APPLICATIONS

The DICOM (Digital Imaging and Communications) images used in radiology are quite huge. Therefore, sending these photos to the cloud or a central server for processing and receiving the machine-learning inference can be quite expensive and time consuming. However, edge-AI makes it possible for the analysis to take place locally, which results in a considerably quicker diagnosis.

17.2.3 RURAL HEALTH

Providing high-quality healthcare in isolated rural regions has always been a difficulty. Despite developments in telemedicine and more freely available health information, medical professionals still struggle to provide quick, high-quality care to patients who reside far from hospitals and have a limited internet connection. Due to connectivity constraints, standard healthcare databases face significant obstacles, but the combination of edge computing applications and IoT medical devices made it easier to overcome such obstacles. Medical workers can access vital patient information, even in areas with poor connectivity, thanks to IoT healthcare equipment, which can increase the reach of existing networks (Kamruzzaman et al. 2022).

17.3   RELEVANT WORK

Due to issues with speed, cost, and privacy, advancing the AI frontier to the edge ecosystem that exists at the last mile of the internet is extremely difficult. When compared with the conventional cloud-based computing paradigm, the physical proximity of the sources for computing and information generation promises several advantages, such as context awareness, low latency, energy efficiency, and privacy protection (Zhou et al. 2019). In contrast to AI, which aims to imitate intelligent human behavior in devices and computers through learning from data, edge computing aims to organise many collaborating edge devices and servers to process the generated data locally. Pushing AI to the edge offers additional benefits to one another in addition to the benefits of edge computing generally. Edge intelligence may function in a cloud-edge-device coordination manner via data offloading rather than implying that the AI model is fully trained or inferred at the edge. Figure 17.1 illustrates how data dumping volume and path length reduce as edge intelligence increases.

The industrial, government, and healthcare groups are devoting a lot of consideration to the development of smart sensors, artificial intelligence, and edge analytics with the integration of cloud computing and their linkage with healthcare. For this analysis, several studies that were recently published – between 2016 and 2021 – were chosen. The objective of a study conducted by researchers S. U. Amin and M. S. Hossain was to analyse the most recent and innovative edge computing frameworks. The objective of this chapter is to thoroughly investigate

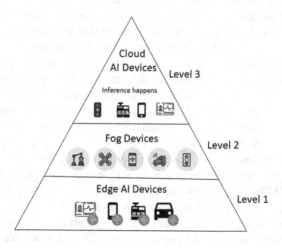

FIGURE 17.1   Levels of increasing edge intelligence.

the application of categorisation in relation to cutting-edge AI and approaches that may be employed for edge intelligence. New diseases like COVID-19 have emerged because of the growing population. According to research by Amin & Hossain 2021, these pandemic illnesses can be controlled by implementing a 5G wireless connection based on technology.

"Ethereum blockchain-based architecture with edge-AI for studying the data at the neof securitytwork edge and for retaining the trace of the parties that are dedicated to access the analytical results, kept in disseminated databases", was detailed by Nawaz and colleagues in research that was published in 2019 (Nawaz et al. 2019). This framework assisted in addressing the increasing problems of security brought on by the inclusion of new coatings in the network design (Nawaz et al. 2019).

A study was undertaken by Tuli et al. (2020) to present a vision for putting in place a comprehensive framework that can accommodate the growing needs of patients and healthcare professionals. The vision also focuses on outlining the theoretical foundation that can provide a significant response to the escalating needs. The approach provided includes every facet of interaction at various levels, blockchain, and AI, for computing and machine learning (Tuli et al. 2020).

Imran et al. (2020) claim that security, latency, bandwidth, and privacy issues may be the main issues with IoT applications. According to a review of research conducted over the previous six years (Imran et al. 2020), the issues related to transmitting data to the cloud and processing it would be made worse by about 20 million IoT devices.

To assess the use of IoT for predicting the solutions for linked healthcare in smart cities, Greco et al. (2020) undertook a review-based analysis. This study offers solutions, from the viability of wearable sensor-based health monitoring to a thorough analysis of the most recent developments in edge computing for connected healthcare.

Pramanik et al. (2017) conducted a study to critically examine the progressive, cutting-edge healthcare industry and to analyse a variety of complex data in several healthcare areas. IoT and 5G wireless connections were two of the most recent advances in linked healthcare that provide the faster speed and low latency. The challenges which patients face when using an ambulance in an emergency were the main topic of Poongodi et al. (2021). The data on heartbeat, temperature, and breathing rate may be successfully employed for quick diagnosis by the ambulance tracking system and patient monitor, as was confirmed after analysing the literature research. Edge-AI has various applications in connected healthcare in smart cities, according to Pazienza et al. (2019). It is essential to address the edge computing architecture so that processing can occur at gateways (edge nodes) or devices (end nodes). It is necessary for applications like critical analysis and medical monitoring because it reduces unnecessary processing and data traffic. Edge-AI has various prospects in smart cities, claim Vyas et al. (2022). Adopting edge-AI for linked healthcare in smart cities may provide a variety of obstacles, as highlighted by (Vyas et al. 2022). Tuli et al. (2020) carried out a study to provide a vision for developing a complete framework that would fulfill the increasing needs of patients and healthcare professionals (Syed et al. 2021).

The main problems with IT applications include a lack of security, latency, bandwidth, and privacy, according to the qualitative secondary study carried out by Imran et al. (2020).

17.4   SECURITY OF EDGE-BASED AI SYSTEMS

Data protection is still essential to guaranteeing the security of AI system operations, regardless of whether computing takes place in the cloud or at the edge. For instance, secure boot updates and integrity checks are unquestionably mission critical. Furthermore, a successful assault would not only have an impact on the security of the data set for applications that directly influence people's lives, like healthcare, but it may also put lives in danger. When preparing for system security, AI system developers must take the training phase into account. This implies that additional associated attack surfaces must be considered in addition to the hardware itself (including the neural network accelerator). These risks include altering or stealing training data; altering or stealing an AI model that has been trained; altering or stealing input data; stealing inference results; or altering outcomes that are utilised for retraining. Malicious assaults can be lessened with the careful application of security measures that use privacy and integrity cryptographic functions. Figure 17.2 shows a representation of an edge-AI system's training through implementation phases.

Interference and stealing of information with the trained model results in a major loss of company resources and confidential information because the entire training process needs a non-trivial amount of time and effort for the acquisition of training data (and for the training period itself). It should therefore come as no surprise that today's designers must prioritise security from the very beginning of the design cycle, given the significance of security for edge-AI in IOT healthcare and the wide range of attack surfaces available to a determined hacker. Additionally, just as AI systems are constantly changing, their security must likewise advance to continue thwarting increasingly sophisticated threats as AI systems become more complex.

A typical first step in enhancing system security is swapping out One-Time Programmable (OTP) memory that uses give off with anti-fuse OTP. Installing a root-of-trust, which typically consists of protected storage, an entropy source (using Physically Unclonable Functions (PUF) and True Random Number Generators (TRNG)), and a unique identity, would be the next, intermediate stage (acting as the foundation for a secure boot flow) as shown in Figure 17.2. The

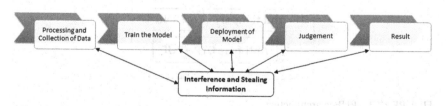

FIGURE 17.2   Phases of system training.

incorporation of a fully functional crypto coprocessor, secure element, or trusted execution environment would be the ultimate step. This kind of secure element can carry out all security and cryptographic operations inside its own, trusted zone of security. It's a constant struggle for designers to incorporate more security modules into a single system. When updating an old product or creating a whole new product line, design architects frequently opt for the simplest but most comprehensive option to integrate. With first-generation designs, integrating several IPs is essentially unavoidable, since the size and feature sets of such security modules/IP will vary depending on the chosen degree of protection. This frequently results in security being seen as top-down, starting with cryptographic algorithms, and concluding with key storage as the final component. However, this strategy poses some significant issues.

When IPs come from different providers, there is additional integration work to be done in addition to creating and maintaining a security border covering multiple IPs.

Even with an edge-AI SoC, ease of integration is crucial when adding security to a system. Power consumption, however, is a special and significant factor for edge-AI-Driven Security Operations (AISoCs) because edge devices are deployed in the field. Unfortunately, this goes directly against the demand for increasingly complex computation-related functions that must be performed at the edge. As a result, people looking for greater performance and reduced power consumption are increasingly drawn to using more advanced process technologies (Hayyolalam et al. 2021).

A growing number of edge-AI SoC designs are using 12/16 nm process nodes, which hit the sweet spot for computation power, current consumption, and cost, according to current market trends. The two significant difficulties previously identified are addressed by PUFsecurity's PUFcc secure crypto-coprocessor IP. PUFcc is built on a hardware root-of-trust (HRoT) that incorporates secure storage and entropy sources. NIST-CAVP- and OSCCA-certified crypto engines are then added, and everything is protected by an anti-tamper shell. Due to PUFcc's ability to offload secure processes that would otherwise burden the main core, system performance is enhanced while power usage is reduced. Figure 17.3

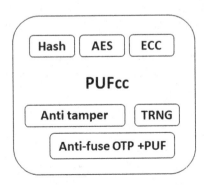

FIGURE 17.3 PUFcc architecture.

depicts the PUFcc architecture. The architecture includes the integrity check and encryption algorithms like AES or ECC.

17.5 IOT HEALTHCARE MONITORING SYSTEM WITH EDGE-AI

Healthcare edge networks have undergone substantial innovation and progress. Based on the literature, we have determined certain fundamental needs and problems that arise when constructing such systems. These same issues are what our solution aims to solve.

Security. Information about a healthcare scenario refers to people's particular medical conditions. These data must be secured since they are extremely important and pose a privacy risk. Even if the IoT devices are believed to be reliable, there is a potential that the data could be intercepted or falsified during transmission over the network. Therefore, it is essential to find a solution to the system's security problem.

Ownership. The information must originate from the legitimate source and not from a hostile device. A system for authentication is therefore required. IoT devices have limited processing and storage capacity. These gadgets contain embedded sensors, but they lack sufficient processing power for data analysis and memory to store the vast volumes of data produced. These duties require outsourcing (Vyas & Gupta 2022).

Response. Health data must be constantly tracked, and any emergency scenario must be quickly discovered and reported to a doctor for prompt treatment. In urgent or dangerous circumstances, such as a heart attack or paralytic stroke, time is particularly crucial. So that he/she can swiftly recommend a plan of action, the doctor must be informed as soon as possible. Therefore, it is best to keep the overall time needed for data transfer, processing, notification, and resolution to a minimum (Vyas et al. 2022).

Data analysis. To find patterns, make diagnoses, and recommend treatments, an intelligent system must be created.

Data communication. For other practitioners to make use of a single system, it is crucial to share the data as well as any crucial conclusions or models produced. High-quality sensors are required to efficiently capture data on heart rate, body temperature, respiration, images, speech, and other factors. Data collection from diverse IoT devices is standardised because each one has different hardware, which also affects the data formats. It's important to comprehend and send the accurate values of data obtained from IoT devices. In this direction, it is vital to standardise the data format.

17.6 CONCLUSION

The cutting-edge technologies edge-AI and the Internet of Medical Things (IoMT) are currently being used in numerous connected healthcare applications in smart cities. The usage of these technologies for linked healthcare monitoring and management can also be very advantageous because it can decrease the amount of labor-intensive human work and improve management performance. The difficulties, possibilities, and uses of edge-AI for linked healthcare in smart cities have been thoroughly analysed in this study. An edge IoT healthcare monitoring system with edge-AI capabilities is the suggested solution for future systems (Vyas 2023). The system's main purpose is to schedule patients in real time. In addition to allocating resources according to a person's health or category, it prioritises the provision of resources, including doctors, medications, ambulance services, blood, intensive care units, and medical equipment like X-ray machines. IoT devices with AI capabilities that are attached to the patient first collect vital indicators. These data can be analyzed and stored on the edge server because it has the processing power and memory needed. The edge node launches a scheduler, immediately monitors the data, and releases medical resources as necessary. If the desired resources are not accessible, an edge controller receives the request and uses peer nodes linked to other hospitals to provide the requested resources. The design makes the resources instantaneously and securely available in this way.

REFERENCES

Amin, S. U., & Hossain, M. S. (2021). Edge intelligence and internet of things in healthcare: A survey. *IEEE Access*, 9, 45–59.

Greco, L., Percannella, G., Ritrovato. P., Tortorella, F., & Vento, M. (2020, July). Trends in IoT based solutions for health care: Moving AI to the edge. *Pattern Recognition Letters*, 135, 346–353.

Gundi, J. (2022). https://www.einfochips.com/blog/how-edge-ai-is-transforming-healthcare/, Accessed on 16 November 2022.

Hayyolalam, V., Aloqaily, M., Özkasap, Ö., & Guizani, M. (2021, June). Edge intelligence for empowering IoT-based healthcare systems. *IEEE Wireless Communications*, 28(3), 6–14. https://doi.org/10.1109/MWC.001.2000345

Imran, H. A., Mujahid, U., Wazir, S., Latif, U., & Mehmood, K. (2020). Embedded development boards for edge-AI: A comprehensive report. https://arxiv.org/abs/2009.00803v1, Accessed on 10 July 2020.

Kamruzzaman, M. M., Alrashdi, I., & Alqazzaz, A. (2022, February 23). New opportunities, challenges, and applications of edge-AI for connected healthcare in internet of medical things for smart cities. *Journal of Healthcare Engineering*, 2022, 2950699. https://doi.org/10.1155/2022/2950699. PMID: 35251564; PMCID: PMC8890828.

Nawaz, A., Gia, T. N., Queralta, J. P., & Westerlund, T. (2019, November). Edge AI and blockchain for privacy-critical and data-sensitive applications. *2019 12th International Conference on Mobile Computing and Ubiquitous Network (ICMU)* (pp. 1–2). Kathmandu, Nepal. doi: 10.23919/ICMU48249.2019.9006635..

Pazienza, A., Mallardi, G., Fasciano, C., & Vitulano, F. (2019, November). Artificial intelligence on edge computing: A healthcare scenario in ambient assisted living. In *Proceedings of the Artificial Intelligence for Ambient Assisted Living (AI-AAL.it 2019)*. Rende, Italy.

Poongodi, M., Sharma, A., Hamdi, M., Maode, M., & Chilamkurti, N. (2021). Smart healthcare in smart cities: wireless patient monitoring system using IoT. *6e Journal of Supercomputing*, 77(11), Article ID 12230.

Pramanik, M. I., et al. (2017, November). Smart health: Big data enabled health paradigm within smart cities. *Expert Systems with Applications*, 87, 370–383.

Syed, S., Sierra-Sosa, D., Kumar, A., & Elmaghraby, A. (2021). IoT in smart cities: A survey of technologies, practices and challenges. *Smart Cities*, 4(2), 429–475.

Tuli, S., et al. (2020, March). Next generation technologies for smart healthcare: Challenges, vision, model, trends and future directions. *Internet Technology Letters*, 3(2), e145.

Vyas, S. (2023). Chapter twelve - Extended reality and edge AI for healthcare 4.0: Systematic study. In Khan, S., Alam, M., Banday, S. A., & Usta, M. S. (Eds.), *Extended Reality for Healthcare Systems* (pp. 229–240). Academic Press. ISBN 9780323983815, https://doi.org/10.1016/B978-0-323-98381-5.00010-6.

Vyas, S., & Gupta, S. (2022). Case study on state-of-the-art wellness and health tracker devices. In Iyer, S. S., Jain, A. & Wang, J. (Eds.), *Handbook of Research on Lifestyle Sustainability and Management Solutions Using AI, Big Data Analytics, and Visualization* (pp. 325–337). IGI Global. DOI: 10.4018/978-1-7998-8786-7.

Vyas, S., Gupta, S., Bhargava, D., & Boddu, R. (2022). Fuzzy logic system implementation on the performance parameters of health data management frameworks. *Journal of Healthcare Engineering*, 2022, 1–11.

Zhou, Z., Chen, X., Li, E., Zeng, L., Luo, K., Zhang, J. (2019). Edge intelligence: Paving the last mile of artificial intelligence with edge computing. *Proceedings of the IEEE*, 107(8), 1738–1762.

Index

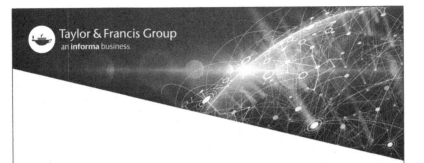

Taylor & Francis eBooks

www.taylorfrancis.com

A single destination for eBooks from Taylor & Francis
with increased functionality and an improved user
experience to meet the needs of our customers.

90,000+ eBooks of award-winning academic content in
Humanities, Social Science, Science, Technology, Engineering,
and Medical written by a global network of editors and authors.

TAYLOR & FRANCIS EBOOKS OFFERS:

A streamlined
experience for
our library
customers

A single point
of discovery
for all of our
eBook content

Improved
search and
discovery of
content at both
book and
chapter level

REQUEST A FREE TRIAL
support@taylorfrancis.com

 Routledge
Taylor & Francis Group

 CRC Press
Taylor & Francis Group